The
GULF COAST
OF FLORIDA
Book

A Complete Guide

Lee County Visitor and Convention Bureau

THE
GULF COAST
OF FLORIDA
BOOK
A Complete Guide

CHELLE KOSTER WALTON

Berkshire House Publishers
Stockbridge, Massachusetts

The Gulf Coast of Florida Book: A Complete Guide
Copyright © 1993 by Berkshire House Publishers
Front cover and interior photographs © 1993 by Greg Wagner except where otherwise credited.
Back cover photographs © Oscar Thompson

Library of Congress Cataloging-in-Publication Data

Walton, Chelle Koster
    The Gulf Coast of Florida book : a complete guide / Chelle Koster Walton
    Includes bibliographical references and index.
      p.   cm. — (The Great destinations series)
    ISBN 0-936399-50-3 (pbk.) : $16.95
    1. Gulf Coast (Fla.)—Guidebooks. I. Title. II. Series.
F317.G8W35   1993
917.5904'43'0916364—dc20   93-34198

ISBN: 0-936399-50-3
ISSN: 1056-7968 (series)

Editors: Editorial Alternatives. Managing Editors: Sarah Novak, Philip Rich. Original design for Great Destinations™ series: Janice Lindstrom. Original design for Great Destinations™cover: Jane McWhorter. Production services by Ripinsky & Company, Connecticut.

Berkshire House books are available at substantial discounts for bulk purchases by corporations and other organizations for promotions and premiums. Special personalized editions can also be produced in large quantities. For more information, contact:

Berkshire House Publishers
Box 297, Stockbridge MA 01262
800-321-8526

Manufactured in the United States of America
First printing 1993
10 9 8 7 6 5 4 3 2 1

The <u>GREAT DESTINATIONS</u> Series

The Berkshire Book: A Complete Guide
The Santa Fe & Taos Book: A Complete Guide
The Napa & Sonoma Book: A Complete Guide
The Chesapeake Bay Book: A Complete Guide
The Coast of Maine Book: A Complete Guide
The Adirondack Book: A Complete Guide
The Aspen Book: A Complete Guide
The Charleston, Savannah & Coastal Islands Book:
  A Complete Guide
The Gulf Coast of Florida Book: A Complete Guide
The Central Coast of California Book : A Complete Guide
  (Fall 1993)
The Newport & Narragansett Bay Book: A Complete Guide
  (Spring 1994)
The Hamptons Book: A Complete Guide (Spring 1994)

The Great Destinations™ series features regions in the United States rich in natural beauty and culture. Each Great Destinations™ guidebook reviews an extensive selection of lodgings, restaurants, cultural events, historic sites, shops, and recreational opportunities, and outlines the region's natural and social history. Written by resident authors, the guides are a resource for visitor and resident alike. Maps, photographs, directions to and around the region, lists of helpful phone numbers and addresses, and indexes.

To Gene and Theresa Koster,
who first instilled in me
a love for the road

Contents

CHAPTER ONE
Mangroves, Man, and Magnates
HISTORY
1

CHAPTER TWO
Blazing the Trail
TRANSPORTATION
29

CHAPTER THREE
Your Place in Paradise
LODGING
45

CHAPTER FOUR
Inspiration by the Sea
CULTURE
71

CHAPTER FIVE
Fruits de mer and de terre
RESTAURANTS & FOOD PURVEYORS
109

CHAPTER SIX
Fun in the Sun
RECREATION
145

CHAPTER SEVEN
Gifts from the Sea
SHOPPING
191

CHAPTER EIGHT
Practical Matters
INFORMATION
214

Acknowledgments

I can't list all of the people upon whose patience and understanding I depended to see me through this project. First dibs on my gratitude must go to my husband, Rob, for not divorcing me; and my son, Aaron, who was particularly helpful with my beach and "especially for kids" research. Thanks to Ron and Mindy Koster, who visited during my most intense stretch of writing-under-deadline, and managed to enjoy the Gulf Coast without me, and with — thankfully — Aaron.

Special thanks to Prudy Taylor Board, who checked my historical facts and who no doubt will cringe at the pirate legends I just couldn't bring myself to omit. Jacey Smith did a superb job of efficiently finishing up on fact-checking before an outbreak of chicken pox hit. Thanks to her, and to the staff at *Lee Living* magazine. Also, my gratitude goes to the staff of Magellan Geographix, who created the maps included herein.

I owe a debt of gratitude to several people who helped me with research: Nancy Hamilton at the Lee County Visitor & Convention Bureau, Kevin Russell at the Sarasota Convention & Visitors Bureau, and Ardath Chamberlain at the Manatee County Convention & Visitors Bureau.

Then there are all the friends and devoted fellow diners who assisted with reviews and suggestions, including Rose Kaley, Tom Estep, and Patty and Charlie Shaffer.

Thanks to photographer Greg Wagner, and to my supportive editors: Sarah Novak, Philip Rich, and Leslie Rich. You all helped to extract the agony of detail work inherent in creating a guidebook, and to make this a joyful undertaking.

Introduction

Morning dawns like a boater's dream. The sky is clear except for a trace of last night's moon: wispy, like a wadded-up cloud. The water seems pulled as tight as cellophane between Sanibel and Pine Islands. It is a morning to wonder why one ever does anything else on days off, but return to the sea. On cue, a family of three dolphins pierces the surface with their fins and their smiles. The show has begun.

In the course of our leisurely, two-hour cruise between Sanibel Island and Boca Grande, we are entertained by leaping sting rays, a school of mackerel, the usual dive-bomb squadron of gray pelicans — and, today, a rare treat— a visiting flock of white pelicans, feeding in the shallows behind Cayo Costa.

At lights-out call, after lunch in a marina-side fish house, beach time on an unbridged island, and a duck-the-afternoon-rains cocktail at an historic island inn, nature's revue reaches its spectacular finale. In the moonless dark, the wake behind our boat sparkles like a watery fireworks display. The Gulf suddenly throws an electric breaker switch. Liquid lightning strikes all around us as our 21-foot Mako powerboat parts the seas. White caps puff like nuclear popcorn.

Scientists call the phenomena *dinoflagellates*. Lay folks call the glowing organisms phosphorescence. Jamaicans call them sea-blinkies. The Ancient Mariner called them death-fires. I call their unpredictable visits to our waters magic: a topsy-turvy, ethereal feeling that someone has transformed the sea into a starry sky, without warning.

Such a perfect day isn't required in order to appreciate fully the Gulf Coast of Florida, but such days do help to remind me why I moved here from longjohn land over a decade ago. Like so many who constitute our hodge-podge population, I escaped, I loved, I dug in. I stayed for the exotic, warm quality of tropical nature. I remain because of the miracles I discover — and watch my toddler son discover — every day.

Chelle Koster Walton
Sanibel Island, Florida

THE WAY THIS BOOK WORKS

ORGANIZATION

For the sake of this book, the Gulf Coast of Florida is defined as that section on the state's western shores often lumped under the heading Southwest Florida. It is bounded on the north by the Manatee River and on the south by Ten Thousand Islands. This guide covers in depth the cities, towns, and communities from Bradenton–Sarasota to Naples–Marco Island.

I have sliced this delectable pie into four geographical regions, north to south: Sarasota Bay Coast, Charlotte Harbor Coast, Island Coast, and South Coast. Within these divisions, towns are listed in alphabetical order.

Eight chapters reveal to readers the multi-faceted world of Florida's glorious Gulf Coast: History, Transportation, Lodging, Culture, Dining, Recreation, Shopping, and Information. Each chapter begins with a regional overview that examines either separately, or in the context of a whole, that particular aspect of Gulf Coast living and vacationing.

A series of indexes at the back of the book provides easy access to information. The first, a standard index, lists entries and subjects in alphabetical order. Next, hotels, inns, and resorts are categorized by price. Restaurants are organized in two separate indexes, one by price, and one by type of cuisine.

LIST OF MAPS
The Gulf Coast of Florida
Gulf Coast Access Maps
Sarasota Bay Coast
Charlotte Harbor Coast
Island Coast
South Coast

PRICES
Rather than give specific prices, this guide rates dining and lodging options within a range.

Lodging prices normally are based on per person/double occupancy for hotel rooms; on per unit for efficiencies, apartments, cottages, suites, and villas. Price ranges reflect the difference in off-season and high-season. Generally, the colder the weather up north, the higher the cost of accommodations along the Coast. Rates can double during the course of a year. Many resorts offer off-season packages at special rates.

Pricing does not include the six percent Florida sales tax. Many large resorts add gratuities or maid charges. Some counties impose a tourist tax as well, proceeds from which are applied to beach and environmental maintenance.

If rates seem high for rooms on the Gulf Coast, it's partially because many resorts cater to families by providing kitchen facilities. Take into consideration what this could save you on dining bills. A star after the pricing designation indicates that accommodations include at least continental breakfast with the cost of lodging; a few abide by the American Plan of serving all meals.

Dining costs are figured upon a typical meal, including an appetizer, salad (extra when the menu is à la carte), entree, dessert, and coffee. To save money at the more expensive restaurants, look in this guide to see which ones offer "early bird specials." Restaurants at some large resorts add gratuities to the tab. This is also customary for large parties at most restaurants, so check your bill carefully before leaving a tip. Satisfied diners are expected to tip between 15 and 20 percent.

Heavy state taxes on liquor served in-house can mount up a drinking tab quickly. Paying as you drink is a wise measure to prevent sticker shock.

PRICE CODES

	Lodging	Dining
Inexpensive	Up to $50	Up to $15
Moderate	$50 to 110	$15 to $25
Expensive	$110 to 180	$25 to $35
Very Expensive	$180 and up	$35 or more

The following abbreviations are used for credit card information:

AE - American Express   DC - Diners Card
CB - Carte Blanche   MC - MasterCard
D - Discover Card   V -   Visa

AREA CODE

One area code covers the Gulf Coast of Florida: 813. Where the area code is omitted, that code applies. Only a few places listed in the eastern section of the Everglades have a different code, and that is so indicated.

TOURIST INFORMATION

Local visitors' bureaus, tourism development councils, and chambers of commerce are quite adept at the dissemination of materials and information about their area. These are listed in Chapter Eight, *Information*.

For information on the entire region and other parts of Florida, contact the Florida Tourism Bureau at 107 W. Gaines St., Suite 432, Tallahasee FL 32399-2000; 904-487-1462.

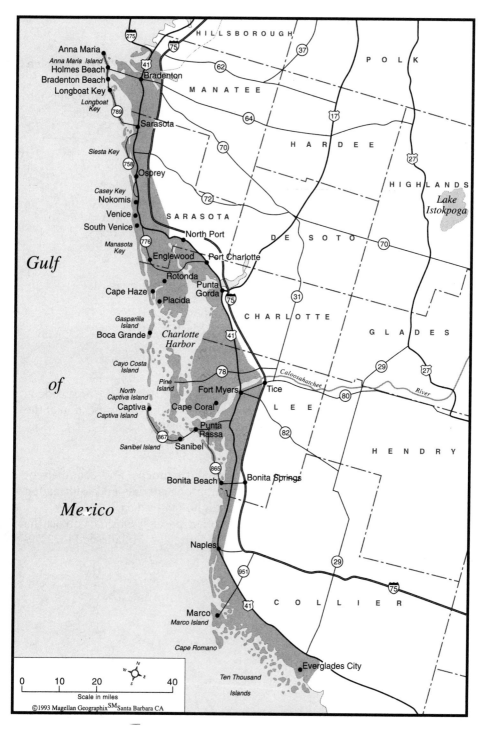

THE GULF COAST OF FLORIDA

The
GULF COAST
OF FLORIDA
Book

A Complete Guide

CHAPTER ONE

Mangroves, Man, and Magnates
HISTORY

The essence of Gulf Coast Florida seems to lie in a balance between two polar extremes: the ultimate both in natural wilderness and in social civility. To understand the region and the richness of its heritage, culture, and environment, one must understand its roots, learn the names, and revel in the legends of its past — a past steeped in romance, adventure, and power.

The story begins with a single mangrove tree, and evolves around man's need to conquer that tree's private world. Enter the main characters: Ambition, Wealth, and Social Grace. How does the story end? Happily, we can hope, with the modern rediscovery of the coast's unique natural and historical heritage.

Commercial fishing continues to sustain Gulf Coast residents as it did in the days of the ancient Caloosa Indians.

NATURAL HISTORY

FROM GRAINS OF SAND

"Each wave helps build a ridge of accumulating sand and shell that runs roughly parallel to the beach. Over a period of hundreds or thousands of years, a ridge may become a barrier island."

—Lynn Stone, Voyageurs Series', *Sanibel Island*, 1991

"On the floor is a straw mat. Under the mat is a layer of sand that has been tracked into the cottage and has sifted through the straw. I have thought some of taking the mat up and sweeping the sand into a pile and removing it, but have decided against it. This is the way keys form, apparently, and I have no particular reason to interfere."
—E.B. White, *On a Florida Key*, 1941.

Billions of years ago, the Florida peninsula existed only as a scattering of volcanic keys, akin to the Caribbean islands. The passing years, silt, and the sea's power eventually buried any evidence of these volcanic origins. What is now Florida remained submerged until some 20 million years ago, when matter build-up brought land to the surface in the form of new islands.

Ice-age sea fluctuations molded Florida into solid land, and islands continued to grow along its fringes. From a single grain of sand or mangrove sprout, they stabilized into masses of sand and forests comprised of leggy roots and finger shoots. As shells and marine encrustations accumulated, islands fell into formation along the Gulf Coast, protecting it from the battering of an abusive, storm-driven sea. Where the islands left gaps, the Gulf's waters scoured the shore to forge inlets, estuaries, bayous, creeks, and rivers. The sea chiseled a mottled, labyrinthine shoreline that kept the Gulf Coast a secret while the rest of the land was tamed.

During its infancy, the region hosted a slow parade of ever-changing creatures. In prehistoric graveyards, modern archaeologists have found mummified remains of rhinoceroses, crocodiles, llamas, camels, pigmy horses, saber-toothed tigers, mastodons, and great wooly mammoths — Florida's first winter visitors at the advent of the Ice Age. Another era brought giant armadillos, tapirs, and other South American creatures. Fauna and flora from these ancient eras survive today: cabbage palms (the state tree), saw palmettos, garfish, seahorses, horseshoe crabs, alligators, manatees, armadillos, and loggerhead turtles.

AN EARLY PICTURE

"In the bay of Juan Ponce De Leon, in the west side of the land, we meet with innumerable small islands, and several fresh streams: the land in general is drowned mangrove swamp.... From this place [Cape Romano, latitude 25:43] to latitude 26:30 are many inconsiderable inlets, all carefully laid down in the chart, here is Carlos Bay, and the Coloosa Hatchee, or Coloosa river, with the island San Ybell, where we find the southern entrance of Charlotte harbour...."

—Bernard Romans, 1775

One of the earliest recorders of Florida native life and topography, Bernard Romans is credited with naming Charlotte Harbor after the queen of England, his adopted homeland, and Cape Romano after himself. Earlier Spanish explorers and Native American vocabulary are responsible for other regional place names.

The Miracle of the Mangrove

The mangrove forest is both a fertile incubator and a marine graveyard, the home of an island construction crew and a vegetative ballet troupe. It is a self-sustaining world marked by vivid contrasts. The Mangrove Coast (as one local historian terms it) is fringed by red, black, and white species of the tree. Red mangroves strut along coastlines, canals, and island leesides, on graceful prop roots. At least they look graceful, until low tide reveals the oysters, barnacles, and tiny marine metropolises that keep them weighed down and seabound.

Further inland, black and white mangroves create thick, impenetrable forests that buffer waves, filter pollutants, send out shoots, and always busily build. Encrustations of shellfish grab algae, silt, and sand, creating rich soil out of decaying materials. Fish, crabs, and mollusks skitter among the roots, nibbling dinner, depositing eggs, and tending to their young. Birds rest and nest in the mangroves' scraggly branches, ready to dive-bomb for the fish on which they feed. Mother trees send their tubular offspring bobbing upon sea currents to find a foothold elsewhere and begin, perhaps, a new island.

The cycle is ancient and ongoing, threatened only by the chain saws of developers. In earlier times, these natural builders were leveled, in favor of cement seawalls. Strict regulations prohibit mangrove destruction today. The crucial role of the mangrove in the survival of Florida's sea life finally has been realized. And cherished.

The harbor was already the center of west coast life when the first explorers discovered it. Its deep waters and barrier-island protection made it most suitable to early aborigines and their predecessors, by creating a pocket of unusually mild climate.

Romans and his contemporaries found the Gulf Coast alive with wild turkeys, black bears, deer, golden panthers, bobcats, possums, raccoons, alligators, otters, lizards, and snakes. Wild boars and scrub cattle roamed, descendants of stock brought by Spanish missionaries. Birds and waterfowl of all varieties filled the skies and backbays, some permanent, some migrant. Majestic ospreys and bald eagles swooped; kites soared effortlessly; sandhill cranes dotted the countryside; wood storks nested; pelicans came in colors of brown, gray, and white; gulls, terns, and sandpipers patrolled seashores; cormorants, ducks, anhingas, ibises, egrets, roseate spoonbills, and herons fed among the mangroves.

Marine life flourished. Manatees effectively cleared waterways, dolphins frolicked in the waves, and mullet burst from bay waters like cannonshot. Tarpon, rays, snapper, snook, flounder, ladyfish, and mackerel churned the back waters. Grouper, triple tail, tuna, and shark lurked in deep waters offshore.

On land, a wide variety of vegetation was found. Sea grapes, mahoes, sea oats, knickerbean, and railroad vine anchored sandy coasts. Thick, impenetrable jungle clogged inland areas. Cabbage palms and gumbo limbo trees stood tallest in the profile. Citrus and date trees sprouted, transplanted from Spain.

Papayas grew, native to the region, along with indigenous flowering shrubs. In hardwood forests, pines climbed skyward and live oaks wore their eerie veils of Spanish moss. Cedars fringed islands along the Sarasota Bay Coast. Ferns and grasses carpeted the marshes. Swamplands hosted great cypress trees with bony knees and armfuls of parasitic plants: mistletoe, orchids, bromeliads, and epiphytes.

Primeval and teeming, Florida held an exotic and mysterious aura. The swamp nurtured all of life, from the Everglades along the lowlands of the Gulf Coast. It was a perfect ecosystem, designed by nature to withstand all forces, except man.

FACELIFTS AND IMPLANTS

With the arrival of the first settlers, the natural balance that existed along the Gulf Coast began to change. The Spanish brought citrus seedlings and livestock. Naturalists and growers introduced specimens from the north and south: mangoes, avocadoes, bougainvillea, hibiscus, frangipani, coconut palms, pineapples, sapodillas, tomatoes, and legumes. For the most part, these exotics proved harmless to the fragile environment.

Three non-native plants brought to the area in the past century have, however, harmed the ecosystem and changed the land's profile. The prolific *melaleuca* tree (or cajeput), *casuarina* (Australian pine), and Brazilian pepper, choke out the native vegetation upon which wildlife feeds, and harm both man and property. Many communities attempt to eradicate these noxious plants, especially the pepper tree.

The complexion of the West Coast was further changed by dredging and plowing. In times when swampland was equated with slimy monsters and slick realtors, developers and governments thought nothing of filling in the wetlands to create more buildable land. This, too, threw the ecosystem off balance. Fortunately, such mistakes were realized before their effects became irreversible. Today government strives to preserve, and even restore, the delicate balance of wetlands.

SOCIAL HISTORY

DATELINE: GULF COAST FLORIDA

The settlement of Florida's southwest coast can be traced like a dateline that begins on the shores of Sarasota Bay in 1841, and ends at Naples in 1887. At first glance, this time frame makes the region look young, without the gracious patina of age and the wrinkles of an interesting past. Common is the belief, in fact, that the Gulf Coast has no history because it lacks Williamsburg's colonial homes and Philadelphia's monuments.

True, the Gulf Coast's earliest settlers left no standing architecture. Termites, flimsy building styles, erosion, and tropical storms saw to that. But these early settlers did leave other proof of their existence, artifacts that date as far back as 10,000 years. If that isn't history, what is?

CALOOSA KINGDOM

A rchaeologists of this century have discovered remnants of early architecture and lifestyles in the shell mounds of the Caloosa and Timucuan tribes, who settled the coastlines more than 2,500 years ago. The Timucuans inhabited the Sarasota Bay Coast for many years and then migrated northward; the Caloosas later moved into the area around Sarasota and were headquartered around Charlotte Harbor.

Evidence of earlier civilizations has been found, placing Florida's first immigrants, possibly from Asia, in the upper Coast regions circa 8,200 B.C. Little is known about these early arrivals except that they used pointed spears.

Archaeological excavations and the writings of Spanish explorers give us a more complete picture of the Caloosa and other tribes who built shell mounds to bury their dead and debris. Popular consensus brings the two tribes to southern Florida from the Caribbean islands, relating them to the peaceful Arawak nation through lifestyle and evidence of sustained contact and trade. Similarities are also found between the Caloosas and South American tribes, leading some historians to consider Florida's tribes to be wayward relatives of the Mayans or Aztecs, given evidence of their great engineering skills. Others trace the connections to trade rather than origin.

The name Caloosa, or Calusa, was used first by Spanish conquerors, who understood the name of the tribe's chief to be Calos. They were said to be heavy-set people with hip-length hair, which men wore in a topknot. When clothed, men wore breeches of deerskin or woven palmetto fiber and women fashioned garments out of Spanish moss. They cultivated corn, pumpkins, squash, and tobacco; fished for mullet and mackerel with harpoons and palmetto-fiber nets; hunted for turkey, deer, and bear with bow-and-arrow, deerbone dirks, and Aztec weapons; and harvested wild sea grapes, fruit, yams, swamp cabbage (hearts of palm), and the coontie root, out of which they pounded flour for bread. Conchs and whelks were fashioned into tools for cooking and raw materials for building. They spent leisure time wrestling, celebrating the corn harvest, and worshipping the sun god.

Great men of the sea, the Caloosas built canoes that would best navigate the currents, and traveled in them to Caribbean islands and the Yucatan. A different style of *pirogue* took them along riverways and bay waters to visit villages of their own tribe, and those of other Nations.

Much knowledge about Caloosa ways comes from the son of a Spanish official stationed in Cartegana. The youngster, Hernando de Escalante Fontaneda, was shipwrecked along Caloosa shores en route to Spain. He lived among the tribe for 17 years, learned its language, and, upon returning to Spain in 1574, recorded its customs.

Information about Caloosa villages comes from the discoveries of Frank Hamilton Cushing, who explored Charlotte Harbor in 1895. He surmised that the Caloosas' piling homes of palmettos had perched upon shell mounds along river banks and coastlines. Terraces and steps bit into the towering mounds, where gardens and courts had been built. Man-made canals up to 30 feet wide connected neighboring villages. Cushing found religious structures atop some of the mounds. Excavations along the Gulf Coast continually provide new information about the region's Native inhabitants and their symbiotic relationship with nature.

SPANISH IMPOSITION

Greed and religious fervor eventually warped this seemingly idyllic picture, and peaceful fishermen became vicious warriors in order to preserve the life they knew. Juan Ponce de Leon first crashed the party in 1513, though conjecture blames early slavers for giving the Caloosas the bad attitude toward Europeans he encountered. Perhaps early slave traders headed north from the Caribbean, to replenish their supplies. Or, perhaps, the Amerindians' early hatred of the *conquistadores* was gained second hand, from trading with island natives. Whatever the reason, however, Ponce was "blacklisted" by the Caloosa shortly after he made his way to Bimini, said to be the land of treasure and a fountain of youth.

Ponce made his first two landings on Florida's east coast. The celebrated Easter-time event went off without a hitch, inspiring the conqueror to name the land after its profusion of spring flowers. However, his second landing, days later, was met by shell-tipped spears and bows-and-arrows. His three wounded sailors were the first Europeans known to shed blood in Florida. Ponce's *San Christoval* continued to the West Coast, where it stopped in the vicinity of Marco Island. Here one native astounded Ponce by speaking to him in Spanish — learned, perhaps from West Indies contacts. Impressed, Ponce allowed himself to be tricked by a marauding Native army in canoes, but escaped with the loss of only one life.

The next stop for Ponce de Leon was an island the Spaniards named Matanza for the profusely bloody battles they there effected. Still treasureless, and middle-aged, Ponce then returned to Puerto Rico to plot a new scheme. In 1521, he set out to establish a Gulf Coast colony as a base for treasure explorations. (His exact landing spot is contested by Punta Gorda and Fort Myers historians, both of whom wish to claim Ponce for their own.) Warned, perhaps by smoke signals, the party that Ponce crashed this time was angry. The

Caloosa's arrows pierced the heavy armor of the Spaniards, killing and wounding many, including the great seeker of youth himself. Rushed to Havana for medical attention, Ponce died there at the age of 60.

Lust for gold overcame common sense as more explorers and invaders followed in Ponce's tragic footsteps. In 1539, Hernando De Soto sailed from Havana and headed up the Gulf Coast seeking, it would seem, a way to confuse future historians of his whereabouts. Three different crew members described the expedition three different ways. The Smithsonian Institution published a report that some locals still refute, which claims De Soto landed first on Longboat Key and then, looking for fresh water, headed toward Tampa Bay. Others are convinced his first landfall was at Fort Myers Beach. De Soto set up his first mainland camp, according to the Smithsonian, at an abandoned Native village at the mouth of the Manatee River, near modern-day Bradenton. Wherever the landing took place, he scoured the Coast for gold, all the while torturing and killing Native Americans who would not, could not, lead him to it.

Sarasota and its environs embrace the Smithsonian study's findings. Some say the name of the town itself, initially written as "Sara Sota", comes from the conqueror. Others prefer a more romantic legend regarding his fictional daughter, Sara. Sarasota's first hotel, in any case, took its name from De Soto. Near Bradenton, a nature park marks the alleged spot of his first landing.

In 1565, Pedro Menendez de Aviles came to the Gulf Coast, searching for a son lost to shipwreck and a group of Spaniards being held captive by the Caloosas. After befriending chief Calos with flattery and gifts, aided by one of Calos' Spanish captives, he built a fort and mission at a spot called San Anton, believed to have been on Pine Island. But Menendez angered and insulted the great chieftain by rejecting his sister as a wife and allying himself with enemy tribes. Sensing Calos' anger, Menendez tricked the leader into captivity and had him beheaded. When Menendez later executed Calos' son and predecessor, along with 11 of his subchiefs, tribesmen burned their own villages, forcing the settlers to bail out in search of food.

The century that followed is considered the Golden Age of the Caloosas. It was marked by lack of European disturbance and great cultural advances, heightened by the input of those Spanish captives who had refused to be saved by Menendez's rescue party, and others who found the Caloosa lifestyle preferable to "civilization."

Eventually, peaceful trading softened the mistrust between Spanish settlers and the Caloosas. The two races went into business together as Cuban immigrants began building their fishing industry around Charlotte Harbor.

The Caloosas had won the war against Spanish inquisitors and impositionists, but were defenseless against the diseases the Europeans brought with them. By the turn of the 19th century, smallpox and other diseases had killed most of the Caloosas; the others were absorbed by inbreeding with the Cubans and newly arriving tribes. The most prominent of the latter were the Seminoles, a mixture of Georgian Creek, African, and Spanish bloodlines. They hold the distinction of being the last tribe to make peace with the U.S. government.

THE VARMINT ERA

"A haunt of the picaroons of all nations," wrote explorer James Grant Forbes in 1772. He spoke of Charlotte Harbor — layover, if not home, for every scoundrel who passed by its island-clotted shores. The Gulf Coast's maze of forbidding bayous and barely navigable waters made it a favorite hideout for escaped criminals, bootleggers, government refugees, smugglers, and — that favorite of all local folk characters — the buccaneer.

Pirate legend colors the pages of local history books in shades of blood red and doubloon gold. Besides willing to residents a certain cavalier spirit, these pirates have left, if one believes the tales, millions of dollars in buried treasure. "...After researching the subject in 1950...then State Attorney General Ralph E. Odum estimated that some $165 million is still buried beneath Florida's sands and waters," reports the *Miami Herald's Florida Almanac*, "$30 million of it originally the property of Jose Gaspar."

Besides the legendary Gaspar, other picaresque names sound along the Gulf Coast: Jean La Fitte, of New Orleans fame; Bru Baker, Gaspar's Pine Island cohort; and a dark soul named Black Caesar, who represented Jose's Sanibel Island contingent. Henry Castor supposedly buried treasure on Egmont Key in the mid-1700s. Local legend places the notorious Calico Jack Rackham and his pirate lover, Anne Bonny, on the shores of Fort Myers Beach for a playful honeymoon. Black Augustus lived and died a hermit on Mound Key, to the south. On Panther Key, John Gomez, Gaspar's self-acclaimed cabin boy, lived to be 122 and sold maps to Gasparillan gold to many a gullible treasure-hunter.

More accurate historical records replace (or at least cohabitate) island pirate havens with crude Spanish fishing *ranchos*, which cropped up as early as the 1600s. The camps provided Cuban traders with salted mullet and roe to eat. They consisted of thatched shacks, some built on pilings in shallow waters, where families lived, according to customs inspector Henry B. Crews, "in a state of Savage Barbarism with no associate but the Seminole Indians and the lowest class of refugee Spaniards who from crime have most generally been compelled to abandon the haunts of civilized life."

Ice-making and railroads changed the direction of fish exportation from southern destinations to the northlands. Punta Gorda, with the area's first railroad station, became the center for the shipment of fresh fish. Major fish-shipping companies built stilt houses for the more than 200 men who harvested their mullet crops. These structures straddled shallows from Charlotte Harbor to Ten Thousand Islands, providing homes for the fishermen and their families until the late 1930s, when modern roads and the burning of Punta Gorda's Long Dock brought the era to a close. Less than a dozen of the historic fish shacks have survived hurricanes, erosion, and the state's determination to tear them down as a public nuisance. They strut the shallows of Charlotte Harbor, in greatest concentration off the shore of North Captiva Island.

"It is highly important that no person should be permitted to settle on the Islands forming 'Charlotte Harbor'... which are of no value for the purpose of agriculture, being in general formed of sand and shells," advised Assistant Adjutant General Captain Lorenzo Thomas in 1844. Nonetheless, out of this era of varmints sprouted a tradition of farming. Coconuts, citrus, tomatoes, and other crops were raised, despite hardship and heartbreak, as plucky pioneers trickled in to coax their livelihood from a hostile environment.

Kingdom of Gasparilla

Of all the rum-chugging and throat-slashing visitors to have set foot upon Southwest Florida's tolerant shores, Jose Gaspar (known by the more properly pirate-sounding name of "Gasparilla") is the one remembered most fondly. Jose set up headquarters, it is said, on Gasparilla Island, where Boca Grande now sits. In his time it was called High Town, where he built his palmetto palace, furnished with the finest of booty. Low Town he placed on a separate island, so as to distance himself from the crude lifestyles of his rowdy shipmates. On Cayo Costa stood Gasparilla's fort.

Legends say Gasparilla got his start as a pirate after some nasty business with the wife of a crown prince. He gave up his cushy position as admiral of the Spanish navy for the hardships of life at sea and in the jungles of late 19th-century Florida.

His address may have changed, but his love of beautiful women did not. He kidnapped the loveliest and wealthiest of them from captured ships and whisked them off to another Gulf Coast island named for its inhabitants — Captiva — until ransom money arrived.

Gasparilla took to High Town the most beautiful of his captives, to woo them with fine wines, jewels, and Spanish poetry. One object of his affection, a Mexican princess named Josefa, would have nothing to do with such a barbarian. Finally, driven to madness by her insults, Gasparilla beheaded his beloved. He carried her body to another key in his island fiefdom, where he buried her with remorse and sand. He named the island Josefa, which, through the years and the twistings of rum-swollen tongues, has been perverted to Useppa. And so the exclusive island is called today.

Nearby Sanibel Island, according to one legend, got its name from the abandoned lover of Jose's gunner. However, variations abound and improve with each telling. The legend began with the ramblings of old "Panther Key John" Gomez, and was perpetuated by railroad press agents and optimistic treasure hunters.

Many serious historians doubt the existence of a man named Gasparilla, but agree that one of the many Gulf Coast pirates may have robbed Gasparilla Island of its name. Others hold tenaciously to the legend, plying coastal sands with shovels and dredges in search of his ill-gotten booty.

YEARS OF DISCONTENT

The bloody years of the Wars of Indian Removal began in 1821, when Andrew Jackson, then governor of the territory, decided to claim northern Florida from the Seminole tribes that wreaked havoc on American settlers. By 1837, fighting had spread to the southern reaches of the peninsula and two forts were built upriver from present-day Fort Myers. The following year, the government reached an agreement with the Seminoles, restricting them to mainland areas along the Charlotte Harbor Coast, Caloosahatchee River, and south.

News of imminent peace prompted Josiah Gates to build a hotel on the banks of the Manatee River, near modern-day Bradenton, in anticipation of the influx of settlers from Fort Brooke (Tampa) the treaty would bring. A modest community rose up around this precursor of the Gulf Coast's resort reputation. Families of soldiers and wealthy Southern planters settled in the area. The latter brought their slaves and built sugarcane plantations on vast expanses of land, which they bought for $1.25 an acre.

Sarasota got its first permanent settler in 1842. William Whitaker, a fisherman, built his home on Yellow Bluffs, overlooking Sarasota Bay. He and his new wife, daughter of one of the Manatee planters, populated the new settlement with ten children and later went into cattle ranching and farming.

The year after the peace treaty was signed, a tribe of Seminoles attacked a settlement across the river from their village, on the same site as present-day Fort Myers. This battle, the so-called Harney Point Massacre, rekindled the war. Fort Harvie was built near the site of the violent attack. Chief Billy Bowlegs led his people in evasive tactics through the wild and mysterious Everglades, but by 1842, the government had captured 230 of his people and shipped them west. Further pursuit was abandoned. Only Fort Harvie and one other fortification remained operational. A new agreement contained the Seminoles along the Caloosahatchee and declared the islands off limits, to protect the fishermen and their families. The treaty made no mention of the swampland, probably because the government considered it useless; the Seminoles assumed the territory was theirs.

By 1848, three years after Florida's admission to the Union as the 27th state, there was a resurgence of interest in the wetlands. The government envisioned drainage projects to create more land, and offered the Seminoles $250 each to relocate out West. When they refused, a systematic plan to conquer them went into effect.

The plan included the repair of Fort Harvie, which was renamed Fort Myers after a U.S. colonel who served for many years in Florida and was about to marry the commanding general's daughter. Manpower was increased there, and the fort was reinforced and enlarged. Scouting parties stalked the Seminoles, but usually found only the remains of abandoned and burned villages.

In December, 1855, soldiers destroyed Billy Bowlegs' prize banana patch, and he and his people retaliated. Fort Harvie then became the center of war activity. The government placed a bounty on the head of any Seminole brought to the fort. It upped its offer to $1,000 per warrior and $100 per woman and child, if they would leave the area. Finally, in 1858, after the enemy had captured his granddaughter and other women of the tribe, Billy agreed. Thus, 37 years of killing and deception were ended. Fort Harvie was abandoned and the remaining Seminoles, mostly of the Miccosukee tribe, dispersed deep into the Everglades. Today they live on reservations, earning a subsistence from tourism, bingo, and fishing. Farmers, planters, fishermen, and cattlemen continued peacefully in their trades after the wars ended, though government vigilance against alliances with the Seminoles forced some of the *ranchos* to close during the war's final years.

In the late 1850s, Virginia planter Captain James Evans bought Fort Myers on the auction block. He brought his slaves to work the fields he envisioned — of tropical fruits, coconut palms, coffee, and other exotic plants. The Civil War interrupted this vision, sending him back to his homeland. Florida joined the Confederacy in 1861. West Coast inhabitants generally remained uninvolved until a federal blockade at Key West cut off supplies.

CATTLE KINGS, CARPETBAGGERS, AND CRACKERS

Jacob Summerlin epitomized the Florida Cattle King. He dressed in a cowboy hat, leather boots, a beard, and trail dust. Having established a steady trade between Florida and ports south before the Civil War, Summerlin was well-positioned to provide the Confederate army with contraband beef. Working with his blockade-running partner, James McKay, Sr., he drove his cattle from inland Florida to Punta Rassa, where the causeway from Sanibel Island makes landfall today. There he sold his scrub cattle, descendants of livestock left by early Spaniards. The U.S. Navy eventually learned of these illegal dealings and stationed itself at Sanibel and Punta Rassa. In spite of that attempt to interrupt their trade, however, the men sold 25,000 steers to the Confederates between 1861 and 1865.

Jacob Summerlin lived by the seat of his pants, driving cattle to Punta Rassa and collecting big bags of Cuban gold, which he spent at the end of the line on drinking and gaming. In 1874, he built the Summerlin House at Punta Rassa, a place where he and his men could bunk, and invest in frivolity the great profits of the business.

The rough, free-and-easy lifestyle of the cowboy (or cow hunter as he was often called) attracted young post-Civil-War drifters. In addition, Summerlin's success lured Civil War officers into the prosperous life of the cattle boss, including Captain F.A. Hendry, founder of an ongoing Fort Myers dynasty. Into the 1900s, the cowboys drove their herds through the streets of downtown Fort Myers, past the homes of wealthy investors and bankers. Between 1870 and 1880, they sold 165,000 head of cattle at Punta Rassa for over $2 million.

Post-war Reconstruction brought other settlers to Florida's West Coast. Judah P. Benjamin, one notable rebel refugee who served as secretary of state to the Confederacy, ducked indictment as a war criminal by hiding out in Florida. His one-week-long refuge at the old Gamble plantation, near Bradenton, ensured that landmark's preservation by the United Daughters of the Confederacy.

To Fort Myers first came the vultures, to pick clean the fort of coveted building materials. Then came men who remembered the old fort in its heyday and hoped to settle with their families in this promised land of plenty. The first settler, Captain Manuel A. Gonzalez, had run a provisions boat from Tampa during the Seminole War. He and his family moved from Key West with another family, named Vivas. Other war officers and refugees settled in and around the ruins of the old fort, planting gardens, opening stores, and living a blissful existence unknown elsewhere in the devastated South.

James Evans returned to find his land comfortably occupied. After struggling in the courts to keep the land out of government hands, he split it with the squatters in exchange for a share of his legal fees. In 1872, the first school was built. County government was centered 270 miles away, in Key West.

Fort Myers' thriving cattle-shipping business precipitated Sanibel Island's first permanent structure, a lighthouse built in 1884. Its caretaker's cottages represent prime examples of Cracker or so-called Old Florida style architecture.

Some historians credit the cow hunters with contributing the name Cracker to early Florida settlers. They say it derives from the cracking of the long whips men used to drive their herds. Others say it originates with the Georgia settler, who cracked corn for his staple hush puppies, corn pone, and fritters.

Though less romantic, the latter theory most likely tells the most truth. Georgians, in fact, did drift down to southwest Florida, most notably the Knight clan, which founded a settlement at Horse and Chaise, named by seamen describing a landmark clump of trees. (The name was changed to Venice in 1888 by developer Frank Higel, who was reminded of the Italian city by the area's many bayous and creeks.)

The Homestead Act, passed in 1862, entitled each settler in Florida to 160 acres of land, provided they built a home and tended the land for five years. The act brought, as it was meant to, a flood of intrepid settlers into the area, from all segments of the Eastern Seaboard. They built rough palmetto huts, burned cow chips to ward off the mosquitoes that carried yellow fever, ate raccoon purloo and turtle steaks, and traveled by foot or boat. They stubbornly outlasted heat, hurricanes, and freezes that stymied a number of enterprises: sugar refining, fish oil production, and pineapple and citrus shipping.

If anything, Florida's cow hunters proved detrimental to the agriculturally-based enterprises associated with the Crackers of the Sarasota Bay region. There they allied themselves with greedy land speculators who dishonestly nullified the beneficial effects of the Homestead Act. By 1883, speculators had discovered a loophole in Florida's land development legislation, namely the Swamp Land Act. It allowed them to purchase overflowed land at rock-bottom prices, while overriding homestead claims. They succeeded in declaring arable property swampland, and ultimately bought up a good 90 percent of present-day Manatee County, much of which had been worked for years by the hardy pioneers. Together, the speculators and the cattlemen fought farmers' protests against free-ranging — the practice of letting herds roam and feed without restriction. A Sara Sota Vigilance Committee formed in opposition and, by the time the fighting ended, two men lay dead.

As thatch homes gave way to wooden farmhouses — a tin-roofed, vernacular style today termed Cracker — West Coast settlements entered a new era, an era that made "riffraff" out of Crackers, rich men out of schemers, and exclusive getaways out of crude, frontier towns.

AT THE DROP OF A NAME

When your first guests are Juan Ponce de Leon and Hernando de Soto, who do you invite next? The standard has been set and it won't do to host just anybody. So began West Coast Florida's tradition for larger-than-life visitors with impressive names and pedigrees, all of whom just as impressively impacted the region's development. Names like Thomas Edison, Henry Ford, Harvey Firestone, John and Charles Ringling, Charles Lindbergh, Teddy Roosevelt, Henry DuPont, Andrew Mellon, Rose Cleveland, and Shirley Temple are among the wide array of Gulf Coast winterers. Their fame and followings greatly accelerated the slow process of frontier discovery. It quickly promoted the Gulf Coast from its stature as crude and backward, to one of avant-garde and exclusive. It brought the "cutting-edge" elite. They set national trends by declaring new hot spots — fresh, wild, unspoiled places about which no one else knew, especially the *paparazzi*. It was they who balanced the very wild Coast with a very civilized clientele. The area's natural endowments of fish, fowl, and game attracted adventurers, fishermen, and hunters with the means to make the long, slow journey.

The first and most influential name in Gulf Coast retrospective is Thomas Edison. Disappointed by the cold winters of St. Augustine, Florida, the ailing inventor embarked upon a scouting cruise along the Gulf Coast in 1885, the same year the town became incorporated. As Edison sailed along the Caloosahatchee River, he sighted a stand of bamboo trees. Then and there he decided to move to Fort Myers. And he wanted that lot.

The bamboo worked well for filament in Edison's light bulb experiments, and the climate bolstered his failing health, helping to add another 46 years to his life. On the banks of the Caloosahatchee the inventor fashioned his ideal winter home (Seminole Lodge), complete with laboratory and tropical gardens. Holder of more than 1,000 patents, the genius experimented with rare plants in his search to produce inexpensive rubber for his friend, tire mogul Harvey Firestone. So enamored with this town was Edison, that he persuaded Firestone to spend winters in Fort Myers. And he set up fellow visionary, Henry Ford, on an estate next to his. Edison, a self-styled botanist, is responsi-

Social residents in early 20th-century Fort Myers — including next-door-neighbor, Thomas Edison — gathered at Henry Ford's winter home for foot-stomping square dances.

ble for the frequently photographed row of royal palms lining the street that eventually ran past his home, McGregor Boulevard, thereby earning the town its nickname, City of Palms.

Meanwhile, the Florida Mortgage and Investment Company — connected with distinctive Scottish names such as the archbishop of Canterbury and estate owner Sir John Gillespie — lured a colony of politically disgruntled Scotsmen to young Sara Sota: a paradise of genteel estates, bountiful orange groves, and cheap land. Or so the brochures promised. Rather than the ready-made manor houses and Garden of Eden the colonists had read about, however, they found food and building materials in short supply. Only by the kindness of the Whitakers and other pioneers did they survive their first month. Then the Gulf Coast's unpredictable winter weather dealt a final, cold blow, causing most of the colonists to return to their homeland. Those who stayed, however, brought life to the struggling village and sparked it with a determined spirit.

Most influential amongst the Scottish ranks was John Hamilton Gillespie, son of Sir John. He built the city's first hotel, the De Soto, became its first mayor in 1902, and is responsible for introducing to Florida the game of golf. Gillespie transplanted the game from his homeland, first by building a two-hole links down Main Street in Sarasota, near his hotel. He later built the area's first real course and clubhouse, nearby.

It was an American woman, however, who finally and firmly upgraded Sarasota's image. At the turn of the century, the name Mrs. Potter (Berthe) Palmer stood for social elitism — not only in her hometown, Chicago, but also in London and Paris, where she kept homes and socialized with royalty. When the widowed socialite decided to visit Sarasota in 1910, hearts palpitated: she could make or break the new town. Enchanted by the area's beauty and the town's quaintness, Mrs. Palmer immediately bought 13 acres that eventually grew into 140,000. She built her home, The Oaks, and a cattle ranch in a community south of Sarasota called Osprey, and from there proceeded to spread the word.

Mrs. Palmer's much publicized love affair with the Gulf Coast drew the attention of John and Charles Ringling, the youngest of the illustrious circus family's seven sons. The two brothers, in a contest of one-upmanship, began buying property around town. They became active in civic affairs, built bridges to Sarasota's islands, and stoked the economy by making the town the winter home for their Ringling Circus. John Ringling especially, with his wife, Mabel, lent Sarasota a new worldliness born of their extensive travels and love of European art.

The fate of the Charlotte Harbor Coast lay mostly in the hands of one powerful man, Henry B. Plant. The West Coast's counterpart to Henry Flagler — builder of the East Coast's railroad and great hotels — Henry B. Plant brought the railway to Tampa, where he built a fabulous resort of his own, always in competition with Flagler. At the same time, Florida Southern Railway extended its tracks to some unknown, unsettled spot in the wilderness of Charlotte Harbor's shores. Its Punta Gorda Hotel reigned shortly as the latest posh outpost for wealthy sportsmen and adventurers, counting Andrew Mellon and W.K. Vanderbilt among its patrons. But in 1897, Plant decided the town's deep-water port and resort posed too much competition for his Tampa enterprises. So he choked the life out of a thriving commercial and resort town by severing the rails, which he now owned, to Punta Gorda's Long Dock.

Another man who influenced the development of the Gulf Coast's discovery and transportation system came to town in 1911. John M. Roach, Chicago streetcar magnate and owner of Useppa Island, introduced Barron Collier to the area. Collier eventually bought Useppa from his friend and there established the Useppa Inn and Izaak Walton Club. Both attracted tarpon fishing enthusiasts the likes of Shirley Temple, Gloria Swanson, Mae West, Herbert Hoover, Zane Grey, and Mary Roberts Rinehart, who then bought nearby Cabbage Key.

Collier went on to transfuse life into the South Coast by underwriting the completion of the Tamiami Trail, stalled on its route from Tampa to Miami. He acquired land throughout the county that today bears his name, after earlier attempts by Louisville publisher Walter Haldeman had failed to put Naples on the map.

Fort Myers enshrines its history with its Mediterranean-style train depot, completed in 1923.

Along the Gulf Coast of Florida, Collier bought more than a million acres, much of it under the infamous Swamp Act. Though he dreamed of development on the scale of Flagler and Plant, anti-corporation outcry, hurricanes, the Depression, and war brought him death before success. His sons inherited his kingdom, which they ruled with a heart for the unique environment their father so loved. Collier's influence led to the discovery of the Gulf Coast as a refuge for crowd-weary stars and illuminati. These islands still are popular with the rich and famous who seek anonymity.

But what about the ordinary people — the Native Americans, fishermen, cattlemen, Crackers, pioneers, and common folk — who loved this land long before it became fashionable to do so? For the most part, they lived side by side with this new brand of resident, called the "winterer" or "snowbird." They became their fishing guides, cooks, and innkeepers. In some cases, their heads were turned by their brush with wealth. In other instances, heightened standards pulled the curtain on crude lifestyles, especially for the cow hunter, whose boisterousness and preference for free-running stock hurried his extinction.

Sometimes the common folk protested big-bucks development; then they became classified as riffraff. The "Cracker" label today, despite those peoples' enriching influence on architecture and cuisine, is considered an insult by some native Floridians.

BOOMS, BURSTS AND OTHER EXPLOSIONS

The Gulf Coast's resort reputation came of age at the turn of the century. Sarasota's De Soto, the Punta Gorda Hotel, Boca Grande's Gasparilla Inn, the Useppa Inn, Fort Myers' Royal Palm Hotel, the Naples Hotel, and the Marco Inn pioneered the hotel field, and hosted visitors in styles from bare bones to bend-over-backwards. They sparked an era touched with Gatsbian glamor, giddiness, and graciousness.

The Gulf Coast's halcyon days peaked in the early 1920s, as the state entered a decade known as The Great Florida Land Boom. Growth came quickly to the young communities of Bradenton, Sarasota, Fort Myers, and Naples. Having struggled for so long to attract residents and commerce, the good people of the Gulf Coast grew dizzy with the whirl of growth and success.

Sarasota's population, according to the 1910 census, was 840; before the 1920s drew to a close, almost 8,400 people called it home. In the meantime, the city shaped itself with schools, sidewalks, streets, a newspaper, a pier, an airfield, and the establishment of its own county, having split from Bradenton's Manatee County. A bridge to Siesta Key created a whole new element to the town's personality by plugging it into the Gulf and attracting a seaside resort trade.

World War I briefly interfered. Prohibition brought to the Coast yet another roguish character in the form of the rumrunner. Homes and hotels popped up like toadstools after a summer rain shower. Increased lodging options opened the Gulf Coast to a wider range of vacationers. No longer a socialite's haven, the average traveler could now afford Florida's Gulf Coast. A new class of winterer known as the "Tin Can Tourist" arrived in force, pulling mobile homes, trailers, and campers. Tourist camps sprang up overnight and Southwest Florida became Everyman's paradise. Real estate profits added to the lure of tourism, and many visitors decided to remain there permanently.

The 1920s created Charlotte County along the Charlotte Harbor Coast. A bridge crossed the Peace River between the pioneer towns of Charlotte Harbor and Punta Gorda, spurring growth and spawning subdivisions by the score.

Fort Myers became the seat of a new county named for Robert E. Lee. Population grew from 3,600 to 9,000 between 1920 and 1930, boosted by the completion of the Tamiami Trail in 1928. Fort Myers grew from a raucous cattle town to a modern city with electricity, telephone lines, and a railroad. The Royal Palm Hotel treated guests to a regal departure from the cow trails that ran adjacent to property. A country club put Fort Myers on the golfing map, and a bridge to Estero Island's beautiful beaches further boosted tourism. Real adventurers took the ferry to Sanibel Island to be accommodated at the Casa Ybel or Palm Hotel.

South of Fort Myers, Survey was renamed Bonita Springs, a farming community. In 1923, Naples (previously a well-kept secret among buyers from such far-away places as Kentucky and Ohio, and distinctive vacationers from upper echelons) became a city just in time to feel the effects of the tourism boom. The same year, Collier County seceded from Lee. The Naples Pier, which had served as a landing point for visitors and cargo since 1887, was upstaged by a railroad depot in 1927.

Gulf Coast skies had never been sunnier. Visitors spent lots of money. Residents prospered. Real estate prices soared. It seemed too good to be true. And indeed it was.

Along the Gulf Coast, the Great Depression affected each community differently. A 1926 hurricane hit Fort Myers, worsening a state of already deepening debt. In Sarasota, John Ringling suffered severe financial losses, from which he never recovered. On the South Coast, however, national economics had little impact upon a surge of awareness sparked by the opening of the Tamiami Trail.

The Depression stymied the full head of steam at which the Gulf Coast had progressed during the 1920s, but in many ways affected the region less drastically than it did other parts of the country. Since it most tragically affected the middle class, wealthy Gulf Coast residents were largely spared. Works Progress Administration (WPA) recovery projects built Fort Myers its Waterfront Park, Yacht Basin, and first hospital. And, despite serious financial problems, Ringling kept his promises to build bridges and an art museum. The WPA funded the building of Bayfront Park, a municipal auditorium, and the erstwhile Lido Beach Casino along the Sarasota Bay Coast.

By the beginning of World War II, Southwest Florida had firmly joined the 20th century with modern conveniences that made it popular among retirees. New golf courses accommodated active seniors, who participated in the civic affairs of their second home communities, often more vigorously than they had in those of their first homes.

Professional golf tournaments took place, first in Naples and then along the Coast, making the area golf's winter home. Spring baseball camps later brought another spectator sport to this land of year-round recreation.

Warmth-seekers turned their attention to the Gulf Coast's islands and beachfronts. Golfing communities and waterfront resorts swallowed up the farming and fishing industries. High-rise condominiums replaced Cracker houses, posh resorts toppled tourist fishing camps, and the Gulf Coast continued to grow — albeit not quite as loudly or erratically as in pre-Depression times.

Some areas learned to control their growth. Sanibel Island served as a model, taking control of its fate after a causeway connected it to the mainland in 1963. It incorporated and introduced measures to protect wilderness areas, as well as limiting the takeover by developers.

The southward expansion of Interstate 75 during the 1970s and 1980s changed the Gulf Coast from a series of towns connected by two-lane roads, to

Manatee County Convention and Visitors Bureau

Sugar built the antebellum plantations along Bradenton's Braden River, perhaps literally in some cases. It is rumored that molasses was mixed into the Gamble Mansion's tabby (seashell) mortar.

The elements — not Yankee soldiers — have reduced Braden Castle, the Tara of the Gulf Coast, to romantic ruins.

communities keeping pace with the world. Communication and transportation systems improved. Commercial development spread out to the freeway corridor, leaving downtown areas to fade in bygone glories. Light industry and winter-weary entrepreneurs relocated. Post-secondary schools worked to prepare local youth for the changing marketplace. Construction and tourism industries continued to fortify. The Gulf Coast seemed to remain untouched by the fluctuations of the American economy. Life was removed from the realities of urban blight. Northerners fled to the Gulf Coast to escape overcrowding, smog, and crime. In decades past, this had caused unnatural development in some of the metropolitan areas. The delicate balance of infrastructure, human services, nature, heritage preservation, and the arts went akilter. The Coast lived very much in the present, deaf to the demands of residents, both human and otherwise.

New trends of eco-tourism and social responsibility finally amplified the voices of the few, who had screamed over the decades for preservation of the environment against tourism and cultural sterility. Sarasota and Naples served as cultural prototypes; Sanibel and Gasparilla islands provided environmental models. The 1990s saw the dawn of an awareness of the fragility of the West Coasts' islands, wetlands, and shorelines. At the same time, interest in the area's past grew, and movements were launched to preserve those architectural treasures spared by the bulldozer. Finally, the dipping economic trend affected the Gulf Coast. Construction slowed its racing pulse and unemployment figures jumped as Northerners arrived, looking for nonexistent jobs in this legendary land of treasure and youth.

All of these factors contribute to a new perspective on today's Gulf Coast. Such economic fluctuations give city planners occasion to pause and rethink. Future growth is being mapped out with more care than ever before. Dying downtown neighborhoods and abandoned Cracker homes are being revitalized, recognized as an important part of the area's heritage. Government is drawing into its blueprints the need for environmental preservation, cultural enrichment, and historic renovation. With economic recovery comes a more enlightened attitude that promises to return the sunshine to Gulf Coast skies, free of the past's blinding clouds. The grain of sand and the mangrove pod, from which this land was wrought, once again influence the future.

MAP OF CHARACTER

The personality of each of the myriad cities, towns, communities, and villages along the Gulf Coast is rooted in an individualized past from which its particular, unique character is tailored.

In **Bradenton** and surrounding mainland communities, two pioneering influences dictated a low-key attitude and light development. The first were the wealthy plantation owners of the 1840s. They made Manatee County the largest area in the state for sugar and molasses production. These aristocratic

Oak-canopied Old Bradenton remembers its past at Manatee Village Historical Park, a collection of vintage structures.

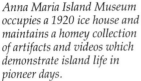

Anna Maria Island Museum occupies a 1920 ice house and maintains a homey collection of artifacts and videos which demonstrate island life in pioneer days.

families set the social standards of the town until the Civil War turned the lucrative sugar industry sour. Nineteenth-century land speculators who exploited Florida's Swamp Act had an opposite, stunting effect on the area's development. By having homestead property dishonestly declared wetlands, they prevented agricultural expansion and delayed its byproduct, the building of railroads.

Most of Bradenton's growth has occurred since 1970, when tourism and shipping into its deep-water Port Manatee became major sources of income. Today, preservation of the Gamble Plantation and original village sites, along with pier and waterfront restoration projects, make Bradenton a vital city, textured with an interesting past.

Fishing, resorts, and heterogeneous neighborhoods mark the flavor of the three incorporated towns of ***Anna Maria Island: Anna Maria, Holmes Beach,*** and ***Bradenton Beach.***

Longboat Key was mentioned often on the maps and journals of early Spanish explorers. It supposedly got its name from the longboats that De Soto's landing party used to come ashore. Aside from one tucked-away village with a salty, local flavor, Longboat Key is known for its prim-and-properness. It,

Circus magic touches Sarasota wherever the Ringling brothers left their mark. Here, a plaque remembers the role of elephants and circus giants in building the town.

The Town the Circus Built

"The circus comes as close to being the world in microcosm as anything I know; in a way it puts all the rest of show business in the shade. Its magic is universal and complex."
—E.B. White, *Ring of Times*, March 22, 1956

Rumor has it that Sarasota's barrier islands of **Bird Key** and St. **Armands Key** came into John Ringling's possession in a poker game. Tales of the circus master's influence on the area's development grow to mythic proportions: elephants that built bridges, midgets who built fortunes, and an eccentric who built himself an Italian palace. However true the legends, John Ringling, during the 20 years after he came to Sarasota to house his circus in winter, demonstrated a three-ring influence over the city and its barrier islands.

After falling in love with the fledgling village and purchasing real estate offshore, Ringling erected his lavish Ca'd'zan (House of John in Italian, modeled after a Venetian *palazzo*). He undertook the construction of a causeway to **Lido Key**, thus filling the areas between existing islands. He dreamed of a city park and shopper's haven on **St. Armands**. For **Longboat Key** he envisioned a Ritz-Carlton. In **Venice**, he established a world-famous clown school. With unbridled fervor, he set out to own a fine collection of baroque art.

The dreams Ringling failed to realize before he died in 1936 were not abandoned. The causeway was completed and donated to the state. St. Armands Circle today is famed for its shops. The skeleton of what was to be the world's finest hotel sat rusting on Longboat Key for years, until reborn as a modern resort. The John and Mabel Ringling Museum of Art encompasses acres of bayside estate. Its collection includes baroque statuary, original Rubens, rose gardens, Ca'd'Zan, a circus museum, and an antique Italian theater.

Aside from John Ringling's concrete legacy to Sarasota, he bequeathed an undying commitment to beauty, fantasy, art, and theater. The circus remains an important industry in Sarasota, with 18 companies now headquartered in the vicinity. Theaters and galleries thrive, thanks to Ringling's patronage of the arts. Without his influence, the entire Coast might well have remained a cultural frontier.

along with **Sarasota** and its bracelet of other keys, acclaim John Ringling as its godfather. He is responsible for putting the area on the cultural map. His arrival in 1911 sparked Sarasota's first land boom.

Remote **Siesta Key** resisted settlement until the turn of the century, when a hotel launched the island's reputation as a restful place. A bridge built in 1917 finally brought permanent residents.

The Webb family first arrived in the Sarasota area in 1867 to plant the seed for a town they named **Osprey** 17 years later. Mrs. Potter Palmer settled here in 1910.

The original village of Venice sat where **Nokomis** does today. It moved south and seaward after the railroad bypassed it in 1922, to a station in the middle of nowhere. Actually an island separated from the mainland by narrow waterways, it reflects the influence of Ringling and other early, in-the-know vacationers.

Casey Key and *Manasota Key* were built on the principle that island real estate should be reserved for the well-to-do. This has kept them pristine and lightly developed. *Nokomis Beach,* at Casey Key's southern end, is a beachy, fishing-oriented resort area, in contrast to its exclusive homes. Likewise, *Englewood Beach,* at the southern tip of twisty, out-of-the-way Manasota, is popular with young people.

On the Charlotte Harbor Coast, *Port Charlotte* is a new city that was built around the Tamiami Trail, principally as a retirement community. Its nearby towns of *North Port, Murdock, Rotunda,* and *El Jobean* constitute inland residential neighborhoods that recently were boosted by the building of a large shopping mall. The spring training grounds of the Texas Rangers baseball club are located there. Along the Coast of Charlotte Harbor, the neighboring towns of *Englewood, Lemon Bay,* and *Placida,* heaped upon ancient Indian mounds, retain an age-old fishing flavor.

The town of *Charlotte Harbor* was settled shortly after the Civil War by farmers and cattle ranchers. Facing it across the Peace River's widest point, *Punta Gorda*'s past is as deeply rooted. The southernmost station for the Florida Southern Railroad in 1886, the deep-water port town enjoyed a bustling era of commerce and tourism before railroad builder Henry Plant decided to shut it down in favor of further developing Tampa Bay. Ice-making, turpentine-stilling, pineapple-growing, and, especially, commercial fishing continued for some time to earn local citizens a living. Today, Punta Gorda works to recover its past glories through downtown and riverfront restoration. Home of Ponce de Leon Park, it hosts subdivisions of modern-day youth-seekers.

Though many barrier islands built their reputation and character on fishing, the cluster around *Gasparilla Island* have one fish in particular to thank for

Neither railroads nor hurricanes could diminish the importance of the Naples Pier to its community. Grown from 600 feet in 1888 to 1,000 feet today, it serves as the town's focal point.

The Burroughs home in old Fort Myers — a Georgian oasis of gentility in a raucous, turn-of-the-century cow town.

their privileged past: the tarpon. Phosphate shipping and legends of bygone buccaneers first caused the area to be noticed. The Silver King drew millionaires to **Boca Grande, Useppa Island,** and **Cabbage Key,** which they hoarded for themselves, keeping growth and development minimal by sheer force of their dollars. These islands, along with privately owned **Little Gasparilla** and **Palm Island,** and mostly state-owned **Don Pedro Island, Cayo Costa,** and **North Captiva,** remain the uncut jewels in the necklace of Charlotte Harbor islands.

Cayo Costa, Pine Island, and the northern regions of Gasparilla, gave birth to the Gulf Coast's legacy of fishing lifestyles, back when the Caloosas lived off the sea. On Pine Island, fishing, crabbing, and shrimping are still a way of life and survival, despite tightening government restrictions that make it less and less profitable. Protected from rampant resort development by lack of beaches, Pine Island clings to old traditions like an oyster to a mangrove prop.

Fort Myers Beach, on **Estero Island,** is also synonymous with Gulf shrimp and fish docks. South of it, the trickle of islands ending with **Bonita Beach** are reminiscent of the Coast's earliest times, with primeval estuaries, intact shell mounds, whispers of buried pirate treasure, and fishing lifestyles.

Cape Coral once was largely a hunting refuge for steel magnate Ogden Phipps, who vacationed in Naples. The second largest city in Florida in area, it was somewhat of a developer's folly. The young city was cleared, canalled, and platted in 1970, and slowly grows into itself, bordered on the east by **North Fort Myers** and on the south by the Caloosahatchee River.

Across the river from North Fort Myers and Cape Coral, **Fort Myers** has grown from its fort status of wartime, into the hub of communication and transportation for the Gulf Coast. Cattle barons gave the community its early wild temperament; Thomas Edison and his class of successful masterminds elevated it above its cow-trail streets.

Out in San Carlos Bay, at the southern extreme of Charlotte Harbor, the islands of *Sanibel* and *Captiva* developed quietly. At various times in their past, the islands supported a lighthouse reservation, citrus and tomato farms, communities of fishermen, and a coconut plantation. From 1910 through 1940, wealthy notables made their way to the islands, intent upon the relative anonymity that the wilds afforded them. Teddy Roosevelt discovered Captiva Island in 1914. Charles Lindbergh and his wife visited often, inspiring Anne Morrow Lindbergh to pen her well-loved seashell analogies in *Gift From the Sea*. Pulitzer Prize-winning cartoonist and conservationist Jay N. "Ding" Darling gained Captiva and Sanibel islands national attention by fighting for the preservation of their natural attributes during his winter visits. He is to thank for developing the islands' environmental conscience.

Spartan by modern standards, Palm Cottage exemplifies gracious living in turn-of-the-century Naples. It was one of the first Gulf Coast structures entirely built of local materials.

A small community along the Tamiami Trail named *Estero,* south of Fort Myers, was created by most unusual circumstances. A 19th-century religious cult called the Koreshan Unity first settled there, led by Cyrus Teed. The Koreshans believed that life clings to the inside of a hollow earth, like coconut meat to its shell. Members practiced celibacy and communal living. They experimented with tropical gardening, bringing to Southwest Florida the mango and avocado. The site of their brief stay has been preserved by the state, together with their buildings and the natural Florida they discovered there.

Bonita Springs adheres to the its early agricultural heritage with a reputation for tomatoes, citrus, and other cash crops. Citrus freeze-outs up north, and the town's navigable Imperial River, created the community first called Survey in 1893. Here Henry Ford maintained a hunting lodge to which he and his Fort Myers friends traveled by horseback. Where the tomato fields end today, upscale golfing communities take root, all surrounding a neighborly little town left frozen in time by dint of the Tamiami Trail's rerouting.

Perched on alabaster sands at the edge of Florida's Everglades, meticulous ***Naples*** transcends its wild setting like a diamond in the rough. Settled by land developers late in its life, this cultural oasis historically appealed to the rich and the sporting. Today, the state's final frontier is known for its million-dollar homes, great golfing, art galleries, world-class shopping, posh resorts, and fine dining. Just around the corner, all this civility is balanced with swampbuggy

Once a trading post, Smallwood's Store today serves as a museum in the secluded Everglades outpost of Chokoloskee Island.

mud races, crop fields, Native American villages, fishing lodges, the few surviving Florida panthers, and the unvarnished wilderness of the *Everglades.*

Neighboring *Marco Island* introduces the swampy, mysterious land of Ten Thousand Islands. Tempered in a rough-and-tumble history, the island, too, boasts its contemporary upscale resorts and good manners. Ancient Indian mounds, clam canneries, and pineapple plantations color the past of its three communities: *Isles of Capri, Marco,* and *Goodland.* The island, which was first settled by the William Collier clan in 1871, has done most of its growing in the past few decades. Between 1960, when plans for a modern bridge were being formed, and 1980, the population increased by 755 percent.

In its historical context, the map of Gulf Coast Florida resembles a patchwork quilt. It blankets its people in warmth, checkers its past with multiple patterns, and layers its character with intriguing textures.

CHAPTER TWO
Blazing the Trail
TRANSPORTATION

The Gulf of Mexico and its great rivers and intracoastal waterways comprise the region's oldest and lowest-maintenance transportation system. From the days when the Caloosas traveled the bays and estuaries in dugout canoes, through the romantic steamboat era, up until 1927 when the railroad to Naples was completed, boat travel

Trolleys, like this one in Venice, are a popular form of coastal transportion for residents and sightseers.

was the most popular means of getting around. Early homes studded waterways, and today face them, rather than facing the roads that accommodate modern-day traffic. Even today, the Caloosahatchee River, which empties into the sea along the Island Coast and connects to the East Coast via Lake Okeechobee, constitutes a major inter-coastal water route.

The railroad first came to Charlotte County's deepwater port in 1886 and created the town of Punta Gorda, much to the chagrin of Fort Myers' leaders, who had tried for years to persuade company officials to extend their Florida Southern Railroad to the Caloosahatchee River. Instead an unsettled location was selected and a fabulous hotel built there — the custom of Florida's great railroad builders of the day. Besides transporting wealthy winterers to the nation's southernmost railroad stop, fresh fish, cattle, and crops were hauled by rail.

A train nicknamed "Slow and Wobbly" ran between Bradenton and Sarasota from 1892 until 1894. The Seaboard Airline Railroad built a more reliable version to Bradenton in 1902. In 1911, it was extended past Venice, and played musical chairs with town names. Infuriated residents of Venice changed the town's name to Nokomis, and the Venice of today sits where that first station was built. The Charlotte Harbor and Northern Railway laid track in 1906 to ship phosphate from inland mines to the deep waters of Boca Grande Pass, off Gasparilla Island. Another exclusive resort came with it.

Fort Myers finally got its first railroad station in 1904. In 1922, the trestles reached Bonita Springs, where trains turned around on a Y for return trips. When the track was finally extended to Naples and Marco Island, the train had to travel backward south of Bonita Springs, after making the Y turn. Famous passengers such as Hedy Lamarr, Greta Garbo, and Gary Cooper rode the rails to vacation at the posh Naples Beach Hotel & Golf Club, one of Florida's first resorts to have greens on the property.

The concept of the Tamiami Trail made headway when, in 1923, a self-formed group called the Trail Blazers followed the proposed route that would connect Tampa and Miami. Mules, oxen, and tractors were used to complete that first motorized crossing of the Everglades. Before the Trail was paved, it had a sand surface. Summer rains caused flooding. Old-timers remember getting out of the car to catch fish in the road while their parents tried to get unstuck. Jarring, muck-crusted ruts made the trip less than comfortable once the rains subsided.

As the Trail's west-coast leg inched toward its destination, it changed the lives of each community it penetrated. Progress was slowed by dense jungles, forbidding swampland, devastating heat, and mosquitoes so thick that they

Ed Frank (second from far right), invented the swamp buggy, an amphibious form of transportation engineered for travel in the Everglades. He poses here in 1947 with his brainchild and hunting buddies.

The Collier County Historical Society, Inc.

covered exposed skin like a buzzing body glove. Builders lived at the work site, and a whole body of legend grew up around the monumental task. War and depletion of funds frustrated the project. A new dredge had to be invented to build the section across the Everglades.

Thirteen years in the building, the completion of the Tamiami Trail in 1928 opened up early communities to land travel, trade, and tourism, and was met with euphoria. Today the Trail, also known as Highway 41, strings together the region's oldest towns and cities, and newer communities have grown up around it.

With the extension of Interstate 75 parallel to its path, the Tamiami Trail has now forfeited its role as the sole intercoastal lifeline. It remains, nonetheless, the backbone of the West Coast. Probing both metropolitan interiors and rural vistas, it provides glimpses of a cross-section of life — as it was and as it is — in Southwest Florida.

For the most part, Highway 41 draws the eastern boundary of the area covered in this book. At the Gulf Coast's northern and southern extremes, it edges close to the shoreline. Its midsection reaches inland, to communities built along harbors and rivers.

I–75 glimpses, at top speed, Gulf Coast life in the 1990s. Although convenient and unriddled by traffic lights, it misses out on the character which the more leisurely pace of the Tamiami Trail reveals. It extends the boundaries of Highway 41's family of communities, and creates new ones. Occasionally, this book will use it as a reference point, especially where attractions along its path merit mention.

GETTING TO FLORIDA'S GULF COAST

BY CAR

Southwest Florida is plugged into Florida's more highly charged areas by both major conduits and small feeders. Tampa lies at the Sarasota Bay Coast's back door, along Highway 41 or I–75. The Tamiami Trail ends here, at its source. The interstate continues northeast and connects to Orlando and the East Coast via Interstate 4. Highway 19 takes up the coastal route in St. Petersburg, heading toward Georgia. Highway 70 cuts across the state above Lake Okeechobee, to connect the East Coast to the Sarasota Bay Coast at Bradenton, and at Sarasota and Punta Gorda via Routes 72 and 17, respectively. These roads delve into Native American reservation territory, Arcadia's cowboy country, and the expansive Myakka River State Park. The route runs jaggedly between the Island Coast, the big lake, and West Palm Beach, following a series of lazy, two-lane roads, such as routes 80, 27, 441, and 98.

Alligator Alley crosses the Everglades with a certain mystique. Once, upon this two-lane toll road, encounters with crossing 'gators and panthers were common. (Tragically, cars inevitably fared the better of the two in such instances.) The state recently completed its connections with I–75 on both ends and widened it to four lanes, with underpasses for wildlife. It is still a toll road and still less than user-friendly. Gas up before you approach — only one fuel station/restaurant exit breaks up the two-hour drive. It reaches the East Coast at Fort Lauderdale. Highway 41 takes you into Miami and branches off into Highway 1 to the Florida Keys.

GULF COAST ACCESS

FROM FLORIDA CITIES

From	To Sarasota Bay	To Island Coast	To SouthCoast
Miami	212 mi./4.25 hr.	148 mi./2.5 hr.	110 mi./2 hr.
Orlando	132 mi./2.25 hr.	167 mi./3.5 hr.	187 mi./3.75 hr.
Daytona	185 mi./3.75 hr.	219 mi./4.25 hr.	241 mi./4.5 hr.
Jacksonville	239 mi./4.5 hr.	311 mi./6 hr.	325 mi./6.25 hr.

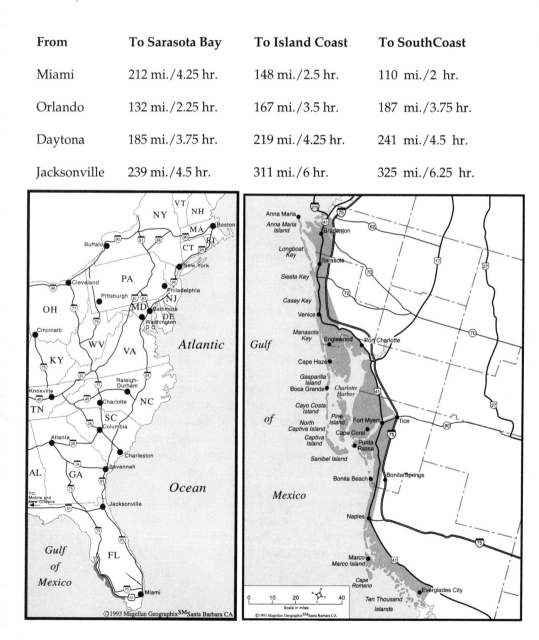

BY PLANE

Two major airports service the Gulf Coast: Sarasota–Bradenton Airport (SRQ), and Southwest Florida International (RSW) in Fort Myers. Both have been granted port-of-entry status. The Sarasota–Bradenton facility gives the best introduction to the region, with shark tanks and tropical orchids from local attractions, a two-story waterfall, and art works from its prolific community.

International airports in Sarasota and Fort Myers promise global transportation networking in years to come.

Small airports and fields in Punta Gorda, Naples, and Marco Island service shuttle and charter flights. North Captiva island has its own landing strip for private planes, and seaplane service is available to some islands.

Sarasota–Bradenton Airport — 359-5200; American, Continental, Delta, Northwest, Trans-World Airlines, United, USAir.

Venice Municipal Airport — 488-2967

Charlotte County Airport — 639-1101

Southwest Florida International Airport — 768-1000; Air Canada, American, American Eagle, American TransAir, Continental, Delta, Northwest, Trans World Airlines, United, USAir.

Naples Municipal Airport (APF) — 643-0733; American Eagle, Comm-Air, Delta, USAir.

Marco Island Airport — 394-3355

BY BUS

Greyhound Bus Lines depots are found along the West Coast at Sarasota (575 North Washington Boulevard; 955-5735), Fort Myers (2275 Cleveland Avenue; 334-1011), and Naples (2669 Davis Boulevard; 774-5660).

BY TRAIN

Amtrak (1-800-872-7245) stops at Bradenton's Manatee County Court House Bus Terminal (Manatee West at 12th Street West) and Sarasota's City Hall Bus Terminal (Lemon Avenue between 1st and 2nd streets).

GETTING AROUND FLORIDA'S GULF COAST

BY CAR

Best Routes:

Tamiami Trail (Highway 41) centerpoints the Gulf Coast's major metropolitan areas and provides north-south passage within and between them.

Sarasota Bay Coast

In Bradenton and Sarasota, Highway 41 runs along bay shores and converges with Highway 301, another major trunk road. Principal through-streets for east-west traffic in this area generally are those with exits off I–75, north to south: Manatee Avenue (Route 64); Carter Road (70); University Parkway; Fruitville Road; Bee Ridge Road; Clark Road (Route 72); and Venice Avenue. To reach the islands from I–75, follow Route 64 or 72.

Bradenton's 75th Street West (De Soto Memorial Highway) skims the town's western reaches close to the bayfront. Streets hiccough through downtown Sarasota, starting and stopping without warning. Main Street runs north-south, crossed by Orange Avenue, one of the neighborhood's longest streets. Bayfront Drive arcs around the water and is home to a lot of the town's action. Bahia Vista intersects Orange at its southern extremes, and constitutes a major route. To cross town from north to south between Highway 41 and I–75, take Tuttle Avenue, Beneva Road, McIntosh Road, or Cattlemen Road. Take Venice Avenue off of I–75 to get to Venice's beaches and old, Mediterranean-influenced neighborhoods. Harbor drives travel north-south along the beaches, with Beach Road and The Esplanade branching off along waterfront communities. Highway 41's business route splits from the Tamiami Trail at Venice, and takes you to the older part of town.

Charlotte Harbor Coast

Highway 41 heads inland, running within miles of I–75 at some points. Getting to the Gulf entails crossing several bodies of water in these parts. Most of the routes qualify as back roads and are listed under that heading.

Island Coast

Bonita Beach is touted as the closest sands to I–75 in this area. Highway 41 again distances itself from its modern counterpart to take you into downtown business districts and past upscale golfing communities. Pine Island Road, Route 78, diverges from the major arteries and scoots mainland, across North Fort Myers and Cape Coral, to reach Pine Island.

On the other side of the Caloosahatchee Bridge, Fort Myers' main east-west connectors are Martin Luther King, Jr. Boulevard, Colonial Boulevard, College

Thomas Edison is credited with planting the flank of royal palms down Fort Myers' prestigious McGregor Boulevard, thereby earning the city its nickname, "City of Palms".

By land or by sea: Drawbridges such as the Sanibel Causeway accommodate Intracoastal Waterway boaters, as well as motorists.

Parkway (which crosses the river between Fort Myers and Cape Coral), Daniels Parkway, and Gladiolus Drive. Traveling roughly from north to south, historic and royal-palm-lined McGregor Boulevard (Route 867) follows the river past the old homes that line it. Summerlin Avenue (Route 869) and Metro

Parkway run parallel, to the east. Tamiami Trail becomes Cleveland Avenue. Take McGregor or Summerlin west (they eventually merge) to get to Sanibel and Captiva Islands, lands of no traffic lights. There's a $3.50 toll for crossing the bridge to Sanibel without a sticker. Periwinkle Way is the main drag and connects to Sanibel–Captiva Road via Tarpon Bay Road. Policemen with white gloves direct traffic at the main intersections during high-traffic hours. The Sanibel–Captiva Road dead-ends at Captiva, with no return route to the mainland, so you must backtrack.

South Coast

Here, Highway 41 (also known as 9th Street) closes in on the sea once again, as it travels through Naples. At Bonita Springs, Old Highway 41 branches off toward the town's business district. Parallel to Highway 41 in Naples, major city dissectors include Goodlette–Frank Road (Route 851) and Airport–Pulling

Art shows and community functions give new life to the Naples Depot, site where celebrities disembarked in the Roaring '20s.

Road (Route 31). East-west trunks are Naples–Immokalee Highway (Route 846) at the north edge of town, Pine Ridge Road (Route 896), Golden Gate Parkway (Route 886), Radio Road (Route 856), and Davis Boulevard (Route 84) in town, and Rattlesnake Hammock Road (Route 864) at the southern extreme.

Alternate Back Road Routes:

The Gulf Coast has many scenic back roads which bypass traffic and plunge the traveler into timeless scenes and unique neighborhood temperaments. These routes are especially good to know when you tire of counting out-of-state license plates during rush hour in high season.

Sarasota Bay Coast

Follow the twisty road through a litany of barrier islands, from Anna Maria in the north to Bird Key at the end. This Route 789 adopts a different name on each island: Ocean Boulevard, Gulf of Mexico Drive, etc. Route 758, along Siesta Key, makes a short, beachy bypass between Siesta Drive and Stickney Point Road. The loop through lovely Casey Key begins between Sarasota and Venice at Blackburn Point Road, off Highway 41, then proceeds north through Nokomis Beach and back to the mainland.

Charlotte Harbor Coast

To reach Englewood from Venice, cross lovely, twisty, out-of-the-way Manasota Key along Route 776. Then follow Routes 775 and 771 back to Route 776 for a scenic drive through the peninsula, separated from the mainland by Charlotte Harbor, or to get to Gasparilla Island. (It costs $3.20 to cross the causeway onto the island.) Keeping straight on 776 takes you more directly to Highway 41. To skirt Highway 41's chain outlet anonymity in the Port Charlotte area, take Collingswood Boulevard off 776 to Edgewater Drive, and back to 41.

Between Charlotte County and the Island Coast, Route 765, or Burnt Store Road, delves into the county's Cracker era: scrub cattle, rusty tin roofs, and old fishermen bobbing cane poles. This connects to Highway 78, which leads to Pine Island when taken west, or Highway 41 and I–75 when followed east. To enter Cape Coral the back way, go east to Chiquita Boulevard, head south to Cape Coral Parkway, then go left.

Island Coast

The back road along the Island Coast's shores plunges you briefly into the frenzied activity of Fort Myers Beach along routes 968 and 865, then carries you along at a more mellow pace as you cross into Lover's Key and Big and Little Hickory Islands. The road returns you to Highway 41 at Bonita Springs.

South Coast

South of Naples, routes numbered 951, 952, and 953 carry you to Isles of Capri, Marco Island, Goodland, and back to Highway 41 just before the Everglades.

CAR RENTALS

Rental agencies with airport offices or shuttle service are listed below:

Alamo:	1-800-327-9633 (SRQ, 359-5540; RSW, 768-2424)
Avis:	1-800-331-1212 (SRQ, 359-5240; RSW, 768-2121; APF, 643-0900)
Budget:	1-800-527-0700 (SRQ, 359-5353; RSW, 768-1500; APF, 643-0086)
Dollar:	1-800-800-4000 (RSW, 768-2223)
Hertz:	1-800-654-3131 (RSW, 768-3100; APF, 643-1515)
National:	1-800-328-4567 (RSW, 768-2100; APF, 643-0200)
Thrifty:	1-800-367-2277 (RSW, 768-2322)

AIRPORT TAXIS/SHUTTLES

Many resorts arrange pick-up service to and from the airport. Taxi and limousine companies operate in most areas. To find which companies service the Bradenton–Sarasota airport, call 359-5225.

Boca Grande Taxi & Limo (964-0455 or 1-800-771-7533) provides 24-hour connections to all Florida airports. For more grandiose arrivals and departures, call *Boca Grande Seaplane* (964-0234).

Pine Island Taxi and Limousine Service (283-7777) provides 24-hour service anywhere.

Sanibel Island Taxi makes airport pick-ups and delivery for Sanibel and Captiva visitors. Call 472-4160. Or contact *Sanibel Island Limousine* at 472-8888.

In the South Coast area, call, *Affordable Limousine Service* at 455-6007 or 1-800-245-6007; *Naples Shuttle* at 262-8982; or *Naples Taxi* at 775-0505. *Admiralty Transportation* (394-4411) services Marco Island for airport service.

BY BUS

The Sarasota Bay Coast boasts dependable public transportation, with discounts for school children and seniors. Buses run every day but Sunday, 6:00 a.m. to 6:00 p.m. For route information, call *Sarasota County Area Transit* (SCAT) at 951-5851 or *Manatee County Transit* at 747-8621 or 749-7116.

The open-air *Sarasota Trolley* does a downtown route every 30 minutes between 9:45 a.m. and 4:45 p.m., Monday through Saturday. Cost: $.25 weekdays, $.05 on Saturdays.

On the Island Coast, city buses follow routes around Fort Myers, Cape Coral, Fort Myers Beach, and south Fort Myers. Call *Lee Tran* at 275-8726.

In season, a guided trolley tour takes visitors to local historical sites, including the Edison and Ford winter homes, Fort Myers Historical Museum, Burroughs Home, and shops. Call 275-8726.

Trolleys provide the only public transportation on Sanibel and Captiva. Call 472-6374 for a Sanibel–Captiva schedule. For information about trolley rides to and around Fort Myers Beach, call 275-TRAM (8726); in Bonita springs call 992-0200. Trolley rides often include guided tours. The *Naples Trolley and Blue Trolley Line* (262-7300) conducts sightseeing and shopping tours in the Naples area. Marco Island's trolley visits 13 different historical sites. Call 394-1600.

BY CARRIAGE

Horse-drawn tours of "The Circle" on St. Armand's Key, and Lido Beach, are available from *Centennial Carriage and Livery* (378-0100, St. Armand's

Circle). **Naples Horse and Carriage Company** (649-1210) provides evening tours of Old Naples, the beaches, and the fishing pier.

BY TRAIN

The **Seminole Gulf Railway** (275-6060), stationed at Metro Mall in Fort Myers, takes dinner trips, Murder Mystery tours, and other excursions throughout the area.

BY WATER

Water no longer provides functional transportation routes. On the Gulf Coast today, boat travel is purely recreational (except for commercial fishermen, of course), using two types of trademark water vessels. The noisy, power-driven airboat is designed especially for the shallow waters of the Everglades. The swamp buggy travels on steel treads as an all-terrain vehicle, built to carry up to 20 passengers. In addition, pontoon boats offer a more conventional way to explore the Everglades.

Speedy, wetlands-efficient airboats are popular for water travel in the Everglades.

Numerous sightseeing tours and charters originate at marinas and resorts daily. Some specialize in fishing, others in shelling or birding. Many include lunch at an exotic island restaurant, while a few serve meals on board. All cater to the sightseer. Most tour operators are knowledgeable about sights on local waterways. These are all listed in the Recreation chapter under *Boating*. Included here are shuttles designed purely to carry passengers to one or more island destination where "by water" is still the only means of arrival.

The **Miss Cortez** (794-1223), an excursion boat out of the fishing village of Cortez near Anna Maria Island, takes visitors to Egmont Key every Tuesday and Thursday afternoon.

The **North Captiva Water Taxi** operates out of Pine Island's Pineland Marina. Service is free to guests. Call 472-9223 for non-guest prices and schedules.

Jensen's Twin Palm Marina (15107 Captiva Dr., Captiva; 472-5800) runs water taxis to Upper Captiva, Cabbage Key, and Cayo Costa.

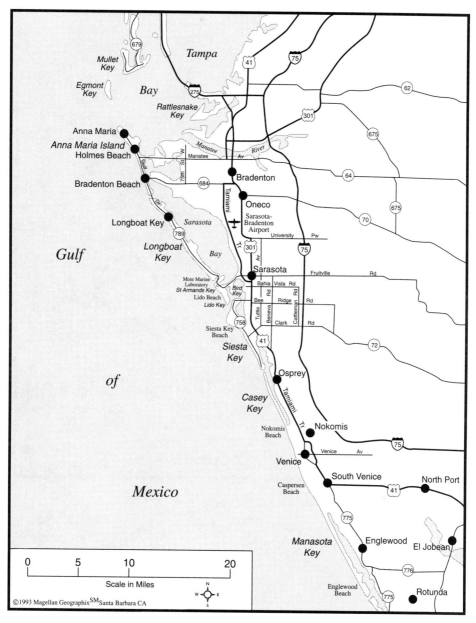

SARASOTA BAY COAST

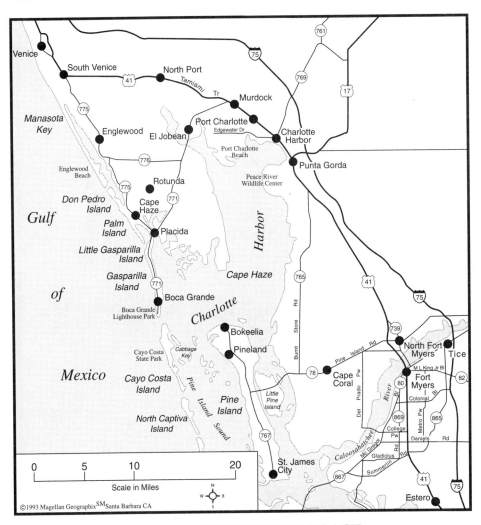

CHARLOTTE HARBOR COAST

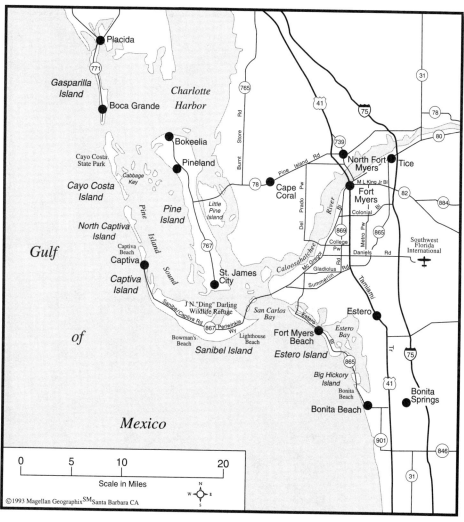

ISLAND COAST

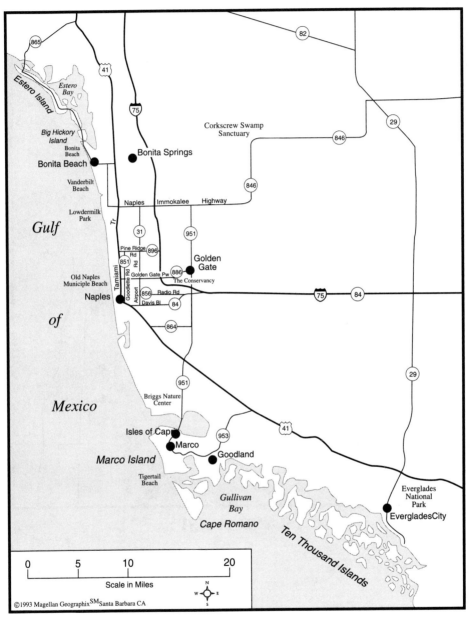

SOUTH COAST

CHAPTER THREE

Your Place in Paradise
LODGING

Maine may boast about its bed-and-breakfasts, Vermont its historic inns, and Colorado its ski lodges. But when vacationers envision Florida, it's the state's many beach-side resorts that flash first through the mental slide projector. The Gulf Coast has perfected this widespread image of sun-and-sand abandonment. Mega-resorts are designed to keep guests (and most of their disposable income) on the property. Not only can you eat lunch, rent a bike, and get a tennis lesson — you can hire a masseur, charter a boat for a sunset sail, play 18 holes of golf, and enroll your children in Sandcastle Building 101. These destination resorts are in business to fulfill a wide

Gingerbread trimmings lend a storybook charm to this 19th-century structure in Bradenton Beach.

range of fantasies, and they spare no effort to achieve that goal.

There are, also, in Florida, the homey little cottages that have held their ground through head-spinning negotiations. Perhaps they lack state-of-the-art architecture and service, but they fulfill other types of fantasies. They appeal to visitors looking for a sense of place. They provide guests with the opportunity to explore more than beaches and on-site lounges, at their own pace and in their own way. They encourage rubbing elbows with the locals, and making those serendipitous discoveries that linger longest in vacation memory banks.

In between the two extremes exist a wide variety of high-rise condos, funky hotels, retirement resorts, mom-pop motels, tasteful bed-and-breakfasts, fishing lodges, and inns. In their variety, they accommodate every stripe of Florida vacationer.

Privately owned second homes and condominiums provide another source of upscale accommodations. Vacation brokers throughout the region are trained to match visitors with such properties. See the section entitled *Home and Condo Rentals*, at the end of this chapter.

The Gulf Coast fills its rooms during the winter season, which begins shortly before Christmas and is reflected by rates which may rise anywhere from 10 to 100 percent above those charged during the off-season. Some resorts schedule their rates based on as many as four different seasons, with the highest rates applying from mid-December through April. Reservations are required during these months. Some resorts and rental services require a minimum stay, especially during the peak season. Hotels traditionally are busiest during students' spring break, when families and college coeds descend *en masse*.

The highlights of Gulf Coast hospitality listed here include the best and freshest in the local industry. While spanning the range of endless possibilities, they concentrate on those properties that break out of the skyscraping, wicker-and-floral mold.

If rates seem high for rooms on the Gulf Coast, it's because many resorts cater to families by providing kitchen facilities. Take into consideration what this could save you on dining bills. A star after the pricing designation indicates that the rate includes at least a continental breakfast in the cost of lodging; a few abide by the American Plan, including all meals in the rate charged.

Pricing codes are explained below. They are normally per person/double occupancy for hotel rooms; per unit for efficiencies, apartments, cottages, suites, and villas. Many resorts offer off-season packages at special rates. Pricing does not include the six percent Florida sales tax. Many large resorts add service gratuities or maid charges. Some counties impose a tourist tax as well, proceeds from which are applied to beach and environmental maintenance.

Rate Categories

Inexpensive	Up to $50
Moderate	$50 to 110
Expensive	$110 to 180
Very Expensive	$180 and up

The following abbreviations are used for credit card information:

AE - American Express	DC - Diners Club
CB - Carte Blanche	MC - MasterCard
D - Discover Card	V - Visa

Federal law mandates that properties with 50 rooms or more provide accommodations for physically handicapped persons. I have indicated only those small places that do not make such allowances.

LODGING — SARASOTA BAY COAST

Bradenton

POINTE PLEASANT B&B
Innkeepers: Joe and Audrey Bach
747-3511
1717 1st Ave. W., Bradenton 34205
Price: Inexpensive*
Credit Cards: No
Handicapped Access: No

On one of downtown Bradenton's twisty and oak-lined streets, where a jut of land into the Manatee River forms Point Pleasant, a stately, colonial-style home smiles welcome with gracious old age and finely manicured lawns. The Bachs' little dog meets you first, and gives you a sniff to make sure you're up to snuff. Having passed inspection, you are shown into the sitting room, dominated by a black marble fireplace which Audrey says has never been used. All of the rooms are tastefully decorated, with Oriental rugs over gleaming hardwood floors, lace curtains, antiques, and lots of unique artwork. The home, built in 1935, now has only two guest rooms (more have been approved, but not yet built), done prettily in chenille and Victorian florals. Guests share a bath. The Bachs serve what they call an "expanded continental" breakfast, which translates into just about anything you want, hold the meat.

Bradenton Beach

DUNCAN HOUSE B&B
Innkeepers: Joe Garbus and Becky Kern
778-6858
1703 Gulf Dr., Bradenton Beach 34217
Price: Moderate*
Credit Cards: AE, MC, V

Scrunched between a breakfast joint and some trailers, across the street from the beach, resides an oasis of whimsy in a tropical state of purple, pink and blue, with carved balusters and scalloped edging — a vision amongst ugliness. Built in the 1800s, this home was moved from downtown Bradenton in 1946 to its present location. Ask the innkeepers to see pictures of the original building, its ferry trip, and their renovation project, which turned a decrepit triplex into a charming, two-room and two-apartment facility. Public rooms are compact and lined with board-and-batten walls. Accommodations include private baths, are spacious, and are dressed in extraordinary antique pieces, cheerful window treatments, and floral wallpaper. Separate entrances lead to the apartments, each with complete kitchen facilities. Gourmet breakfast and beach access add to this bed-and-breakfast's special qualities.

Holmes Beach

**HARRINGTON HOUSE
B&B**
Innkeepers: Jo and Frank
 Davis
778-5444
5626 Gulf Dr., Holmes
 Beach 34217
Price: Moderate to Expen-
 sive*
Credit Cards: MC, V

One of Florida's loveliest and best-maintained bed-and-breakfasts, Harrington's beachfront adds to the allure of this homey, historic inn. Built in 1925 of local coquina rock and pecky cypress, with Mediterranean flourishes, the home was refurbished recently by the Davises with casual elegance and magic touches. Each of the seven rooms is named — Renaissance, Birdsong, Sunset, etc. — with a needlepoint door sign. Room sizes vary, from spacious with a king-sized bed, to comfortably cozy. Each guest room has its own bath, refrigerator, and TV. An eclectic collection of antique, hand-picked furniture is meant to enhance comfort. A dramatic cut-stone fireplace dominates the sitting room, where taped classical music is interrupted only by an occasional piano solo. Guests enjoy full, home-cooked breakfasts at individual tables, amid Victorian pieces and filmy white curtains. Outdoor areas include decks, a pool, a wide beach, and charmingly colorful landscaping around picket fences and arched alcoves.

Lido Key

**HALF MOON BEACH
CLUB**
General Manager: Shelley
 Lederman
1-800-358-3245 or 388-3694
2050 Ben Franklin Dr.,
 Sarasota 34236
Price: Expensive
Credit Cards: AE, D, DC,
 MC, V

Half Moon's stretch of beach is so romantic that people come here to get married, or shoot commercials. During the winter months repeat business, comfortable social areas, and the sheer intimacy of the property, lends to it a community feel. Two neo-art-deco buildings form roughly a half moon and hold 86 guest rooms, efficiencies, and suites, all with refrigerators, coffee makers, and hair dryers. Contemporary Florida-style appointments grace the rooms and public areas, but the beach is the British-owned resort's best feature. Everything draws you outdoors, including an indoor restaurant that overlooks the pool, bike rentals, a beach sundeck with thatch cabanas, well-tended grounds, volleyball, shuffleboard, and dramatic sunsets.

Longboat Key

**COLONY BEACH AND
TENNIS RESORT**
General Manager: Kather-
 ine Klauber Moulton
1-800-426-5669 (U.S.); 1-
 800-282-1138 or 383-6464
 (Florida)
1620 Gulf of Mexico Dr.,
 Longboat Key 34228

The Colony is ranked among Florida's finest resorts, as a place where you could hide indefinitely behind security gates, without ever having to face the real world. It stakes its reputation on topnotch tennis and dining. Its 21 tennis courts are state-of-the-art soft surface, including ten which use a revolutionary underground watering system

Court sports and family fun are the focus of Colony Beach & Tennis Resort, on Longboat Key. Various special programs both train and entertain children.

Colony Beach & Tennis Resort

Price: Very Expensive
Credit Cards: AE, CB, D, DC, MC, V

known as Hydro-Court. The Colony Restaurant, one of the property's four dining spots, consistently wins awards. The 13-acre resort occupies a stretch of private beach that recently was re-nourished. It boasts its "Kidding Around" recreational programs, which take young guests to the courts, beach, pool, and off-property attractions. The Colony's 235 privately owned units range from a high-rise penthouse to tony beach houses, but most are one- or two-bedroom suites. All units contain modern kitchen facilities and bright, tropical color schemes. Guests have free use of tennis facilities, as well as a spa, and a health club with an aerobic studio. A golf-around program allows the sports-minded to sample the best of Sarasota's links.

HOLIDAY INN
General Manager: Gary Dorschel
1-800-HOLIDAY or 383-3371
4949 Gulf of Mexico Drive, Longboat Key 34228
Price: Expensive to Very Expensive
Credit Cards: AE, CB, DC, D, MC, V

There's less starch in the attitudes of Longboat Key's northern end than at its southern end. The Holiday Inn here is classier than the average hotel chain standard, but still is more easy-going than the island's secured properties, in its south. One of its two swimming pools is contained inside the Holidome, an indoor recreation center complete with whirlpool, shuffleboard, and ping pong. Other recreation centers around a wide and luxurious beach with a cabana, sailboat rentals, and a beach bar. There's also an outdoor swimming pool, sauna, tanning salon, four lighted tennis courts, two indoor bars, and two restaurants. Rooms and suites — 146 in all— provide comfortable accommodations with above-standard furnishings.

John Ringling's dream — a luxury resort on Sarasota's barrier islands — is realized at the 400-acre resort at Longboat Key Club.

The Resort at Longboat Key Club

LONGBOAT KEY CLUB
General Manager:Gary Rogers
1-800-237-8821 (U.S. and Canada); 1-800-282-0113 or 383-8821 (Florida)
301 Gulf of Mexico Dr., P.O. Box 15000, Longboat Key 34228
Price: Expensive to Very Expensive
Credit Cards: AE, CB, DC, MC, V

Located where John Ringling built the foundation for his doomed Ritz-Carlton in the 1920s, a community resort today thrives on 400 acres of gulf-front property. One 18-hole and three nine-hole courses attract serious golfers. Two tennis centers and a complete array of bicycles, rafts, sailboats, boogie boards, kayaks, and snorkeling gear provide plenty of activity options. In all, there are 38 Har-Tru tennis courts, plus an Olympic size swimming pool and a kid's club. Six dining rooms range in style from formal to poolside. Classy touches and sunbelt motif grace the open public areas, as well as the 233 condominium suites and 1,700 guest rooms, which occupy seven buildings with bayfront, golf course, or lagoon views — all behind security gates. Special attention to detail, such as twice-daily cleanings, refrigerators, preferred seating program at local entertainment centers, and complimentary use of exercise facilities, earn Longboat Key Club all its stars, diamonds, and accolades.

Nokomis Beach

SEA GRAPE MOTEL
Owner: Gerry Weaver
484-0071
106 Casey Key Rd. Nokomis 34275
Price: Inexpensive to Moderate
Credit Cards: MC, V
Handicapped Access: No

Nokomis Beach is a fisherman's mecca. The Sea Grape addresses that reputation with its prime location on the Gulf-accessible backbay, directly across the street from the beach. Six boat docks and five units accommodate guests and their vessels. The rooms and fully-stocked efficiencies recently were modernized with tile baths, updated kitchenettes, ceiling fans, and contemporary furnishings. Nothing elaborate, but clean, comfortable, and — most important — close to the fish.

Sarasota

HAMPTON INN
General Manager: Robert
  Lewis
1-800-HAMPTON or
  351-7734
5000 N. Tamiami Tr.,
  Sarasota 33234
Price: Moderate*
Credit Cards: AE, CB, D,
  DC, MC, V

Lined up between Sarasota's airport and main attractions are a string of hotels and motels of the chain or family-owned variety. This particular link in the chain provides a most pleasant and convenient experience in motor lodging. I liked its continental breakfast and ever-brewing coffee pot. Plus there's a pool and a workout facility. Rooms are clean and nicely decorated — and quiet, despite highway traffic.

HYATT SARASOTA
General Manager: Tom
  Sullivan
1-800-233-1234 or 366-9000
1000 Blvd. of the Arts,
  Sarasota 34236
Price: Expensive to Very
  Expensive
Credit Cards: AE, CB, D,
  DC, MC, V

The pinnacle of mainland lodging in Sarasota, the Hyatt appears somewhat dated from the outside. So much for first impressions. Inside unfolds a world of modern decor, contemporary comfort, and bayside splendor. Spaciousness and good taste characterize the 12-story hotel's 297 rooms and 12 suites. Boat slips, a marina, and a waterfront restaurant direct focus to the bay. Inside, a soaring atrium makes way for a clubby lounge and formal dining room with windows on the water. Seven lighted tennis courts, a full fitness center, a swimming pool, and close proximity to the Sarasota Quay and downtown attractions make this longstanding landmark a favorite for business travelers and vacationers. In the summer, the Hyatt is known for its live jazz sessions on Sundays.

Siesta Key

BANANA BAY CLUB
Owners: Hannah and
  Robert Spencer
346-0113
8254 Midnight Pass Rd.,
  Siesta Key 34242
Price: Moderate to Expensive
Credit Cards: No
Handicapped Access: No

Banana Bay Club called to me as I drove by it. Among all of the high-rise condos and beach clubs on Siesta Key, this one seemed to stand out. One thing different about this island property is that it occupies not a beach, but the shoreline of a quiet, tidal lagoon bird sanctuary, traveled only by canoes and rowboats. When the manager described the seven guest units as very Floridian, I prepared myself for yet another rattan-and-floral rubber-stamp job. But lo and behold, there was nothing ordinary about this interior scheme. Safari patterns, colored bed sheets, European-style kitchen cabinets, splashy boldness, and individual style marked the difference. "We use the word pizazz a lot," the manager told me, "and immaculate." Confirmed! Accommodations range from a studio apartment to a two-bedroom house, and include a small heated swimming pool. Bikes, boats, and fishing equipment are available free of charge. Units are stocked with more than just the necessities, and the staff provides those small, special services that mount up to the forgotten art of gracious hosting.

CRESCENT HOUSE B&B
Innkeepers: Paulette & Bob
   Flaherty
346-0857
459 Beach Road, Siesta Key
   34242
Price: Moderate*
Credit Cards: No

If you enjoy feeling as though you are a guest in a friend's home, this is your kind of place. Interesting, antique pieces add to its charm. The home is vintage 1920s, which means lots of lovely latticework, shake siding outside, and a wonderful fireplace inside. It also means small rooms that show their age. An antique pump organ in the jalousied Florida Room plays only when the humidity is high (which occurs fairly regularly in these parts), and a key lime tree out back provides a squeeze for your refreshments. An outdoor hot tub and sundeck add to the amenities. Each of the four guest rooms holds a television and air conditioning unit; baths are shared. Breakfast is self-serve on a lace-covered and venerable dining room table.

Venice

BANYAN HOUSE
Innkeepers: Chuck and
   Susan McCormick
484-1385
519 So. Harbor Dr., Venice
   34285
Closed: August
Price: Moderate (two-night
   minimum)*
Credit Cards: No
Handicapped Access: No

In the mid-1920s, architects designed Venice to underscore its Italian nomenclature. Homes and buildings were modeled upon north Mediterranean styles. The town's first community swimming pool was located in the backyard of one of the original homes, next to a fledgling banyan tree. Today that small pool, with its Greek goddess fountain and now-sprawling tree, are located next to a bed-and-breakfast inn known as the Banyan House. Classic statuary, fountains, multi-hued blossoms, a tree-house sundeck, courtyard, hot tub, and red tile-roofed Iberian home share the property. Four rooms, each with a private bath, exert their individual personality, but with a little less panache than the public rooms. The Palm Room has a fireplace, the Laurel Room country-style appointments, the Tree House a sunny sitting room overlooking the pool, the Palmetto Room a balcony and separate entrance. All units contain at least a small refrigerator — three are efficiencies. The owners also rent out five apartments, separate from the bed-and-breakfast. Deluxe continental breakfast, featuring Susan's homemade specialties, is served in a courtyard-side solarium off the formal sitting room. The latter is furnished with an antique Italian fire-

Banyan House's Italian facade fits with Venice's original Mediterranean development of the 1920s.

place, a circa-1890 hoopskirt bench, and other Victorian period pieces. Pecky cypress, wood beam ceilings, terra cotta slate tiling, and wrought-iron banisters are all original. Free bicycle usage permits guests to explore old Venice's nearby shopping mecca and beach.

INN AT THE BEACH
General Manager: Steve C. Korn
1-800-255-8471 or 484-8471
101 The Esplanade, Venice 34285
Price: Moderate to Expensive
Credit Cards: AE, CB, D, DC, MC, V

This modern resort was built to include Mediterranean architectural overtones and contemporary Florida comfort and decor. Located across the street from the public access to Venice Beach, many of its 44 units overlook the Gulf. Turquoise tones inside and out are reminiscent of the sea. Rooms are decorated in pastels, with above-standard wood furnishings, stylish lamps and torchieres, and non-private balconies or porches. Lattice, thatch, and terrazo mark the Florida character of the two-story building. Accommodations include rooms, efficiencies, and one- or two-bedroom suites. A small pool with a sundeck is tucked away in back, near the parking lot.

LODGING — CHARLOTTE HARBOR COAST

Boca Grande

GASPARILLA INN
General Manager:
Steve Seidensticker
964-2201

With subtle grandeur, the Gasparilla Inn sits upon a throne of lush greenery. Dressed in pale yellow clapboard with white columns, Georgian porticos and Victorian sensibilities, it has

Prim and proper, Gasparilla Inn hosts the Social Register crowd during the winter season, has it as since 1913.

5th St., & Palm St., Boca Grands, 33921
Closed: Mid-June through mid-December
Price: Expensive to Very Expensive*
Credit Cards: No

been, since 1912, a town anchor and social emblem. The region's oldest surviving resort, it first opened its doors as a retreat for families such as the Vanderbilts and DuPonts, whose descendants still winter there. If you try to reserve a room during the "social season" (December through April) and you aren't "the right kind of people," you could be turned away even if rooms are available. Not that accommodations are ultra-elegant. The 140 rooms and cottages reflect the era of their inception, with understated furnishings. A wood-and-wicker dining room, a beauty salon, an 18-hole golf course, a croquet lawn, tennis courts, a beach club with fitness facilities, and two pools provide amenities. It's said that Gasparilla Inn, in quiet Boca Grande, is where Palm Beach socialites came to escape charity balls and the perpetual fashion show of their winter residences. The inn does not advertise, but depends upon its reputation for top-of-the-line service to attract guests.

Cape Haze

PALM ISLAND RESORT
President: Dean L. Beckstead
1-800-824-5412 (U.S.); 1-800-282-6142 or 697-4800 (Florida)

A true island getaway in grand style, Palm Island is a slab of sand above Gasparilla Island, devoted to a private resort with villa lodging. One must boat in; there's an hourly ferry from the resort's mainland marina, ensconced by its two-level suite buildings. Old Florida-style island villas come

7092 Placide Rd., Cape
   Haze 33946
Price: Very Expensive
Credit Cards: MC, V

with fully equipped kitchens, laundries, one to three bedrooms, exquisite appointments, and screened porches overlooking more than two miles of deserted beach. The 160-unit property (counting the mainland accommodations) has five pools and 11 tennis courts, plus a restaurant and bar, island store, full-service marina, boat rentals, charter service, bicycle and watersports equipment rentals — all of the makings for an "I'm never leaving this island" vacation. What it doesn't have is roads, cars, stress, and rigorous time schedules.

Manasota Key

**MANASOTA BEACH
   CLUB**
Owners: Robert and Syd-
   ney Buffum
Managers: Jim and Dee
   Dee Buffum
474-2614
7660 Manasota Key Rd.,
   Englewood 34223
Closed: Mid-May through
   mid-November
Price: Expensive to Very
   Expensive*
Credit Cards: No

A tiny, low-impact sign whispers "Manasota Beach Club." And though it occupies 25 acres of Manasota Key, the rest of the resort is just as unobtrusive. The non-advertised property preserves the island's natural attributes with a low-key attitude, wooded paths, and deserted beach. I saw a pileated woodpecker while there, and guests have reported 92 other species about the grounds. Fifteen cottages, the dining room, and a library exude Old Florida charm. The resort appeals to the "sink into oblivion" type of vacationer who wishes to hide out amongst its natural, gnarly vegetation. (There are no televisions in the units.) The property, which has a summer camp feel to it, also appeals to the sportsperson, with three tennis courts, a swimming pool, bocce ball, shuffleboard, basketball, horseshoes, croquet, bicycling, sailing, windsurfing, and charter fishing. A private 18-hole golf course nearby is available to guests. During social season (January through mid-April), cottages are shared by guests who receive three meals a day on the American Plan. During November, December, and late April, the resort rents entire cottages with kitchens, and provides no meals.

LODGING — ISLAND COAST

Bonita Beach

**BONITA BEACH
   RESORT MOTEL**
General Manager: Eric
   Mohlenhoff

B onita Beach has a reputation for recreational fishing. Its earliest lodging accommodated intrepid sportsmen, and the island still boasts a

992-2137
26395 Hickory Blvd.,
   Bonita Springs
   33923–3790
Price: Moderate. Credit
   Cards: AE, MC, V

lion's share of motels designed around marinas and backbay locations. Bonita Beach Resort is one of the few close to the Gulf. It spreads its 20 units between the main drag and the bay, with lots of room for customers to dock, a boat ramp, pontoon rentals, and a playground. There's nothing plush or fancy about the room furnishings. They are clean, air-conditioned, and completely adequate for someone whose mind is set on finding the prime fishing hole. Some have kitchens, some water views.

**THE BEACH & TENNIS
   CLUB**
General Manager:Betty
   Brown
1-800-237-4934 or 992-1121
5700 Bonita Beach Rd. SW,
   Suite 3103, Bonita
   Springs 33923
Open year-round
Price: Inexpensive to Moderate
Credit Cards: No

A string of five high-rise buildings and a complex of 10 Har-Tru tennis courts make up this property, across the street from the bleached-blond sands of Bonita Beach. Each one-bedroom, privately owned apartment has a balcony with a view of either the gulf or backwaters. They are modernly equipped with full kitchens, sleeper sofas, and dining and living rooms. Two heated swimming pools, a children's pool, beauty salon, restaurant, shuffleboard courts, tennis pro shop, and laundry complete the amenities.

Cabbage Key

CABBAGE KEY INN
Innkeepers: Rob & Phyllis
   Wells
283-2278
PO Box 200, Pineland
   33945
Price: Moderate to Expensive
Credit Cards: MC, V

Cabbage Key appeals to vacationers seeking an authentic, Old Florida experience. Built on an unbridged island atop an ancient shell mound, the inn and its guest accommodations are reminiscent of the 1930s, when novelist Mary Roberts Rinehart used native cypress and pine to construct a home for her son and his bride. Rinehart's own cottage, furnished with some of her belongings and other period pieces, is for rent along with four others, mostly all two-bedroom, all rustic. Six guest rooms each claim their own unpretentious personality. The restaurant and currency-papered bar attract boaters and water tours for lunch, but the island shuts down to a whisper come sundown.

One of Florida's great destination resorts, South Seas Plantation is named for the coconuts and limes which were once farmed at the northern end of Captiva Island.

Captiva Island

SOUTH SEAS PLANTA-TION
General Manager:Fred L. Hawkins
1-800-237-3102 (U.S.);
1-800-282-3402 or 472-5111 (Florida)
P.O. Box 194, Captiva Island, 33924
Price: Expensive to Very Expensive
Credit Cards: CB, D, DC, MC, V

S outh Seas is one of the great destination resorts of Florida, where it ranks as a standard for top-quality accommodations and service. It's one of those places where you can enter through the security gates and one week later leave, without ever having gone off-property. Celebrities crave its privacy and discretion. South Seas realizes any type of getaway dwelling you could imagine, from tennis villas, to beach cottages, to harborside hotel rooms — nine different types of accommodations in all. The plantation monopolizes a third of the island with 600 guest units, both privately owned and otherwise, three restaurants (only one of which is open to the public), lounges, shops, a nine-hole golf course, fitness center, yacht harbor, 18 swimming pools, 21 tennis courts, watersports equipment rentals and lessons, excursion cruises, organized activities for children and teenagers, and two and a half miles of augmented beach. A free trolley takes guests wherever they want to go on the property. Rooms are furnished with quality, stylish pieces, and appointments. Everything is carried off with a South Pacific theme and attention is detailed.

'TWEEN WATERS INN
General Manager:Jeff Shuff
1-800-223-5865 (U.S.); 472-5161 (Florida)
Captiva Island, 33924

T ween Waters spans the gap between historic lodging and modern super-resort. It remains quaint and true to its heritage in spite of its size — 126 rooms, cottages, efficiencies, and apartments, plus restaurants, a marina, tennis courts, and swimming pool. Named for its location between two

Price: Expensive to Very
    Expensive
Credit Cards: D, MC, V

shores at Captiva's narrowest stretch, it lies across the road from a length of beach that remains lightly populated because it lacks public parking facilities. Its marina is one of the island's watersport centers, with charters, tours, boat and canoe rentals, and the marina-side Canoe Club restaurant. Its lounge provides the island's nightlife, and is located next to the main dining room. Built early in the decade, when wildlife patron "Ding" Darling kept a cottage there, the property shows its age graciously, with glints of old Florida architecture and attitudes.

Fort Myers

**DRUM HOUSE INN BED
    & BREAKFAST**
Innkeepers: Jim and
    Shirley Drum
332-5668
2135 McGregor Blvd., Fort
    Myers 33901
Price: Moderate to Expen-
    sive*
Credit Cards:No

The Drum House provides the quintessential bed-and-breakfast experience. with its historic setting, cozy atmosphere, interesting location, congenial hosts, and furnishings that evoke memories of grandma's house. Known in historical literature as North Fort Myers' Dowling home, it was built at the turn of the century and moved, in 1946, to its present location in the heart of historic Fort Myers. The Drums first opened their doors as a refurbished bed-and-breakfast in January, 1992. By spring, five guest rooms and their private baths, a sitting room/conservatory, a sunny breakfast nook, and a TV room were outfitted with years' worth of the Drums' passion for antique-collecting. The inn is full of historic furnishings — a grandfather clock, vintage buffets, rocking chairs, canopied beds, unique sherry sets, lamps, floor radios, china basins, wood figurines, and even flapper-era clothes in the closet. Breakfast is continental style, roses are fresh, and the Thomas Edison Winter Home is within walking distance.

**SHERATON HARBOR
    PLACE**
General Manager: Rolf
    Werner
1-800-325-3535 or 337-0300
2500 Edwards Dr., Fort
    Myers 33901
Price: Moderate to Expen-
    sive
Credit Cards: AE, CB, D,
    DC, MC, V

The tropical air that dominates the Sheraton's decor is touched with Gatsbian elegance. The marble-pillared, two-story lobby overlooks the city yacht basin, as do the majority of rooms. Of its 420 units, 187 are harborside suites; 82 city suites. The suites continue in the vein of revived art-deco motif with a tropical floral interpretation, stylized lamps, and comfortable, well-used armchairs. One of the resort's two swimming pools is wrapped around a tiki bar, and surrounded by a marine-life mural and cascading waters. A small fitness center, an outdoor pool, a restaurant, lounge, and gift shop fill the creature-comfort bill at this high-rise hotel which manages to bring to its guests both modern comforts and a sense of place.

Sheraton Harbor Place commands a seaworthy view of Fort Myers' Yacht Basin.

Fort Myers Beach

DAYS INN AT LOVERS KEY
General Manager: Pamela Pratt
1-800-325-2525 or 765-4422
8701 Estero Blvd., Fort Myers Beach 33931
Price: Moderate to Expensive*
Credit Cards: AE, D, MC, V

Not to split hairs, but this 14-story skyscraper actually occupies Black Island; Lover's Key fronts it. At the very tip of Black Island, to be exact, it overlooks the waters of Big Carlos Pass and Estero Bay, renowned for its dolphin populations. A small, unspectacular patch of sand tries to make up for lack of beach with many varieties of available watersports equipment. The 104 rooms come with kitchens, balconies, and water views — the hotel's best asset. Continental breakfast and complimentary sunset drinks are included in the price. A waterside cafe serves breakfast, lunch, and dinner in a casual atmosphere.

PINK SHELL BEACH & BAY RESORT
General Manager: John Naylor
1-800-237-5786 or 463-6181
275 Estero Blvd., Fort Myers Beach 33931
Price: Moderate to Very Expensive
Credit Cards: AE, D, MC, V

Every sort of lodging imaginable is available at Fort Myers Beach. There are chains, and small, mom-and-pop places. Upscale accommodations congregate in tall condo buildings or time-share villages. The range is wide, to fit all budgets. One single resort pretty well covers that range all within its own 12 acres. The nicest thing about Pink Shell is that it occupies — practically monopolizes — the island's north end, where traffic slows to a trickle and the sugary sands span wide. Something of an island landmark since the 1950s, it was bought and spruced up a few years ago in a way that maintains its old island character while upgrading typical Fort Myers Beach style. Many of the 176 units dwell in endearing stilt cottages, with up to three bedrooms and less-than-cutting-edge accoutrements. Yet they are appealing in the way they willfully remain one step behind the times. Multi-storied buildings contain one- and two-bedroom apartments and modern efficiencies. The resort broke ground in 1993 on a new building that will hold over 40 luxury suites. Guests, many of whom have been coming here for years, have access to two swimming pools, a wading pool, two Har-Tru tennis courts, a restaurant, beach bar-and-grill, and wide-ranging recreational opportunities and programs on both waterfronts, including water taxis and tours. The Pink Shell is a world of its own. Guests meet at weekly cocktail parties and catch up on fellow vacationers via a newsletter.

SANIBEL HARBOUR RESORT & SPA
General Manager: Bob Moceri
466-4000
17260 Harbour Pointe Dr., Fort Myers 33908
Price: Expensive to Very Expensive
Credit Cards: AE, D, DC, MC, V

Stunningly beautiful for a property this size, the public areas at Sanibel Harbour capitalize on Florida style and a spectacular location. Not really on Sanibel Island as the name suggests, the resort's 240 rooms, 80 condos, three restaurants, two outdoor swimming pools, high-tech tennis courts, spa facilities, and beach are located on a chin of land across the bay from the island, a bay known as Sanibel Harbour. Ninety-five percent of the units have water views, either on the bay or nearby estuaries. One of the bars has a 280-degree view of the sea, with a lovely, breezy cocktail patio that spills

All that's missing from Sanibel Harbour Resort's Gatsbian setting and Old Florida demeanor is the bootleg gin.

Sanibel Harbour Resort

out from it. The Promenade Cafe, which serves spa and regular lunches, is set on a porch atop a waterside pool that brings to mind exotic Roman baths. The resort began as the namesake tennis facility for Jimmy Connors, with flanking condo towers and a world-class spa. Guests — for a fee — have access to an entire menu of fitness gadgetry, counseling, racquetball, classes, and special services (the most unusual being the unique BETAR bed of speakers — a form of mental, resonance massage). Rooms, suites, and condos, in their light-wood and tropical motif, instill the sea's sense of space, lots of space. Rentals and charters for on-the-water adventure include a private canoe trail, island tour boat, and sailing lessons. Kids Klub takes youngsters to the movies, on nature hikes, and provides them with a variety of other activities.

North Captiva

SAFETY HARBOR CLUB
General Manager:Jack Hunt
472-1056
P.O. Box 2276 Pineland 33945
Price: Expensive to Very Expensive (three day minimum)
Credit Cards: No

No roads. No cars. No bridges. Perhaps North Captiva is best described by what it isn't. A favorite off-shore hideaway for connoisseurs of unspoiled places, the Safety Harbor private club offers accommodations (with a three-day minimum) in one of 33 two-bedroom townhouses clustered on the harbor, or in a privately owned home. All are designed for minimal intrusion upon nature, but furnished fashionably and with all the necessities. Townhouses sleep up to six; homes up to eight. Guests take a ferry from Pine or Captiva Island — their last opportunity for "reasonable" supplies. (Bring all your own groceries, because the tiny general store is understandably high-priced.) The club includes a swimming pool, freshwater lake, two tennis courts, beach pavilion with lending library, docking, and miles of undeveloped beach on the Gulf. People get around on foot, bicycles, or golf carts. (You can rent all of these — except feet, of course — on-island). An airstrip welcomes small planes. Three restaurants stay open year-round but on a fluctuating schedule. It really is the ultimate in natural tranquility and relaxation. The focus is the beach, sea, and boating. The most activity occurs around sunset, when residents and guests gather for cocktail hour at the club. Club rules mandate "no wing-tip shoes or ties allowed. Watches are not recommended."

Sanibel Island

ISLAND INN
Innkeepers: Gary and Diana Ruppel
1-800-851-5088 or 472-1561
P.O. Box 659, Sanibel Island 33957

Sanibel's only historic lodging brandishes all the refinement of Florida's great old inns and hotels, but without the snobbery. It has the same congenial and relaxed atmosphere Granny Matthews, a Sanibel matriarch of renown, elicited at the

Price: Moderate to Expensive*
Credit Cards: AE, D, MC, V

turn of the century when she entertained the whole island — even guests from other resorts — at Saturday night barbecues. She also initiated the Sanibel Shell Fair as a way to keep guests busy, and hosted it in the lobby, where white wicker, French doors, and a lattice-edged dining room now give an immediate impression of immaculate spaciousness and island graciousness. During the winter season (November 15 to April 30) it's an American-Plan resort; off-season it's a bed-and-breakfast. Cottages and lodges house 56 units, all with a view of gentle Gulf waves lapping at a shelly beach. Cottages have one or two bedrooms; lodges contain hotel rooms, either with kitchens or refrigerators only, which can be combined into suites. The innkeepers don't pretend to furnish extravagantly; all is done in uncontrived old island style. That does not mean to imply shoddiness. The Island Inn is owned by a non-profit corporation of 156 families which reinvests all profits for constant upgrading. Decor is cheerful and comfortable, and it is impeccably maintained. Outside each lodge room door sits a wooden table where, in season, guests display their shell finds for others to peruse and admire. The atmosphere is saturated with conviviality. Though no alcohol is served in the dining room, cocktail parties are hosted nightly by guests or management. Outdoors, native vegetation landscapes tin-roofed structures. A butterfly garden frames a croquet court, a swimming pool sits squarely on the beach, and a putting green is in the works.

THE CASTAWAYS
General Manager: Michael G. Byrne
1-800-375-0152 or 472-1252
6460 Sanibel–Captiva Rd., Sanibel Island 33957
Price: Moderate to Expensive
Credit Cards: D, MC, V

The Santiva area that lies before the bridge to Captiva Island is unique to Sanibel. It demands less than the island's more exclusive beaches and their properties. Here a barefoot and ultra-carefree attitude prevails. With its marina and cottage style, The Castaways embodies my vision of what a Florida beach vacation should be. For those who shun the traffic of nearby Turner's Beach, which some of the cottages border, many of the accommodations hide bayside where the preoccupation is fishing. The forty units are spread out between the two waterfronts with lots of room in between. The one- to three-bedroom, weathered, blue-gray cottages provide clean, comfortable, and ample — if somewhat dated — accommodations. A small swimming pool and watersports equipment rental concession complement an ideal location.

SUNDIAL BEACH & TENNIS RESORT
General Manager: Brett Smith

Sundial promises the perfection of a worry-free vacation. Sanibel's fine shelling beach is the focus of the resort, which takes its name from one species of shell. Thirteen tennis courts contribute

1-800-237-4184 or 472-4151
1451 Middle Gulf Drive,
  Sanibel Island 33957
Price: Expensive to Very
  Expensive
Credit Cards: AE, D, DC,
  MC, V

their part to the nomenclature, but recreation of all sorts is provided. The resort has five heated swimming pools, 10 jacuzzis, bike-and-beach rental concessions, game rooms, and children's programs. The lavish main building houses two restaurants — one overlooking the Gulf, the other serving Japanese food — and shines with Caribbean elegance. Less stylish, low-rise condo buildings are camouflaged by well-maintained vegetation and hold 230 fully equipped units decorated in hot pink, sea foam green, and natural wicker. They take advantage of Gulf or garden views. Given its high level of service, the Sundial is one of the area's least pretentious, most comfortable properties, especially for families.

LODGING — SOUTH COAST

Bonita Springs

SHANGRI-LA
Innkeeper: John Cheatham
992-3811
P.O. Box 2328, Bonita
  Springs 33959
Price: Moderate (three-day
  minimum)*
Credit Cards: MC, V

There's a mysterious aura about Shangri-La. It appears as a bright, white vision of 1920s-style Mediterranean architecture amidst a rather plain, somewhat shabby downtown section of Bonita Springs. Townspeople don't really know what to think about it; rumors range from its being a religious retreat to a manatee research facility. Shangri-La, in fact, has nothing to do with spirituality. Or manatees, for that matter. It is a health resort, but the emphasis is on natural diet. Exercise programs, beach trips, tennis and basketball courts, a swimming pool, shuffleboard, rowboats, paddleboats, and retreat-like surroundings are conducive to the good health Shangri-La promotes, but hygiene education is the main thrust. Guests check in to one of 60 units, of which 12 are suites, for a minimum of three days to learn how founder R.J. Cheatham lived 24 years longer than expected by the doctors who diagnosed him with cancer. He credited his survival to natural diet, and opened Shangri-La to share his discoveries. Meals consist of fresh fruits, vegetables, nuts, grains, and distilled water. The squeaky clean kitchen uses no animal products or byproducts, oils, or processed foods. The eight-acre property wraps around tranquil Oak Creek. Some of the buildings date back to the town's earliest development. The sulphur spring that gives the town its name was walled by a later owner who purported its healing qualities. These days the spring, still surrounded by glass cubes and whitewashed cement, sits dormant most of the year because of the area's lowering water table. A his-and-her solarium allows guests to sunbathe *au naturel*. Rooms are void of televisions and phones, but are comfortable, clean, and air-conditioned, some with vintage fixtures and bathroom tiles, some with shared baths. Everything is low-key; no one forces health upon you, and John Cheatham (R.J.'s son) is a young, personable fellow with strong convictions, but certainly no fanatic.

Everglades City

ROD & GUN CLUB
Innkeeper: Marcella
    Bowen
695-2101
200 Broadway, Everglades
    City 33929
Price: Inexpensive
Credit Cards: No
Handicapped Access: No

Steeped both in history and outdoorsmanship, this circa-1850 lodge crowns a modest town that serves as the South Coast's gateway to the Everglades. The club's main building dates back to 1850, when it was built as luxury pioneer housing. The Old South-style mansion came under the ownership of the county's namesake, Barron Collier, who turned it into a fisherman's and hunter's haven during the 1920s. A sportsman's lodge in its finest sense, its cypress walls are still decorated with mounted tarpon and tools of the fishing trade. Forty rooms occupy cottages scattered around the white clapboard lodge, with its wraparound veranda and yellow trim. The rooms are furnished for function rather than luxury. The club's boat-in restaurant with screened porch specializes in local delicacies and will cook your catch for a nominal fee. The swimming pool is wisely screened to keep out mosquitoes, that most abundant species of Everglades wildlife.

The lodge at Everglades City's Rod & Gun Club blends Southern charm with wilderness sportsmanship.

Naples

THE EDGEWATER BEACH
General Manager: John Ayres
1-800-821-0196 (U.S.); 1-800-282-3766 or 262-1243 (Florida)
1901 Gulf Shore Blvd. N., Naples 33940
Price: Expensive to Very Expensive
Credit Cards: AE, DC, MC, V

Edgewater hints at New Orleans style with lacy, white iron balusters on two of its three buildings. Its 124 one- and two-bedroom suites are spacious, convenient, and appointed in tropical decor. The floor plan of each includes a full kitchen (with microwave), living/dining area, and private patio or balcony. Guests can dine in the award-winning Crystal Parrot, or poolside under stylish canvas and wood umbrellas. There's an on-site exercise room and opportunities for other recreation nearby, including golf privileges at several local courses.

INN BY THE SEA B&B
Innkeeper: Catlin Maser
649-4124
287 11th Ave. S., Naples 33940
Price: Moderate to Expensive*
Credit Cards: MC, V
Handicapped Access: No

Though the sea is actually a few blocks away, this circa-1937 structure is located in Old Naples, at the threshold of the celebrated Third Street South shopping district. The first thing that strikes you is how good the place smells, owing to baskets of potpourri amid the country-style decor. A stenciled stucco fireplace dominates the sitting room, with its melange of wicker and stuffed furniture. Guests will get a kick out of reading the framed Star clipping in the dining room, which spills the news about Innkeeper Catlin's former life as wife of TV actor ("Major Dad") Gerald McRaney. She vows to hang a plaque above it attesting that she neither broke the story to the gossip mills, nor did she hang the article. Washed pine furniture continues the country theme in the same room, where guests partake of Catlin's "tropical breakfast" — fresh-baked goods, fruit. and juice. Darkly stained Dade pine lines ceilings and floors, and trims stucco walls throughout the smallish rooms. The five guest rooms are named for local islands and designed with individual appeal. The Gasparilla room has lace curtains and a quilted coverlet on the bed. Captiva is done like a beach cabana. Sanibel's bed is canopied; its windows shaded with sand-colored Bahamian blinds. Keewaydin and Bokeelia are suites. All have private baths.

KEEWAYDIN ISLAND
General Manager: Oscar Velez
1-800-688-1935 or 262-4149
260 Bay Rd., Naples 33940
Price: Expensive to Very Expensive*
Credit Cards: AE, MC, V

This flashback to old Florida, island style, is reminiscent of gracious eras of seclusion and wilderness. A five-minute ferry ride for Naples' mainland takes one back fifty years, to a world away — an unbridged, 2,200-acre island known for its shelling and birding. The main lodge, built in 1935, sets a sports-haven tone with cathedral wood ceilings, a majestic stone hearth, and warm wood furnishings. Forty-six cottages, one- to nine-bedroom, furnish all the comforts except a telephone and television, which would be too contrary to the mood. All meals are provided and tennis, sailing, windsurfing, and fishing create diversions for non-vegetative types.

The Naples Pier and old Naples Hotel, grandaddy of Gulf Coast resorts, circa 1958.

The Collier County Historical Society, Inc.

NAPLES BEACH HOTEL
& GOLF CLUB
Owners: The Watkins
    Family
General Manager: Michael
    Watkins
1-800-237-7600 or 261-2222
851 Gulf Shore Blvd. N.,
    Naples 33940
Price: Moderate to Very
    Expensive
Credit Cards: AE, CB, D,
    DC, MC, V

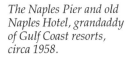he doyenne of Naples resorts, it combines the best of the area — its beaches and its golf — into a three-generation tradition at the heart of the town. The 18-hole golf course hosts the Florida State PGA Seniors Open. Har-Tru tennis courts, a heated pool, Beach Klub for Kids, and watersports equipment rentals vie for off-the-course recreational hours. The hotel's lobby, Everglades Dining Room, and 315 guest rooms and suites are done in wicker, palm-frond-and-hibiscus fabric patterns, and Florida style. Accommodations overlook the palm-studded beach or lush golf course.

THE REGISTRY
RESORT
General Manager: Jerry
    Phirion
1-800-247-9810 or 597-3232

Luxury with beach casualness: The Registry fits Naples like a gold lamé wetsuit. Its distinctive red-capped tower, villas, and 15 Har-Tru tennis courts dominate north Naples' pristine, mangrove-

The Registry Resort introduces pampered pleasures to the natural environment of North Naples beaches and estuaries.

475 Seagate Dr., Naples 33940
Price: Very Expensive
Credit Cards: AE, CB, D, DC, MC, V

fringed estuaries. The resort's style is impressive from the moment you enter the front door into a marble and crystal lobby. Outside is a boardwalk that rims the gulfside and leads to shops and restaurants. Downstairs there's a pool with a Flintstone's feel and a long bridge to the beach. Tram service is available along the wooden walk that traverses tidal bays to Clam Pass Recreation Area, a three-mile stretch of fairly secluded sands. Special packages and programs address environmental awareness. Fifty tennis villas edge the courts; another 474 rooms and suites overlook the Gulf and are furnished with a mini-bar, spaciousness, and class. The Registry owns a nearby 27-hole golf course, and provides shuttles to and fro. Three heated pools include jacuzzis; the health club contains a sauna and steam baths. Seven restaurants and lounges range from casual to the world-class Lafite.

THE RITZ-CARLTON
General Manager: John Conway
1-800-241-3333 or 598-3300
280 Vanderbilt Beach Rd., Naples 33963
Price: Very Expensive
Credit Cards: AE, CB, D, DC, MC, V

The gold standard for regal accommodations, Naples' Ritz molds Old World elegance to Old Florida environment. Each of its 463 units faces the Gulf by way of a U-shaped configuration. Guest rooms and suites are dressed in fine furniture, plush carpeting, and marble bath areas. Accommodations include honor bar, refrigerator, bathrobes, hypoallergenic pillows, telephones in the water closet,

An entourage of royal palms intimate the regal, Old World elegance of The Ritz-Carlton in Naples.

The Ritz-Carlton of Naples

clothes steamers, and private balconies overlooking the hotel's unique back-yard. In the courtyard, fountains and groomed gardens exude European char-acter. Classic arches, stone balusters, and majestic palm-lined stairways lead to a boardwalk that takes you through a completely different world of Florida estuarine life, via a self-guided flora tour. The tour ends at golden Vanderbilt Beach, where a beach bar serves refreshments and provides guests with chaises and cabanas. The hotel's approach facade looms majestically classic, with top-hatted valets to park your car. Inside, oversized vases of fresh flowers, heavy chandeliers, cabinets filled with priceless china, 19th-century oil paintings, vaulted ceilings, and crystal lamps detail Ritz extravagance. Other amenities and services that earn the Ritz its five stars and five diamonds include a formal dining room, afternoon tea service, grill, cafe, pool, lounge, ballroom, jacuzzi, six tennis courts, off-property golf facilities, fitness center, beauty salon, masseuse, children's programs, sailing, bicycle and jet ski rental, shops, trans-portation services, and twice-daily maid service.

Marco Island

**RADISSON SUITE
BEACH RESORT**
General Manager: Derrick
Barnett
1-800-333-3333 or 394-4100

Along the island's stretch of shell-strewn beach, the Radisson accommodates guests in typical Marco high-rise style, with 269 roomy suites and hotel rooms. The suites come in the one- or two-

600 S. Collier Blvd., Marco Island 33937
Price: Expensive to Very Expensive
Credit Cards: AE, CB, D, DC, MC, V

bedroom variety, and hold a completely equipped kitchen. All units have private balconies and comfortable furniture. Microwaves, refrigerators, and coffee makers provide all guests with in-room dining options. A gulfside dining room, grill, and tiki bar fill in when cooking is out of the question. Active guests enjoy a heated free-form pool, two tennis courts, a jacuzzi, water-skiing, kayaking, sailing, tubing, jet-skiing, fishing, sailing, cruising, biking, and golf on three nearby courses.

HOME & CONDO RENTALS

Sarasota Bay Coast

Betsy Hills Real Estate (778-2291; 419 Pine Ave., Anna Maria 34216) Private homes and cottages on Anna Maria Island.

Florida Gulf Coast Vacations (1-800-237-2252, or 778-4800; Paradise, Inc., 3001 Gulf Dr., Holmes Beach 34217) Condominiums, cottages, duplexes, and apartments on Anna Maria Island.

Longboat Accommodations and Travel (1-800-237-9505; 4030 Gulf of Mexico Dr., Longboat Key) Carries more than 300 waterfront properties.

Charlotte Harbor Coast

DCR Rental Management (1-800-741-8484, 624-0500; 24901-8 Sandhill Blvd., Punta Gorda 33983) Condos, homes, beach villas, and golf course units, furnished and unfurnished.

Island Coast

Grande Island Real Estate (1-800-551-7788; 472-5322; 1630 Periwinkle Way, Suite C, Sanibel Island 33957) Sanibel, Captiva, and Boca Grande rentals.

Vacations in Paradise (1-800-237-8906; 481-3636; 8250 College Pkwy. #102, Fort Myers 33919) Privately owned homes and condos, and deluxe hotel accommodations throughout the region and on Marco Island.

South Coast

Bluebill Properties, Inc. (1-800-237-2010, 597-1102; 9060 Gulf Shore Dr., Naples 33963) Rentals from Fort Myers Beach to Marco Island.

RV RESORTS

Sarasota Bay Coast

Royal Coachmen Resort (1-800-548-8678, 488-9674; 1070 Laurel Rd. E., Nokomis 34275–1699) 376 sites with a wide variety of available activities: game room, clubhouse, card room, social events, Olympic pool, tennis, shuffleboard, exercise trail, fitness center, miniature golf, pool tables, softball, basketball, volleyball, horseshoes, playground, ping pong, and tropical bird exhibit.

Sarasota Bay Travel Trailer Park (794-1200; 10777 44th Ave. W., Bradenton 34210) Located on the bay with full hook-ups.

Charlotte Harbor Coast

Punta Gorda RV Resort (639-2010; 3701 Baynard Dr., Punta Gorda 33950) 208 grassy sites with full hookups, some on canals and Alligator Creek for fishing and boating.

Island Coast

Groves Campground (466-5909; 16175 John Morris Rd., Fort Myers 33908) Close to Sanibel Island, with full accommodations and swimming pool.

Pine Island KOA (283-2415; 5120 Stringfellow Rd., St James City) 371 sites, pool, saunas, hot tub, exercise room, tennis court, shuffleboard, and fishing.

Red Coconut RV Resort (463-7200; 3001 Estero Blvd., Fort Myers Beach, 33931) Right on the beach, but packed in a bit tightly; offers full hook-ups, on-site trailer rentals, laundry, shuffleboard, cable TV, and car rentals.

South Coast

Chokoloskee Island Park (695-2414; P.O. Box 430, Chokoloskee 33925) Fisherman's paradise with easy access to the Everglades and Gulf; full-service marina, tackle shop, guide service, boat rentals, ramps, and docks. Overnight or seasonal RV sites with complete hook-ups.

Port of the Islands RV Resort (1-800-237-4173, 394-3101; 20 miles southeast of Naples on Tamiami Trail) Location convenient to Ten Thousand Islands on the waterfront. Ninety-nine hookup sites, with laundry, boat ramp, and marina.

Rock Creek Campgrounds (643-3100; 3100 North Rd at Airport Road, Naples) Two hundred sites for RVs only, with full hookups, pool, laundry, and shade trees. No pets.

CHAPTER FOUR
Inspiration by the Sea
CULTURE

One of Southwest Florida's great contradictions is that it lies more to the North than to the South on the cultural map. To the north, or inland, you will find Deep South cookery, clog dancing, bluegrass music, and traditional southern arts. In Southwest Florida, however, the midwestern and eastern U.S. influences are most noticeable. For many years, certain coastal areas were in a cul-

One of Pine Island's vernacular architectural gems awaits restoration on Main Street, Bokeelia.

tural limbo, void of any strong artistic or regional identity. The Coast's large retirement population includes many people involved in the arts, whose efforts in diverse media provide infinite variety. One of the few arts that residents can truly call their own is shellart — which in its highest form can be stunning and delicate — and in its lowest, can result in some pretty tacky shell animals. The Miccosukee Indians in the Everglades contribute the only authentic, indigenous art with their colorful weaving, stitching, jewelry, and other age-old handicrafts.

Besides Native American influences, enclaves of ethnicity sprinkle the map with exotic, Old World flavor. The Scots who settled Sarasota in its youth are largely responsible for the area's abundant golf courses. An Amish farm settlement outside of town brings its home-cooked flavors to the local dining scene.

The populations of Cape Coral and North Fort Myers include many elements — Italian, Jamaican, German, and Hispanic — who share their customs at social clubs, restaurants, festivals, and other functions. Throughout Fort Myers, Afro-Americans, Asians, East Indians, and other nationalities heighten the cosmopolitan flavor.

Affluent residents of Naples share a county with impoverished migrants, many of whom work at the nearby Immokalee agricultural center. The influences of Haitian, Puerto Rican, Jamaican, and other Caribbean peoples are finding their way into the mainstream.

Flashes of Southern spirit and Cracker charm do brighten the Coast's less resorty areas, in particular Bradenton, North Fort Myers, Pine Island, Bonita Springs, and Everglades City.

In areas where the wealthy settled early on, culture arrived with them. At first eager to escape the metropolitan ways for the simplicity of life on the beach, these also wanted access to serious theater and fine arts, and so ensured their existence. Sarasota most benefited from generous cultural endowment via the Ringling brothers. Not only did the Ringlings bring circus magic to a quiet frontier town, but also they exposed the pioneers to the wonders of European art and architecture. In their wake, they left a spirit still palpable and entirely unique to the Gulf Coast. Art schools and theater groups breed a freshness, vitality, daring, and air of the avant-garde unusual for a town its size.

Siesta Key, especially, has an atmosphere that has attracted writers, artists, and actors since folks began settling there: mystery writer John D. MacDonald and Pulitzer Prize-winning author MacKinlay Kantor settled on the island in the past; abstract artist Syd Solomon, sculptor Jack Down, and Pulitzer Prize-winning cartoonist Mike Peters live there today. Other cartoonists and artists, as well, have found the area conducive to creativity. Hagar the Horrible's Dik Browne and Garfield's Jim Davis live on Longboat Key. Surrealist Jimmy Ernst, son of Dada master Max Ernst, spent much time on Casey Key. Artist Thornton Utz still has a home in the area.

The islands of the Charlotte Harbor and Island Coast region have inspired their share of creative minds, too. Singer Jimmy Buffett frequents Cabbage Key and Captiva Island. His brand of beachy folksong is the closest thing the Coast has to home-grown music. Part Caribbean, part country, it extols the virtues of sailing, sunning, and drinking rum. Other Gulf Coast musicians include rock stars Glenn Frey, Brian Howe, Elton John, Brian Johnson, and Cliff Williams, and jazz musician Michael Franks.

On Sanibel and Captiva, the illustrious roll call began in the 1920s with Charles and Anne Morrow Lindbergh, and Edna St. Vincent Millay, whose original manuscript for *Conversation at Midnight* burned in a hotel fire. Today Robert Rauschenberg, a maverick in the field of photographic lithography, is the Island Coast's impresario. Internationally renowned artist Rene Miville lives on Pine Island, where the village of Matlacha begins to etch its place on the artistic map with restored architecture and gutsy galleries.

Fort Myers is coming into its own slowly, in terms of culture, having suffered an image problem from being sandwiched between the arts centers of Sarasota and Naples. The latter excels in architectural, visual, and performing arts in a quieter, less revolutionary way than Sarasota.

All in all, the cultural scene of Southwest Florida unfolds a colorful, multitextured umbrella that encompasses everything from classical opera, to hand-carved sculpture, to Teddy bear collections, to rock concerts on the beach.

For up-to-date information on Sarasota Bay Coast events, performances, and exhibitions, call the Arts Line, 359-ARTS. On the Island Coast, call 433-INFO to learn about arts and festivals.

ARCHITECTURE

If one overall style were chosen to represent Gulf Coast architecture, it would have to be Mediterranean — specifically Italian and Spanish-mission versions. Cracker architecture runs a close second.

Southern European and North African influences are found primarily in public and commercial buildings constructed during the boom years of the Roaring Twenties, when they were lumped together under the label of Mediterranean Revival. It reveals itself in stucco finish, mission arches, red barrel-tiled roofing, bell towers, and rounded step facades. Re-revived, new Mediterranean post-modernism serves as a popular style for upscale housing developments and commercial enterprise. It updates Mediterranean Revival and blends with it elements of tropical styles adopted from the Cracker era.

Pure Cracker style began as folk housing. From the vernacular, single-pen home — a wood-frame, one-room house featuring a shady veranda, tin roof, and board-and-batten siding — grew more sophisticated interpretations of the style. Gothic characteristics, Victorian embellishments, Palladian accents, and New England influences caused the humble Cracker house to evolve into a trendy, modern-day version termed *Old Florida*. Boxy and stilted, its most distinctive characteristics include a tin roof and wide, wraparound porch.

The latest influence on the Cracker house comes from the Caribbean and the Bahamas, via the Keys. Since indigenous West Indian styles are greatly similar to Cracker, especially in their suitability to tropical weather, the relationship was inevitable. The result: sherbet colors and hand-carved fretwork — used as much for ventilation as for decoration — add charm and whimsy to the basic unit.

Like the Cracker home, the Seminole Indian's chickee hut conformed to tropical climate with high-peaked roofs, wide overhangs, and open sides. Today, the thatched roofing, which is the chickee's most distinctive feature has become an art form. Still a popular style of housing for the Miccosukees of the Everglades, the chickee has evolved as a trademark of the Gulf Coast watering-hole tradition known as tiki bars.

With the mid-1920s migration of the "tin can tourist," the mobile home replaced the Cracker house on the low end of the architectural totem. Mobile home parks still provide low-cost housing, mostly to part-time winter residents.

A popular residential style of the 1970s, the concrete-block ranch, was built to withstand hurricanes. Flooding regulations of the 1980s raised these upon pilings; lattice and fretwork added interest. Art deco returned later in the decade as Miami Beach's Art Deco District attracted attention.

Today's Gulf Coast cities are seasoned with period styles and spiced with contemporary theory that strives for compatibility with nature. Use of screened porches, windowed Florida rooms, and lots of sliding doors let the outside in, to enhance our unique and enviable climate and environment.

Sarasota Bay Coast

In the Bradenton area, the Greek Revival style of plantation house has left its impression. The best example of it survives grandly at the Gamble Plantation Mansion. Pioneer styles are preserved at the Manatee Historical Village, including a Cracker Gothic farmhouse and early brick store. In downtown Bradenton, you'll find prime Mediterranean influence at the pink Riverpark retirement hotel and the later-generation Pier Restaurant.

On Bradenton Beach one finds the highest concentration of "beach shack architecture." Located from Anna Maria Key to Marco Island, these anything-but-shacky abodes were so named by the wealthy visitors to the region. The Duncan House Bed-and-Breakfast is one example of this style, spruced up in Caribbean motif.

On Longboat Key, resorts and mansions are more modern. In the village once known as Longbeach, one finds a return to comfortable, older styles, with a bit of New England charm.

Sarasota's downtown and bay areas hold a smorgasbord of old European style, from the lavish Italian-inspired Ca'd'Zan at Ringling Estates, to the Spanish Edwards Theater which, renovated, houses the Sarasota Opera. John Ringling Towers is one of the town's finest examples of boom-time architecture. It awaits rehabilitation in a combined city and county effort. Fine examples of old, residential architecture are found on the fringes of the downtown area.

In the 1950s, Sarasota revolutionized local architecture by developing a contemporary style suitable to the environment. Examples of the Sarasota School of Architecture are spread throughout the area, most notably at Summerhouse Restaurant on Siesta Key.

Often overlooked, Venice houses many architectural treasures created in the 1920s, when the Brotherhood of Locomotive Engineers chose it for a retirement

Venice Little Theatre echoes the town's neo-Mediterranean motif.

center and subsequently built a model city there in North Italian style. Two shining examples are the Park Place Nursing Home at Tampa Avenue and Nassau Street — originally the Hotel Venice — and the nearby Venice Centre Mall, erstwhile San Marco Hotel and Kentucky Military Institute. The length of West Venice Avenue reveals stunning homes in the prevailing, Mediterranean Revival style.

Mango Tours (952-9378) offers weekly walking tours, every Saturday morning, of Sarasota's historic architecture. Admission is $4.00 for adults and is free for children under 12 years old.

Charlotte Harbor Coast

In the smaller towns around Charlotte Harbor, single examples of historic character appear serendipitously, in the midst of concrete block homes. Downtown Englewood, a destination off the beaten path of the Tamiami Trail, holds a few such treasures. One, a quaint clapboard church of stark, puritan style, houses the Lemon Bay Historical Society. The community's first church, it was built in 1926 to accommodate the Methodist circuit preacher who traveled from Nokomis.

Punta Gorda spreads its architectural prizes along Marion Avenue and Retta Esplanade. Hollander House is the jewel of the old riverfront district.

Boca Grande's most noteworthy examples are four historic churches, each with its own style, located in a four-block area downtown. The Catholic Church takes inspiration from Spanish missions. The others occupy early-century, wood frame buildings and serve Episcopal, Baptist, and Methodist congregations.

A few blocks away, on Tarpon Avenue, old Cracker homes slump comfortably in a district sometimes called *Whitewash Alley*. For a taste of wealthy eccentricity, check out the Johann Fust Library on Gasparilla Road. It was built of native coquina, cypress, and pink stucco, by former residents.

Island Coast

Fort Myers is home to some lovely architecture downtown, and along McGregor Boulevard. Thomas Edison's home was, perhaps, Florida's first pre-fab structure. Because wood and materials were scarce (most newcomers made do with palmetto huts), Edison commissioned a Maine architect to draw up plans and construct sections of the home to be shipped down and pieced together on site. Downtown, the Richard Building, circa 1924, boasts an Italian influence, while the court house annex superbly represents Mediterranean Revival. The new Harborside Convention Center echoes the motif in modern times.

Pine Island possesses the best, most concentrated collection in the area of preserved vernacular architecture, especially in Matlacha. Pineland's mound-squatting homes are also prime examples, occasionally dressed up with lattice-work and vivid paint jobs.

Henry Ford named his winter estate in Fort Myers The Mangoes, for the tree prevalent in his orchard. He so loved mangoes that he had the fruit shipped to him at his summer residence in Michigan.

In Bokeelia, the entire Main Street is designated an historic district. Notice especially the Captain's House on Main Street, a fine example of slightly upscale folk housing of the early 1900s, with French Provincial elements. Turner Mansion, nearby, represents a higher standard of living and is reminiscent of New England styles.

The club at Useppa Island, which non-guests can view only by boat, holds a prime collection of Old Florida styles, both traditional and revival.

Side trips down shell-named streets such as Coquina Drive and King's Crown take you into Sanibel Island's residential areas, where styles range from renovated Cracker cottages to stately Victorian mansions. Even art deco dwellings are popping up, despite islanders' attempts to keep out what they call incompatible styles. Caribbean architecture takes hold here, with its shining example and trend-setter, the Matsumoto Gallery, a restored Cracker-style beach home in eye-popping shades.

Indian mounds and Cracker houses make for a scenic, history-saturated drive through the community of Pineland, on Pine Island.

South Coast

In Naples, commercial architecture is marked by style and panache, not to mention the architectural beauty of the homes and resorts. Banks and insurance companies seem to compete for virtuosity. It's truly a land of visual allure. Pelican Bay developments provide examples of a new residential style, and provide a contrast with old-money Port Royal.

Old Naples, that neighborhood in the vicinity of the pier, has held on to some real treasures, including the tabby-mortar Palm Cottage, the old Mercantile (now home to Wind and the Willows boutique), the Old Naples building at Broad and Third, and the Mediterranean-style Plaza, nearby. In the same neighborhood, on Gordon Drive, pay attention to the charming board-and-batten Cracker survivors.

In Everglades City, recreational vehicles and cement-block boxes typify the fishing-oriented community. The Rod & Gun Club, built in 1850, stands out and dresses the town in Southern flair. The Indian-perfected style of thatch housing prevails through the Everglades, and serves as trendy beach-bar motif at the ritziest resorts throughout the coastal region.

Tiki Islander Cruises (262-7577, Tin City, 1200 Fifth Avenue South, Naples), provide sightseeing tours of Naples' mansions aboard a South Island-style, thatch-topped vessel. Tours depart at 11:00 a.m., and 2:00 and 4:00 p.m. daily. The cost is $12.00 per person for adults, and $8.00 for ages 12 and under.

Today, Naples has a reputation for palatial mansions and lush landscaping.

CINEMA

FILM

Sarasota Bay Coast

FSU/Asolo Conservatory Burt Reynolds Wing for Motion Picture, Television and Recording Arts for the Performing Arts (351-8000; 5555 N. Tamiami Tr., Sarasota) A Florida State University film training facility within the Asolo Performing Arts Center, sponsor of the annual Sarasota French Film Festival. (See the listing for *Cultural Events*, later in this chapter.)

Sarasota Film Society (388-2441; Sarasota) Group devoted to screening quality international films year-round, currently at mainstream theaters, but with plans to build its own facilities.

Island Coast

Island Coast locations have provided settings in various contemporary movies: North Captiva in the remake of *Cape Fear*, Sanibel Island in *The Return of the Living Dead* and Fort Myers in *Coup de Ville.*

Film Society of Southwest Florida (481-8333; William Frizzell Cultural Centre, 10091 McGregor Blvd., Fort Myers) is an arm of the Lee County Alliance of the Arts, that screens non-mainstream films.

MOVIE THEATERS

Sarasota Bay Coast

Perhaps Sarasota cinema's greatest claim to fame occurred when the curtain recently came down on PeeWee Herman's career in a local theater.

Bradenton 8 (794-2300; Cortez Plaza, 4425 14th St. W., Bradenton)
Cinema 10 (371-2210; Sarasota Crossing Plaza, Sarasota)
Venetian 6 Theatres (493-5855; Venetian Plaza, 1733 Tamiami Tr. S., Venice)

Charlotte Harbor Coast

Cinema Center 8 (624-3334; 19190 Toledo Blade Blvd., Port Charlotte)
Promenades Cinema (627-3700; 3280-9 Tamiami Tr., Port Charlotte)

Island Coast

Bell Tower East, North, and West (433-3100; Daniels Pkwy. and U.S. 41, Fort Myers)

Coralwood 10 (574-6006; Coralwood Mall, Del Prado Blvd., Cape Coral)
Island Cinema (472-1701; Bailey's Shopping Center, 535 Tarpon Bay Rd., Sanibel)
Northside Drive-In Theater (995-2254; 2521 N. Tamiami Tr., North Fort Myers)

South Coast

Pavilion (598-1211; The Pavilion Shopping Center, N. Tamiami Tr., Naples)
Towne 6 Cinema (793-0006; 3855 Tamiami Tr., Naples)

DANCE

From country clog dancing to classic ballet, participatory and spectator dancing along the Gulf Coast of Florida reflect the diverse origins and social milieux of its people.

Sarasota Bay Coast

Babiak Dance Ensemble (966-1847; 1742 Joyce St., Sarasota) Folkloric, costumed dance performance.
Bradenton Ballroom (351-6466; Airport Mall, 8251 Route 301, Bradenton) Participatory ballroom, country western and line dancing.
Sarasota Ballet (366-6740) Classic and interpretative dance performances are staged at the Sarasota Opera House and Van Wezel Performing Arts Center, from August through March.
Sarasota Scottish Country Dancers (755-6212; 6481 Prospect Rd., Sarasota) One evidence of the town's Scottish heritage.
Town and Country Ballroom (954-8696; Town & Country Shopping Center, 501 N. Beneva Rd., Suite 620, Sarasota) Participatory ballroom dancing.

Island Coast

Caloosa River Cloggers (542-2066; Fort Myers Activity Center, 2646 Cleveland Ave., Fort Myers) Perpetuators of a southern/mountain folk dance performed usually at festivals.
Hall of Fifty States (334-7637; 2254 Edwards Dr., downtown Fort Myers) Hosts ballroom and country-and-western dancing.
Shalom Folk Dancers (267-0834; 6315 Presidential Ct., Fort Myers) Israeli and ethnic dancing lessons.
Southwest Florida Dance Theatre (275-3131; 2084 Beacon Manor Dr., Fort Myers) Ballet and interpretative dance for adults and children, renowned for its programs for underprivileged students.

ESPECIALLY FOR KIDS

Sarasota Bay Coast

BISHOP PLANETARIUM
746-4131
201 10th St. W., Bradenton

Saturday morning programs for students K–3, including a Children's Starshow and hands-on program in adjacent South Florida Museum.

THE GULF COAST WORLD OF SCIENCE
957-4969
717 N. Tamiami Tr., Sarasota
Admission: $1.50

A hands-on museum with fossils, giant bubbles, reptiles to pet, planetarium, echo chamber, computers, sensory games and gift shop. Closed Monday and Tuesday.

SARASOTA JUNGLE GARDENS
355-5305
3701 Bayshore Rd., Sarasota

Exotic bird and reptile shows, shell and mounted butterfly collections, a playground with a jungle theme, a small petting zoo, monkeys, flamingos, swans, wallabies, and other live animals make this the area's favorite children's attraction. Peaceful, jungly gardens appeal to others. (See the *Gardens* section, later in this chapter.)

VAN WEZEL SATURDAY MORNINGS FOR KIDS
953-3366
777 N. Tamiami Tr., Sarasota

Cinderella, *101 Dalmatians*, and other kiddy classics take the stage each Saturday morning at 10:30. November–May.

Island Coast

THE CHILDREN'S SCIENCE CENTER
997-0012
2915 NE Pine Island Rd., Cape Coral

Encourages visitors of all ages to touch and interact with the exhibits. It includes hands-on projects constructed by local students, traveling and permanent shows, and computer, science, and outdoor games.

IMAGINARIUM
332-6666
Dr. Martin Luther King Jr. Blvd. and Evans Ave., Fort Myers

To be completed by Summer, 1994, this touch-and-taste facility will occupy an historic water plant, making use of pumps, pipes, tanks, and dials to learn about weather and other scientific phenomena. Exhibits will encourage participation and use of the imagination.

South Coast

**COLLIER AUTOMO-
TIVE MUSEUM KIDS
PROGRAMS**
643-5252
2500 S. Horseshoe Dr.,
  Naples

Offers Saturday morning FUNshops, where children 4–7 can learn about physics, chemistry, and creative thinking in two-hour, hands-on workshops. Summer Science Camp runs in one-week day sessions for children ages 6–12.

**JUNGLE LARRY'S ZOO-
LOGICAL PARK**
262-5409
1590 Goodlette Rd., Naples
Admission: $10.95 adults;
  $6.95 children 4–15

Very much a children's attraction; true animal lovers may bristle at the small cages. A wide variety of animals can be seen via narrated tram, free boat ride, or on foot. Some, like the cavy, cassowary, and tiglon (half tiger, half lion) are quite unusual. Tiger, alligator, and elephant shows are included in the price of admission; elephant rides cost an extra $2.50 per person. The 52-acre grounds are attractively maintained with the lush vegetation of its so-called Caribbean Gardens (see Gardens). The petting zoo is one of the best I've experienced, with deer, donkeys, goats, and pot-belly pigs that eat out of your hand.

**TEDDY BEAR MUSEUM
OF NAPLES**
598-2711
2511 Pine Ridge Rd.,
  Naples

On its own, this attraction begs for children. (See listings for museums in this chapter.) Volunteers host a Saturday morning story hour and monthly puppet shows.

GARDENS

Sarasota Bay Coast

**SARASOTA JUNGLE
GARDENS**
355-5305
3701 Bayshore Rd., Sara-
  sota
Admission: $8 for adults;
  $4 for children 3–12

Largely a kiddy attraction, plant lovers will enjoy its botanical gardens and tropical jungle. Winding paved paths lead easily through the grounds' 16 acres, 100 varieties of palms, and countless species of indigenous and exotic flora, all identified. Private nooks and bubbling brooks make this a lovely spot for quiet reflection, especially in the early mornings before the throngs arrive. Exotic birds and other attractions are gravy to the connoisseur of nature. (See *Especially for Kids* in this chapter.) Snack bar and gift shop.

**MARIE SELBY BOTANI-
CAL GARDENS**
366-5730
811 S. Palm Ave., Sarasota
Admission: $6 for adults;
$3 for children ages 6–11

A 1920s residence on Sarasota Bay occupies 10 acres, planted in gardens that wow plant lovers with plots of palm, bamboo, award-winning hibiscus, tropical food plants, herbs, and other exotic flora. Selby is world-renowned for its collection of 6,000 orchids in a lush rainforest setting. Best times to visit are the Christmas season, when poinsettias and greenery festoon the grounds and their historic home, and in April, when the blooming orchids inspire a festival.

Island Coast

**FRAGRANCE GARDEN
OF LEE COUNTY**
432-2000
Lakes Regional Park, 7330
Gladiolus Rd., Fort Myers

Still under construction by volunteers, this garden at the park's west end is being built primarily for the disabled, though the general public also will enjoy this one-of-a-kind attraction. For the visually impaired there are pungent herbs, fragrant vines, and signs in Braille. To accommodate the physically handicapped, volunteers are building paved paths and planting vegetation at wheelchair height. Vined arbors will be built wide enough for easy wheelchair access.

South Coast

CARIBBEAN GARDENS
262-5409
1590 Goodlette Rd., Naples
Admission: $10.95 adults;
$6.95 children 4–15.

These tropical gardens, today the setting for Jungle Larry's Zoological Park (see *Especially for Kids*), were planted in 1919 by Dr. Henry Nehrling, a botanist who brought his private collection to Naples. After he died, a Naples developer restored and expanded the doctor's 3,000-plus specimens and opened the gardens to the public in 1954. Besides native vegetation, exotics such as tamarinds, kapoks, orchids, carambolas, and pink tabulia flourish in wetlands and on hammocks. Free tram and boat rides.

HISTORIC HOMES AND SITES

Sarasota Bay Coast

BRADEN CASTLE PARK
746-7700
27th St. E. and Route 64,
Bradenton
Hours: Sunrise to sunset

At the juncture of the Manatee and Braden rivers antebellum memories crumble at a site recognized by the National Register of Historic Sites. Short of spectacular, the ruins are chain-linked with "Keep Out Danger" signs posted. They hide at the center of a compact neighborhood of old, popular architecture. A marker tells the story of the Braden Plantation.

CA'D'ZAN
359-7500
Ringling Estate, 5401 Bay
  Shore Rd., Sarasota
Closed: Major holidays
Hours: Daily 10–5:30
Admission: $8.50 for
  adults, $7.50 for seniors
  55 and over; covers
  entry to all Ringling
  attractions. Children 12
  and under accompanied
  by an adult admitted
  free; Florida students
  and teachers admitted
  free with proper I.D.

Using the Doges Palace in Venice as a model, Circus King John Ringling spared no expense building a monumuent to success and overindulgence in the 1920s. He imported styles, materials, and pieces from Italy, France, and around the world to embellish his so-called (in Venetian dialect) "house of John." Baroque, Gothic, and Renaissance elements contribute to a breathtaking and ornate look of opulence in the 30-room, $1.5 million mansion on the bay.

DE SOTO PARK
792-0458
75 St. NW, Bradenton
Hours: 8–5:30

Somewhat off the beaten path, this is a place where you can imagine yourself back in the 16th century among conquistadores in heavy armor trying to survive among irate Native Americans, mosquitoes, and sweltering heat. Cement plaques and a half-mile-long, interpretive, audio-guided trail, tell the story of Hernando De Soto's life, times, and adventures here, where supposedly he first breached the shores of the Florida mainland. A visitors' center holds artifacts and shells, and a video presentation is available. In the winter, rangers dress and play the part of 16th-century inhabitants, demonstrating methods of weaponry and food preparation.

**DOWNTOWN
  BRADENTON**
9th Street and Route 64

Signs direct you to the Riverfront Cultural Oasis — a grand name for a very humble, somewhat decrepit historic district which is, for some reason, quite loveable in its unpretentiousness. Old Main Street and the city yacht basin are the area's backbone. It includes some very interesting architecture, a great museum, and a few yuppy bars for business and government workers. Locals are trying hard to pump new life into a river town that died with the automobile. Right now things are pretty quiet and most of the residents live in retirement hotels. Visit the antique shop on Main Street and have lunch at the Pier, then stroll around nearby Point Pleasant for a taste of Bradenton's oak-laden homeyness and heritage.

GAMBLE PLANTATION STATE HISTORICAL SITE
723-4536
Route 301 near I–75 in Ellenton
Closed: Tuesday and Wednesday
Hours: Sunrise to sunset
Admission: $2 adults; $1 children 6–13 for mansion tour only; no admission into park

Major Robert Gamble, originally from Scotland, learned about sugar planting in Virginia before he moved to the Manatee River. He cleared 1,500 acres of jungle using his slave labor, and built an 1840s home in Greek Revival style. The mansion's crowning touch — 18 Greek columns —he constructed of oyster shells, sand, and (some believe) molasses, to concoct a mortar known as tabby. The spacious palace, by local standards, was inhabited by bachelor Gamble alone, but served as the area's social hub until the major was forced to sell it in 1856, due to hurricane, freeze, and market losses. In 1925, the mansion was rescued from continued neglect by the United Daughters of the Confederacy. The site was declared a Confederate shrine for its role in sheltering Confederate Secretary of State Judah P. Benjamin as he fled for his life after the Civil War. The United Daughters donated the monument to the state a couple of years later. Visitors can tour the home.

HISTORIC SPANISH POINT
966-5214
500 N. Tamiami Tr., Osprey
Hours: 9–5 Mon.–Sat.; 12–5 Sun.
Admission: $4 adults; $2 children 6–12; under age 6 free

This historic site spans multiple eras of the region's past — 2150 B.C. through 1918. Its importance lies not only in its historical aspects, but also in environmental and archaeological importance. Assembled on the 30-acre Little Sarasota Bay estate, once owned by socialite Mrs. Potter Palmer, are prehistoric Indian shell and debris mounds, the relocated homestead of the pioneering Webb family, Mrs. Palmer's restored gardens, a late Victorian pioneer home, an early cemetery, a rebuilt chapel, a reconstructed citrus packinghouse, and an archaeological exhibit. Local actors give living history performances Sundays during the winter season. Guided tours and tram rides are available on some days.

MANATEE VILLAGE HISTORICAL PARK
749-1800, ext. 4075
6th Ave. E. & 15th St. E., Bradenton
Closed: Saturday year-round and also Sunday during July and August
Hours: 9–4:30 weekdays; 2–5 Sundays

Several buildings with local historical significance have been restored and moved to a pleasant, oak-shaded park strongly representative of Bradenton's wooded and winding neighborhoods. The County Court House is the oldest, completed in 1860. Others include a circa-1889 church, a Cracker farmhouse, a one-room schoolhouse, a smokehouse, and a general store of the early 19th century. A museum of artifacts, photographs, and hands-on exhibits for children is located in the general store. The Stephens House is stocked with period kitchen items, furniture, and farm implements. The staff wears historically accurate dress. Across the street is the Manatee Burying Ground, which dates from 1850 and is appropriately eerie, with strands of Spanish moss straggling from craggy oaks. All in all, it's a romantic site, grossly underrated and lightly visited — only schoolchildren the day I was there.

ROSEMARY CEMETERY
Tenth St. and Central Ave.

Colorful epitaphs and distinctive headstones mark the graves of early Sarasota pioneers in the town's oldest cemetery. It was restored recently by the Sarasota Alliance for Historic Preservation.

Charlotte Harbor Coast

PONCE DE LEON
 HISTORICAL PARK
End of Marion Ave.

A shrine commemorates Ponce de Leon's supposed 1513 landing here, and his subsequent death by Indian attack. The park is a wildlife and recreational area, but lightly visited.

Punta Gorda commemorates Ponce de Leon's first landing on Florida's West Coast with a monument and park on Charlotte Harbor.

**BOCA GRANDE LIGHT-
   HOUSE**
964-0375
Gasparilla Island State
   Recreation Area, Gulf
   Blvd.
Hours: Tours the last Sat-
   urday of each month
   and by prior arrange-
   ment for groups.

This 1890 structure was renovated in Old Florida style and put back into service in 1986, after 20 years of abandonment. It is the most photographed and painted landmark on the island.

Island Coast

BURROUGHS HOME
332-1229
2505 First St., downtown
   Fort Myers
Hours: Tours conducted
   every hour on the hour
   10–4 Mon.–Fri.
Admission: $3.18 adults,
   $1.06 children 6–12.

Mona and Jettie Burroughs, in 1918 dress, host the living history tour at Fort Myers' first luxury residence. Tour guides in period costume assume the playful characters of two sisters who once occupied the Georgian Revival-style mansion, built in 1901. They'll invite you to add a few stitches to the afghan they're knitting for the war effort, then take you back in time to when cowboys drove their cattle past their home, and the Henry Fords hosted square dances. Authentically restored furniture and appointments provide a charming backdrop to this improv pageant on the banks of the Caloosahatchee River.

CHAPEL-BY-THE-SEA
11580 Chapin, Captiva
   Island

This quaint, interdenominational church is a popular spot for interdenominational Sunday services, weddings, and seaside meditation. Many of the island's early pioneers have been laid to rest in a cemetery beside the chapel.

FISH SHACKS
Pine Island Sound at Cap-
   tiva Rocks, east of North
   Captiva

The last legacies of the region's early commercial fishing enterprises brave weather and bureaucracy to strut the shallows along the intracoastal waterway. The one at the mouth of Safety Harbor on North Captiva is most noticeable. It once served as an ice house. Several others can be seen if you look east. Privately owned and maintained as weekend fish homes for local enthusiasts, most are listed on the National Register of Historic Places and serve as a picturesque reminder of days gone by.

**KORESHAN STATE HIS-
   TORIC SITE**
992-0311
Tamiami Trail, Estero
Hours: 8:00 a.m.–sunset

Contained within a state park, this site has restored the customs and ways of the early 1900s religious cult that settled on the banks of the Estero River. Under the leadership of Cyrus Teed,

Admission: $3.25 per vehicle

whose name in Hebrew is Koresh (no relation to the late David Koresh, leader of the Branch Davidians), members of Koreshan Unity were well-versed in practical Christianity, speculative metaphysics, functional and aesthetic gardening, art, Koreshan Cosmogony, and occupational training. Their most unusual theory held that the earth lined the inside of a hollow globe that looked down into the solar system. Teed and his followers envisioned an academic and natural Utopia. They planted their settlement with exotic crops and vegetation. They built a theater, a communal mess hall, a store, and various workshops, all of which have been restored or reconstructed to tell the strange story of the Koreshans, who lost steam upon the death of their charismatic leader in 1908. Surviving members lecture at the Koreshan Unity Foundation and library across the road from the park (992-2184).

SANIBEL CEMETERY
Off bike path on Middle Gulf Dr., not accessible by car

No signs direct you to it — just follow the path and you'll come across a fenced plot with wooden headstones announcing the names of early settlers — a wonderful, quiet place to ponder times past.

SANIBEL LIGHTHOUSE
At the southeast end of Periwinkle Way, Sanibel

Built in 1884, it was one of the island's first permanent structures. Once vital to cattle transports from mainland, it functions still as a beacon of warning and welcome. The lighthouse and Old Florida-style lightkeeper's cottage were renovated in 1991.

Sanibel's oldest landmark, its historic lighthouse, was built in 1884 as a guiding light for cattle transports.

Lee County Visitor and
Convention Bureau

The tropical gardens at Thomas Edison's historic winter estate in Fort Myers add dimension to a visit.

THOMAS EDISON WINTER ESTATE/ FORD HOME
334-3614
2350–2400 McGregor Blvd., Fort Myers
Hours: 9–4 Mon. through Sat.; 12:30–4 Sun.
Admission: $10 adults; $5 children 6–12
Edison Home only: $8 adults; $4 children 6–12

Nowhere in the U.S. will you find the homes of two such important historical figures sitting side by side. This site is so much more than just a couple of preserved houses, however. It is a slice of Floridiana, Americana, and Mr. Wizard, all rolled into 17 riverside acres. The tour begins across the street under the nation's largest banyan tree, a gift from Harvey Firestone. The tree, 400 feet around, poses outside of a museum that contains many of Edison's 1,000-plus patented inventions — the phonograph, children's furniture, the movie camera, and the light bulb — as well as the 1907 prototype Model T Ford his friend and wintertime neighbor, Henry Ford, gave him. Edison's late-1880s home hides in a jungle of tropical flora with which Edison experimented. Actually there are two homes, identically built and connected with an arcade. One contained the Edison's living quarters; the other, guest quarters and the kitchen. (Mr. Edison was bothered by the smell of cooking food, the guide may tell you.) His laboratory, full of dusty bottles and other ancient gizmos, sits in the backyard among reflecting pools and gardens. The

Friendship Gate separated Edison's estate from Ford's. "The Mangoes," as it was called, in honor of the fruit orchards the car manufacturer so loved, seems humble compared to its neighbor. Recently, it was returned to its turn-of-the-century heyday, with furnishings true to the period and the Fords' simple tastes.

South Coast

INDIAN HILL
Scott Drive, Goodland

Marco Island, though rich in natural and historic heritage, hides it well among 20th-century trappings. Witness Indian Hill. On your own (the trolley tour will take you there), you'll have to search to find it, and when you do, only a barely noticeable plaque marks the spot. Southwest Florida's highest elevation at 58 feet above sea level, attained by ancient Caloosa Indian shell mounds, it now holds a ritzy neighborhood called the Heights, which feels briefly like San Francisco.

PALM COTTAGE
261-8164
137 12th Ave. So., Olde
  Naples
Closed: Weekends and late
  summer to early fall
Hours: 2–4 or by appoint-
  ment

Land was selling for $10 a lot when Naples founder, Walter N. Haldeman (no relation to H.R. Haldeman of Watergate fame) built a winter home for fellow worker, Henry Watterson. Haldeman, publisher of the *Louisville Courier Journal*, had discovered the exotic beaches and jungles of Naples in 1887, and then proceeded to buy up land and sing its praises. His enthusiasm persuaded winter escapees from Kentucky and Ohio to visit, including Watterson, his star editorial writer. The cottage Haldeman built for his friend was made of Florida mahogany and a certain type of tabby mortar consisting of seashells burnt over a buttonwood fire. It was one of the first buildings in southwest Florida to be constructed of local materials. Before reaching its present museum status, the cottage — rather spartan by modern standards — knew many lives. If the walls could talk at Palm Cottage, as it eventually came to be known, they would tell of wild parties with the likes of Gary Cooper and Hedy Lamarr in attendance. The Collier County Historical Society now has its headquarters there.

SMALLWOOD STORE
695-2989
360 Mamie St., Chokolos-
  kee Island, south of
  Everglades City
Closed: Wednesday and
  Thursday off-season
Hours: 10–5
Admission: $2.50 adults;
  $2 seniors; children
  under 12 free

An historic throwback to frontier days in the 'Glades, this museum preserves a Native American trading post of the early 1900s. Splintery shelves hold ointment containers, old Coca-Cola bottles, hardware supplies, and hordes of memorabilia. This was the site of a Jesse James-era murder popularized in Peter Matthiessen's novel, *Killing Mr. Watson*.

MUSEUMS

Sarasota Bay Coast

ANNA MARIA ISLAND MUSEUM
778-0492
402 Pine Ave., Anna Maria
Closed: Monday, Friday and Sunday; June through August
Hours: 10–noon
Admission: Donations accepted

A homey little museum inside an ice house of the 1920s, it holds photos, maps, records, books, a shell collection, a turtle display, and vintage videos. Next door sits the old jail, worth a laugh with its humorous graffiti.

BELLM CARS & MUSIC OF YESTERDAY
355-6228
5500 N. Tamiami Tr., Sarasota
Hours: 8:30–6 Mon.–Sat.; 9:30–6 Sun.
Admission: $7.50 adults; $3.75 children 6–12

Displays of antique cars and musical instruments combine under one roof. The museum collection includes 1,200 antique, mechanical, and musical instruments, featuring songs from the 1890s through the 1920s. Browse among 175 classic and antique cars, plus a blacksmith shop and livery stable.

RINGLING CIRCUS GALLERIES
355-5101
Ringling Estate, 5401 Bay Shore Rd. off Tamiami Tr., Sarasota
Closed: Holidays
Hours: Daily 10–5:30
Admission: $8.50 for adults, $7.50 for seniors 55; covers admission to all Ringling attractions. Children under 12 free; Florida students and teachers free with proper I.D.

The Circus Museum was Florida's way of saying "thank you," back in 1948. Its re-creation of Big Top magic paid tribute to a man many believed invented the circus; a man who bequeathed to the city — along with the giddy world of the circus — a legacy of exotica, sophistication, and art appreciation. In 1989, the museum underwent a half-million dollar renovation, with world-class museum designers at the reins. No longer a mere museum, the displays are now called galleries. It was upscaled and upgraded to the high standards of art maintained by Sarasota. The new Circus Galleries reflect Ringling's seemingly contradictory interests. Fine arts displays counterbalance high wire exhibits. Black and white photography is juxtaposed with gilded fantasy. Tasteful cloth mannequins model plumed and sequined costumes. Dutch prints depict bareback riders, striking a perfect

The John & Mabel Ringling Museum of Art, one of the circus's most enduring legacies to Florida.

equilibrium between circus raucousness and the art of form. A favorite display is the collection of antique calliopes and circus wagons.

SOUTH FLORIDA MUSEUM
746-4131
201 10th St. W., Bradenton
Closed: Monday and
   major holidays
Hours: 10–5 weekdays, 1–5
   weekends
Admission: $5 adults;
   $2.50 children 5–12

The two-story museum scans Florida history, with a focus on Native American life and Civil War days. The star of the museum is Snooty, the oldest manatee born in captivity in the United States. Other highlights include life-size Native American dioramas, replicated early Spanish buildings, and an authentic bald eagle nest atop a cypress tree. The Bishop Planetarium adjoins the facility with a 50-foot hemispherical dome, laser shows, and other special effects.

South Florida Museum is the pride of downtown Bradenton, with Snooty the Manatee the starring attraction.

Charlotte Harbor Coast

**MUSEUM OF CHAR-
LOTTE COUNTY**
639-3777
260 W. Retta Esplanade,
Punta Gorda
Closed: Sunday
Hours: 10–5 Tues.–Fri.;
12–5 Sat.

Five galleries scan local history and exhibit African and American animals, and changing displays.

Island Coast

**THE BAILEY-
MATTHEWS SHELL
MUSEUM**
395-2233
Sanibel–Captiva Rd., Sani-
bel Island

To be completed in late 1993, it will underline the island's shelling reputation by providing an educational and research facility. The museum's exhibits will trace the natural and social history of shells, and showcase Sanibel specimens, both common and rare. Until completed, a temporary, preview headquarters is open at 2431 Periwinkle Way.

**CAPTIVA HISTORY
HOUSE**
472-5111
Entrance to South Seas
Plantation resort, Cap-
tiva
Closed: Monday and Sat-
urday
Hours: 10–4

This new museum occupies a 1920s cottage that originally served as a plantation worker's home, back when key limes were farmed. Through photographs, memorabilia, and story boards, the museum relates the history of Captiva Island, from prehistoric man through the farming and fishing eras of the early 1900s.

**FORT MYERS HISTORI-
CAL MUSEUM**
332-5955
2300 Peck St., Fort Myers
Closed: Saturday
Hours: 9–4:30 Mon.–Fri.;
1–5 Sun.
Admission: $2 adults; $.50
children under 12

Housed in a restored railroad depot, the museum's displays take you back to the days of the Caloosa Indians with scale models, graphic depictions, and historical IQ games. Other exhibits include rare glass and art collections, a circa-1930 private rail car, and changing attractions.

**ISLAND HISTORICAL
MUSEUM**
472-4648
850 Dunlop Rd., near City
Hall, Sanibel Island
Closed: Sun.–Tues.
Hours: 10–4

Occupying an historical Cracker-style abode, once the home of an island pioneer, this bite-size museum dwells on Sanibel's modern history of homesteading, citrus farming, steamboating, and tourism, with photos and artifacts. It remembers the Caloosa era with a dugout canoe and other

A classic example of a Cracker house in its most basic form can be viewed at the Fort Myers Historical Museum.

signposts of the times. The original Bailey's General Store, circa 1927, was moved to the site in 1993 as a kickoff to establishing a Pioneer Village on the grounds.

MUSEUM OF THE ISLANDS
283-1525
5728 Sesame Drive, Pine Island Center, Pine Island
Closed: Mon.–Wed. off-season
Hours: 1–4
Admission: Donations accepted

Occupying the old Pine Island library at Phillips Park, it concentrates on the area's Caloosa heritage. In 1992, the museum unveiled a shell mound replica, modeled after one excavated on the island. Continue on to the settlement of Pineland to see time standing still upon intact Native American mounds.

South Coast

COLLIER AUTOMO-TIVE MUSEUM
643-5252
2500 S. Horseshoe Dr., Naples
Closed: Monday
Hours: 10–5
Admission:$6 adults; $3 children 5–12

If you like to look at money in the form of expensive collector cars, you will love this museum. Unlike most museums I've seen devoted to race-car history, this one spells class all the way, housed in a garret-like gallery, with track lighting that makes polished chrome sparkle, and flawless paint jobs. A short film introduces you to the history of the sport, but is the least spectacular aspect of the tour. Vintage race and sports cars are tastefully displayed, along with engine blocks under glass. Signs tell you everything you'd want to know about such classics as the 1907 Renault, 1929 Mercedes-Benz, 1934 MG, 1934 Alfa Romeo, and 1938 BMW. Highlights include the country's first Ferrari, a Bentley collection, and a 1914 Rolls-Royce Silver Ghost, all from private collections, some 75 in all. Children like the 1984

March Indy car, into which they can climb and play out fantasies, but generally it's a no-touch exhibit. Knowledgeable men in business suits provide guided tours and information upon request. An outdoor waterside cafe offers limited food.

COLLIER COUNTY MUSEUM
774-8476
3301 Tamiami Trail E., Naples
Closed: Weekends
Hours: 9–5
Admission: Donations accepted

The most unique aspects of this house of history include a typical Seminole village, a vintage swamp buggy, an archaeological lab, and a steam locomotive situated outdoors in a two-acre park. Inside, the exhibits take you back 10,000 years, with prehistoric fossils and Native American artifacts.

TEDDY BEAR MUSEUM OF NAPLES
598-2711
2511 Pine Ridge Rd., Naples
Closed: Monday and Tuesday
Hours: 10–5 Wed.-Sat; 1–5 Sun.
Admission: $5 adults; $3 teens and seniors; $2 4–12 years old

Home to more than 2,100 teddies, this cuddly museum showcases collector, antique, and limited edition bears, including a signed first edition copy of A.A. Milne's *Winnie the Pooh*. The collection began as one woman's penchant for the stuffed animals, and is whimsically displayed: bored bears at a board meeting, bears on parade, etc. A gift shop sells bears and fine gifts.

MUSIC AND NIGHT LIFE

SARASOTA BAY COAST

Sarasota dances with action throughout the week, and especially on weekends. Besides local bands and chorales, both well-known and up-and-coming stars appear in theaters and nightclubs. Many restaurants host live entertainment in cabaret style. Cores of activity include downtown's bohemia, the neon-bright Sarasota Quay, and posh St. Armands Circle. Check the *Ticket* insert of the *Sarasota Herald-Tribune* and *Bradenton Herald's Weekend* every Friday to learn what's happening in the clubs throughout the area.

Sarasota

Club Bandstand (954-7625; 300 Sarasota Quay, Fruitville Road at Tamiami Tr.) The setting is pure discotheque with a nostalgia theme. Live bands perform some nights.

Florida West Coast Symphony (953-4252, 709 Tamiami Trail N., Sarasota) Besides classical symphony concerts, this group sponsors various related ensembles, including a string quartet, wind quintet, brass quintet, new artists' quartet, youth orchestra, and pops series.

Friends of Florida Folk (377-9256, 1625 Verda Verdi, Sarasota) A musical group specializing in Florida folk music; performs free monthly concerts on City Island.

The Gator Club (366-5969; 1490 Main St., downtown) One of the hottest places downtown, with live music weekends.

Jazz Club of Sarasota (366-1552, 290 Coconut Ave., Bldg. 3) This organization dedicates itself to the perpetuation and encouragement of jazz performance by presenting various monthly and annual events, Saturday jazz jams, clinics, workshops, and youth programs, with a musical instrument lending library.

Limerick Junction (366-6366; 1296 First St., downtown) An Irish pub atmosphere with skits and musical routines on weekends; musicians and open-mike nights throughout the week.

Old Heidelberg Castle (366-3515; Route 301 and Fruitville Rd., Sarasota) Known more for its trampoline and German music shows than for its food, this landmark features the Happy Austrians every night but Monday.

Paradise Cafe (955-8500; 1311 First St.) The kingpin of downtown Sarasota's cabaret scene, it headlines the musical group *Panache* and its musical revue, in an art-deco atmosphere.

Sarasota Blues Society (388-1837) Weekly jams, monthly concerts with renowned artists and an annual festival.

Sarasota Concert Band (955-6660, 73 Palm Ave. S., #224, Sarasota) This ensemble's members (over 50 of them) perform at Van Wezel Hall from October through May, and at outdoor concerts throughout the Sarasota Bay Coast.

Top of the Quay (953-9444; 310 Sarasota Quay, Fruitville Road at U.S. 41) Stages musical shows and revues, with or without dinner.

Siesta Key

Beach Club (349-6311; 5151 Ocean Blvd.) Amid the atmosphere of a rowdy college bar, it hosts local rock, jazz, and reggae groups nightly.

St. Armands Key

Cafe New Orleans (388-2629; 328 John Ringling Blvd., St. Armands Circle) In a cabaret setting, single artists and small jazz or bluegrass bands perform most nights.

ChaCha Coconuts (388-3300; 417 St. Armands Circle) Contemporary music and dancing nightly.

The Patio (388-3987; Columbia Restaurant, 441 St. Armands Circle) Spirited with youthful dance energy and popular music nightly.

Venice

Crow's Nest (484-9551; 1968 Tarpon Center Dr.) Features live jazz musicians and singers on a changing calendar.

CHARLOTTE HARBOR COAST

Port Charlotte

Charlotte Symphony Orchestra (625-5996; Port Charlotte Cultural Center Theater, Aaron St.)
Gatorz Bar & Grill (625-5000; 3816 Tamiami Tr.) Live music throughout the week: jazz and top-forty.

Punta Gorda

Charlotte County Memorial Auditorium (639-3777; 75 Taylor St.) Waterfront host to Broadway plays, big band and swing orchestras, and national stars.

ISLAND COAST

Friday's *Gulf Coasting* supplement to the *News-Press* covers the entertainment scene on the Charlotte Harbor, Island, and South coasts, with emphasis on the Island Coast.

Captiva Island

Crow's Nest Lounge (472-5161; 'Tween Waters Inn, Captiva Rd.) Live contemporary dance bands Tuesday through Sunday. The one and only hot spot for Sanibel and Captiva residents and guests.

Fort Myers

Club Mirage (275-9997; 4797 Cleveland Ave.) A bopping, youthful place with DJ or live music Monday through Saturday.
Harborside Convention Hall (334-4958; 1375 Monroe St.) The new hub of activity, which is drawing more nighttime interest to the downtown area. It hosts prominent entertainers and musicians.
Peter's La Cuisine (332-2228; 2224 Bay St., downtown) In a restored warehouse above a restaurant, it spotlights blues bands in a setting laden with atmosphere.

Fort Myers Beach

The Bridge (756-0050; 708 Fisherman's Wharf) A popular spot with boat-in and drive-in bar-flies, featuring lively dance music outdoors on the docks.

Lani Kai Island Resort (463-3111; 1400 Estero Blvd.) The premier party spot on the Beach, with live entertainment nightly, and during the day on weekends, at rooftop or on the beach.

The Reef (463-4181; 2601 Estero Blvd.) Rowdy, rock-n-roll bar with scheduled jam nights.

North Fort Myers

Guantanamera (656-3505; 4400 Hancock Bridge Pkwy.) Salsa, meringue, and other live island/Hispanic entertainment.

Sanibel Island

Jacaranda Patio Lounge (472-1771; 1223 Periwinkle Way) Live music nightly in a variety of genres.

SOUTH COAST

Naples

Club Oasis (774-9399; 2023 Davis Blvd.) Live music nightly, from reggae to country.

Riverlights Restaurant (775-7772; 1355 Fifth Ave. S.) One-man band and groups Monday through Saturday.

Vanderbilt Inn (597-3151; 11000 Gulf Shore Dr. N.) Live music, indoors and at the Chickee Bar on the beach.

SPECIALTY LIBRARIES

Sarasota Bay Coast

Arthur Vining Davis Library (388-4441; Mote Marine Laboratory, 1600 Ken Thompson Pkwy., City Island) Gathers research for lab scientists. Open to the public for reference.

John and Mabel Ringling Museum of Art Research Library (355-5101; 5401 Bay Shore Rd., Sarasota) Specializes in 17th-century Dutch, Flemish, and Italian paintings.

Verman Kimbrough Memorial Library (351-4614; Ringling School of Art and Design, 2700 N. Tamiami Tr., Sarasota) Art history and instruction.

Selby Public Library (951-5501; 1001 Blvd. of the Arts, Sarasota) The region's central library, it schedules cultural events throughout the year.

Island Coast

C.R.O.W. Wildlife Library (472-3644; Sanibel-Captiva Rd., Sanibel Island)

Talking Books Library (995-2665; 13240 No. Cleveland Ave., North Fort Myers) Library for blind and physically handicapped with books on tapes or records.

THEATER

In grand performing halls and intimate playhouses, the Gulf Coast parades an ongoing bill of entertainment across its stages. From Broadway troupes to community casts, the following listings name places and faces that make up the local drama scene.

Sarasota Bay Coast

Anna Maria Island Players (778-5755; Pine and Gulf Dr., Anna Maria) Year-round community theater.

Asolo Center for the Performing Arts (Box office 351-8000, tours 351-9010, ext. 4806; 5555 N. Tamiami Tr., Sarasota) The Asolo tradition began in Italy in 1798, with a theater built in the queen's castle. It ended up on the Ringling Estate in 1949, where it was reconstructed and, in 1965, designated State Theater of Florida. In the early 1980s a new center was built, incorporating into its interior design another dismantled, historic European theater — a Scottish opera house circa 1900. Carved box fronts, friezes, and ornate cornice work from the old theater decorate the new. Opened in 1989, it hosts the Asolo Theatre Company and is open for free touring when not being used for rehearsals.

Cabaret Club (366-9796, Sarasota) Schedules a rotating repertoire of musical and other entertainment at clubs throughout Sarasota's downtown theater and arts district, with dinner and drinks available.

Florida Studio Theatre (366-9796; 1241 N. Palm Ave., downtown Sarasota) A major testing ground for budding playwrights and new works, this professional troupe presents seven productions during its December–August season, and a summertime New Plays Festival. (See the *Cultural Events* section in this chapter.)

Golden Apple Dinner Theatre (366-5454; 25 N. Pineapple Ave., downtown Sarasota) Year-round, musical dinner entertainment here, and at the **Venice Golden Apple Dinner Theater** (484-7711; Best Western Resort Inn, 447 U.S. 41 Bypass, Venice).

Sarasota's Opera House occupies a restored structure from the area's Mediterranean architectural era of the 1920s.

Manatee Players Riverfront Theater (748-5875; 102 Old Main St., Bradenton) Manatee Players do community theater here.

Sarasota Opera at A.B. Edwards Theatre (953-7030; 61 N. Pineapple Ave., downtown Sarasota) Don't even try to park or dine downtown on opera opening nights during the February–March season. The Gulf Coast's only opera company's opening galas are popular events that require ticket purchase months in advance. It occupies a beautifully restored Spanish mission-style structure in the Theatre and Arts District. In operation for more than 30 years, the troupe stages all the classics. Night and Sunday matinee performances. You can tour the facility (and see the chandelier from the set of *Gone With the Wind*) for $2.00.

Theatre Works Inc. (952-9170; 1247 First St., downtown Sarasota) Professional comedies, musicals, and dramas October through May in an historic, intimate setting at Palm Tree Playhouse.

Van Wezel Performing Arts Hall (953-3366; 777 N. Tamiami Tr., Sarasota) It's that purple eye-catcher that radiates outward like a scallop shell on the shores of Sarasota Bay, designed by the Frank Lloyd Wright Foundation. If it's worth seeing, it's at Van Wezel. Tickets should be purchased at least a

The sculpture Applause *greets visitors to Sarasota's Van Wezel Performing Arts Center.*

month in advance. It hosts name comedians, musicians, and dance groups; Broadway shows; major orchestras, ethnic music, and dance groups; chamber and choral music; and Saturday children's shows. Home of the Florida West Coast Symphony and the Florida Symphonic Band.

Venice Little Theatre (488-2419; 140 W. Tampa Ave., downtown Sarasota) A community theater company from Venice performs a September–June season of seven mainstage shows in a Mediterranean Revival structure.

Charlotte Harbor Coast

Charlotte Players (627-4434; Port Charlotte Cultural Center, 2280 Aaron St., Port Charlotte) Community theater.

Lemon Bay Playhouse (475-7547; 353 W. Dearborn, Englewood) Home of the Lemon Bay Players' community theater group.

Lee Island Coast

The Arcade Theatre (332-6688; 2267 First St., downtown Fort Myers) The glory of the 1920s playhouse has been restored and advanced to the 21st century. In season, professional troupes perform popular comedies and musicals, plus other special events.

Barbara B. Mann Performing Arts Center (481-4849; Edison Community College campus, 8099 College Pkwy SW, Fort Myers) Host to major Broadway shows, musical performers, and dance troupes. Its state-of-the-art sound system provides infrared headsets for the hearing impaired.

Clairborne & Ned Foulds Theater (939-2787; William Frizzell Cultural Centre, 10091 McGregor Blvd., Fort Myers) Operated by Lee County Alliance of the Arts as an indoor and outdoor stage for recitals, concerts, and workshops. The professional troupe, The Company, performs in the intimate indoor theater from Fall through late Spring.

The name of Sanibel's oldest playhouse is restored from its former life as a one-room schoolhouse for pioneer children.

Cultural Park Theatre (574-0465; 528 Cultural Park Blvd., Cape Coral) A major arts complex that houses the local arts' league, an historical museum, a gallery, a community theater, and arts and crafts organizations. In its role as theater, it seats 189 and hosts concerts and local groups such as the Players Guild and Jellybean Players.

Old Schoolhouse Theatre (472-6862; 1901 Periwinkle Way, Sanibel Island) Installed in the charming setting of an historic schoolhouse circa 1896, this theater-in-the-round has served for years as the island's cultural mainstay. Recently updated, it hosts J.T. Smith Musical Productions, a professional troupe, in season; and Off-Beach Players, a community theater, during the summer.

Pirate Playhouse (472-0006; 2200 Periwinkle Way, Sanibel Island) Professional actors present mainstage comedies, musicals, and drama, in two seasons at a new theater-in-the-round.

South Coast

Naples Dinner Theatre (597-6031; 1025 Piper Blvd., Naples) Live professional musicals and comedies with complete dinner; evening shows and matinees.

Naples Playhouse (263-7990; 399 Goodlette Rd. S., Naples) Home of the Naples Players, a community theater troupe that has been entertaining year-round for 40 years.

Philharmonic Center for the Arts (597-1900; 5833 Pelican Bay Blvd., Pelican Bay, Naples) Both the 77-piece Naples Philharmonic and the Miami City Ballet base themselves at "The Phil," as locals call it. Completed in 1989 at a cost of more than $17 million, it hosts audiences of up to 1,222 for Broadway shows, touring orchestras, chamber music, and children's productions.

Philharmonic Center for the Arts, in Naples.

VISUAL ART CENTERS

The canvas of Gulfshore arts reveals a complex masterpiece, layered with the diverse patterns and local color of its many communities. Sarasota, with its backdrop of artistic types dating back to avid collector John Ringling, leads the Coast to avant-garde heights. Flocks of wildlife and other eclectic galleries make a name for Sanibel Island in cultural circles. Like its Italian namesake, Naples serves as the region's aesthetic trendsetter, with gallery-lined streets, which host artists of both national and international stature. In the smaller communities, a sense of the artistic emerges in off-beat galleries and art association halls that deepen the hues of the Gulf Coast art scene with character and folk heritage.

The following entries introduce you to opportunities for experiencing art, either as an appreciator or a practicing artist. A listing for commercial galleries is included in the *Shopping* chapter.

Sarasota Bay Coast

Read the *Sarasota Arts Review* for openings, and changing exhibitions.

ARTarget (953-2482; 522 S. Pineapple Av., downtown Sarasota) Dedicated to both new and established professional artists who address current issues and themes.

Artists Guild of Anna Maria Island (778-6694; 5414 Marina Dr., Holmes Beach) Features changing exhibitions in various media by Gulf Coast artists.

Art League of Manatee County (746-2319; 209 Ninth St. W., Bradenton) Classes and demonstrations in all media; sales gallery.

The Fine Arts Society of Sarasota (953-3366; Van Wezel Performing Arts Hall, 777 N. Tamiami Tr., Sarasota) Van Wezel houses a permanent collection of Florida artists' works. The Society conducts tours weekdays, November through April.

The John and Mabel Ringling Museum of Art (355-5101; 5401 Bay Shore Rd., Sarasota) Sarasota's pride and joy, this is not only an art museum, but also the nucleus of tourism activity and the heart of the local art community. It shares its 66-acre bayfront estate with Ringling's extravagant Ca'd'Zan Palace (see *Historic Homes*), a circus museum (see *Museums*), antique Italian theater (see *Theater*), a rose garden, and a Big-Top-shaped restaurant. Designated the State Art Museum of Florida, the collection specializes in late Medieval and Renaissance Italian works. The Old Masters collection contains five original Rubens tapestries, as well as Spanish Baroque, French, Dutch, and northern European works. The museum continually adds to its collection American and contemporary works. The lushly landscaped courtyards feature reproduction classic statues and Italian decorative columns which Ringling originally purchased for the hotel he wanted to build on Longboat Key. Admission is charged every day but Saturday and covers all property attractions.

Longboat Key Art Center (383-2345; 6860 Longboat Dr. S., Longboat Key) Fairly well hidden from mainstream traffic, here is a find for the buyer and would-be artisan. A gallery sells works, mostly by Florida artists. Changing exhibits feature local, emerging, and experimental artists. A crafts shop sells wares made at the center's surrounding workshops, where classes are taught in basketry, watercolor, jewelry making, metal-craft, pottery, and more.

Manatee Community College Fine Art Gallery (755-1511 ext. 4251; 5840 26th St. W., Bradenton) Features works of major artists.

Sarasota Visual Art Center (365-2032; 707 N. Tamiami Tr., Sarasota) Three exhibition and sales galleries feature the paintings, jewelry, sculpture, pottery, and enamelware of local and national artists. Art instruction and demonstrations are available.

Sarasota County Arts Council (365-5118; Sarasota) The Council supports local artists and organizations through grants, marketing, advocacy, and educational programs.

Selby Gallery (359-7563; 2700 N. Tamiami Tr., Sarasota) Exhibits the works of contemporary local, national, and international artists and designers, in conjunction with the Ringling School of Art and Design.

Charlotte Harbor Coast

Arts & Humanities Council (639-8061; 1601 W. Marion Ave., Suite 203, Punta Gorda) Hosts art displays and events.

Boca Grande Art Alliance (964-0177; 421 Park Ave., Boca Grande) Sponsors art shows and encourages arts for children.

Visual Art Center (639-8810; Maud St., Punta Gorda) Exhibit halls, gift shops, library, darkroom, and classes.

Island Coast

BIG Arts (395-0900; 900 Dunlop Rd., Sanibel Island) Home of Barrier Island Group for the Arts, a multi-disciplinary organization. Art shows are scheduled regularly at the facility.

Cape Coral Arts Studio (4522 Coronado Pkwy., Cape Coral) Art shows rotate through this polygon-shaped studio; classes and lectures are available.

Cultural Park (574-0465; 528 Cultural Park Blvd., Cape Coral) Home of the Cape Coral Arts League, Cape Coral Council for Arts and Humanities, and the Southwest Florida Craft Guild, it rotates gallery exhibits and offers classes and workshops.

Gallery of Fine Art (489-9313, Edison Community College, 8099 College Pkwy., Fort Myers) Exhibits works of nationally and internationally renowned artists.

Lee County Alliance of the Arts (939-2787; William Frizzell Cultural Center, 10091 McGregor Blvd., Fort Myers) Operates a public gallery, and conducts classes and workshops.

South Coast

The Art Gallery at the Registry Resort (597-8001; 475 Seagate Dr., Naples) Rembrandt, Renoir, Rockwell: the gallery carries the crème de la crème of artists.

Art League of Marco Island (394-4221; 1010 Winterbery Dr., Marco Island) Workshops, gallery, and gift shop.

Naples Artcrafters (455-7083, Naples) Artisan group that sponsors arts-and-crafts shows.

Naples Art Association (262-6517; 970 Fifth Ave. S., Naples) Workshops, classes, and gallery for local artists.

Philharmonic Galleries (597-1900; Philharmonic Center for the Arts, 5833 Pelican Bay Blvd., Pelican Bay, Naples) Exhibitions of well-known works, and guided tours.

CULTURAL EVENTS

For sports events and tournaments, please refer to the *Recreation* chapter. Food festivals are listed in the chapter on Dining.

Sarasota Bay Coast

A.D.A.S. Art Walk (953-5757; downtown Sarasota) Sponsored by the Art Dealers' Association of Sarasota, this event occurs twice yearly, for one day in early November and one day in early March.

Anna Maria Island Festival of Fine Arts (778-7155; Holmes Beach City Hall grounds) Hosts art exhibitors for two days in early December.

Children's Art Festival (355-5101; Ringling Museum of Art) Two days, late March.

Cine-World International Film Festival (388-2441, Sarasota) Screens 20 to 30 films from around the world for one week in early November.

Cortez Commercial Fishing Festival (794-1249; Coquina Beach Bayside Park, Bradenton Beach) Food vendors, country music, clogging dancers, arts-and-crafts, and educational exhibits describing the community of Cortez's 100-year-old fishing industry. One day, mid-February.

Creators & Collectors Tour (388-1444, Sarasota) Tour the homes and collections of major local artists and art collectors, hosted by the Fine Arts Society for two days in late February.

De Soto Celebration (747-1998) Held in various locations in and around Bradenton, it commemorates Hernando De Soto's discovery of the region. A reenactment of the 1539 landing highlights the events. One week in late April.

Discover the Past Festival (966-5214; Historic Spanish Point, Osprey) Living history vignettes, historical craft demonstrations, horse-and-buggy rides, canoe trips, food, and entertainment at this center of local history for two days in late November.

Downtown Arts Festival (951-2656, downtown Sarasota) Not your average open-air collection of mediocre and semi-tacky crafts, Sarasota puts together a classy gathering of top-notch artisans from around the world for two days in mid-February.

Historic Homes Tour (951-1547; Sarasota) Sponsored by the Alliance for Historic Preservation. One day in early February.

Manatee Heritage Days (741-4070) Celebration of local history and traditions throughout Bradenton and Manatee County, including guided tours of historical attractions and handicraft demonstrations. One week in late March.

Medieval Fair (355-5101, Ringling Museum of Arts grounds, Sarasota) The event of the year, this fair is a culmination of Sarasota's flair for art, theater, food, and circus, all within the atmosphere of a 15th century flashback. Four days in early March.

National Historic Preservation Week Festival (951-1547; Sarasota) Tours of historic homes, walking tours, and festivities.

Project Black Cinema International Film Festival ((957-7944) September.

St. Armands Circle Salebration (388-1554, St. Armands Circle) Two days, first weekend in October.

Sarasota Arts Day (365-5118; downtown Sarasota.) A gala confluence of Sarasota's visual and performing arts that spills from the galleries and theaters onto outdoor stages and sidewalks. January.

Sarasota Blues Festival (388-1837; Sarasota Fairgrounds) Blues musicians of world renown. One day in early September.

Sarasota French Film Festival (351-9010 ext. 4600; 5555 N. Tamiami Tr., Sarasota) This week-long event is the only one of its kind in the United States. It features world premieres of contemporary French films. The festival opens and closes with fanfare and parties, attracting participants from around the world. Industry seminars, panel discussions, and appearances by French film illuminati fill the week.

Sarasota Festival of New Plays (366-9017; Florida Studio Theatre, downtown Sarasota) Premiers the works of emerging playwrights from Florida and around the nation, launching many mainstage productions.

Sarasota Jazz Festival (366-1552; Van Wezel Hall, Sarasota) Big-name jazz players lead a slate of big bands and jazz combos. First weekend of April.

Sarasota Music Festival (953-4252; 709 N. Tamiami Trail, Sarasota) Presents classical and chamber music by students and faculty from music schools around the world. Sponsored by the Florida West Coast Symphony, it also provides classes for participants. The public is welcome at the performances. Three weeks in June.

Sarasota Sailor Circus (955-8417; 2075 Bahia Vista, Sarasota) There's still circus in the blood of many Sarasota families. Annually, students from grade three to 12 perform professional circus feats. Two weeks beginning in late March.

Shark's Tooth and Seafood Festival (488-2236; Venice) A bacchanal of seafood bounty, it gets its name also from its reputation among sharks-tooth collectors. August.

Siesta Fiesta (349-3800; Siesta Key) Two days in late April.

Springfest (778-2099) A celebration of the arts in Manatee County: ballet performances, plays, watercolor demonstrations, poetry readings, concerts, laser shows, and crafts exhibits. One week in mid-March.

Venetian Sun Fiesta (488-2236; Venice) A celebration of food, folks, and fun. One week in October.

Charlotte Harbor Coast

International Fall Festival and Yankee Peddler Fair (627-2568; Bon Secours–St. Joseph Hospital grounds, 2500 Harbor Blvd., Port Charlotte) Ethnic crafts and foods, with children's carnival. November.

Ponce de Leon Reenactment (637-1343; Ponce de Leon Park, Punta Gorda) A staging of the conqueror's first landing on the Gulf Coast. March.

Punta Gorda Days (Punta Gorda) Community celebration. Early April.

Punta Gorda Waterfront Festival (639-3720; Gilchrist Park, Punta Gorda) Water activities, alligator wrestling, children's art fair, music, and crafts.

Salute to the Arts (Throughout Charlotte County) Showcases performing and visual arts. One week in late October.

Island Coast

Best Southwest Festival (574-0081; Cape Coral Yacht Club, Driftwood Pkwy., Cape Coral) Live music, a western saloon, a casino, dancing, and a taste fair. One day in late April.

BIG Arts Fair (395-0900; Sanibel Community Center, Sanibel Island) Juried arts-and-crafts exhibits. Thanksgiving weekend.

Cape Coral Winter Festival (549-6900; Cape Coral) Ball, teen dance, parade, marathon, barbecue, pub crawl, jazz, and art exhibits. Nine days in late February to early March.

Christmas Luminary Trail (472-1080; Sanibel and Captiva islands) Luminary candles light the path down Sanibel and Captiva's commercial areas, where businesses stay open and dole out free drinks and food. One weekend in early December.

Cracker Festival (North Fort Myers) Reenactments of Civil War days. One weekend in early March.

Edison Festival of Light (334-2550; Fort Myers) Commemorates the birthday of Thomas Edison, culminating in a spectacular, lighted, night parade. Two weeks in early February.

Edison/Ford Homes Holiday House (275-1088; Edison/Ford Complex, Fort Myers) Miles of light strings, and period and seasonal exhibits draw crowds to this popular attraction. December.

Festival of India (939-2787; Lee County Alliance of the Arts, Fort Myers) Ethnic food and entertainment. March.

Greek Festival (481-2099, Greek Orthodox Church, 8210 Cypress Lake Dr., Fort Myers) Ethnic food and music. Two days in late February.

Hispanic Heritage Festival (335-2332; Lee Civic Center, North Fort Myers) A celebration of Hispanic culture which centers in the North Fort Myers and Cape Coral areas, featuring ethnic food, music, dance, and crafts. One day in October.

Indian Exposition and Powwow (455-2171; Lee Civic Center, 11831 Bayshore Rd., North Fort Myers) Native Americans from 100 tribes meet for dance contests, arts-and-crafts shows, and alligator wrestling. Three days in early April.

International Fine Art Auction (939-2787; Alliance of the Arts, Fort Myers) Old and contemporary masterworks on the block. One day in late March.

Jazz on the Green (481-2011; Dunes Golf and Tennis Club, Sanibel Island) Name jazz artists and food from local restaurants. Two days in early October.

Koreshan Unity Lunar Festival (992-2184; Koreshan State Historic Site, Estero) Arts-and-crafts shows and tours of the site. April.

Lee Sidewalk Arts & Crafts Show (334-6626; downtown Fort Myers) More than 250 artisans. Two days in mid-January.

Munich in Cape Coral (939-5050; German-American Club, Cape Coral) Cape Coral celebrates its strong German heritage with Oktoberfest activities. Two weekends in October.

Pan-American Festival (939-3007) A round-up of North, Central, South American, and Caribbean culture held throughout Lee County. One week.

Riverview Art Festival (433-5040; Cape Coral) Live music, food, and the work of over 150 artists and craftspeople on display. Two days in early January.

Sanibel Festival (472-4682; Sanibel Island) Classical music presentations, including free Bach on the Beach by The Woodwind Quintet. March.

Seniors Festival (275-1881) Free concert, games competitions, a gala ball, and a two-day expo at Harborside Convention Hall. One week in late January.

South Coast

Festival of Lights (649-6707; Third Street Plaza, Naples) Holiday street-lighting festivities. Late November.

Fifth Avenue Festival of the Arts (598-0300; Fifth Avenue, Naples) The work of 200 celebrated artists on display. March.

Indian Arts Festival (394-3397; Collier–Seminole State Park, south of Naples) Three days in mid-February.

Naples Tropicool Fest (262-6141) A celebration of Naples' emerging spirit of youth, it features rock and jazz bands, canoeing contests, art exhibitions, and concurrent food festivals. Two weeks in early May.

CHAPTER FIVE
Fruits de mer and de terre
RESTAURANTS & FOOD PURVEYORS

The first Europeans discovered a veritable Garden of Eden along Florida's Gulf Coast. The seas were teeming with Neptune's bounty, and exotic fruits and vegetables flourished on land. In fact, some locals adhere to a theory that this was the original Paradise, and that it was a sweet, luscious mango instead of the apple that caused Eve's downfall. Hence, the fruit's name: *Man! Go!*

In truth, mangoes are not native to Southwest Florida. However, they grow bountifully along with many other tropical products like pineapples, bananas, carambola (star fruit), lychees, avocadoes, coconuts, and

King Neptune's bounty in the raw at Skip One Seafoods in Fort Myers.

sapodillas. Citrus fruit is, of course, the region's most visible and profitable crop, particularly oranges. Key lime trees grow in profusion as well. Practically year-round producers, they are a standard part of any good Florida cook's landscaping scheme. Here, as in the Florida Keys, where the tree got named and famed, key lime pie is a culinary paradigm, and each restaurant claims to make the best. In the finest restaurants with the most extravagant dessert menus, key lime pie inevitably outsells the rest. The classic recipe, created by Florida cooks before refrigeration, uses canned, condensed and sweetened milk, and is elegant in its simplicity. The most important factor is the freshness of the limes — sometimes a problem for restaurants since the fruit does not lend itself to commercial farming. One sure sign of an inauthentic version is the color green. The key lime turns yellow when ripe and, unless the cook adds food coloring, should impart a buttery hue to its pie.

Historically, crop farming has provided coastal residents with economic sustenance. Weather conditions bless farmers with two growing seasons for most ground crops. As land becomes too valuable to farm, agriculture pushes inland. Bonita Springs, where thousands of acres remain devoted to tomatoes, and Pine Island, known for its tropical fruits, are the final bastions of the agricultural tradition.

Seafood is most commonly associated with Gulf Coast cuisine, including some culinary delicacies unique to Florida. The stone crab, our prize catch (Florida author Marjorie Kinnan Rawlings once described their taste as "almost as rare as nightingales' tongues,"), are in season from October 15 through May 15. Restaurants serve them hot, with drawn butter, or cold, with tangy mustard sauce. Their aptly named shells are usually pre-cracked, to facilitate their enjoyment. Stone crabs can be eaten and enjoyed free of guilt. Since only one claw of the shellfish is taken, and regenerates itself in time, no stone crab is asked to give its life to a seafood-gluttonous cause.

The Gulf shrimp is an emblem of local cuisine. Its poorer cousin, the rock shrimp, gets less publicity because of its hard-to-peel shell. More economical and with a flavor and texture akin to lobster, it's certainly worth tasting.

Restaurants change their menus, or at least their daily specials, according to what's in season and the local catch. Grouper, the most versatile food fish in the area, traditionally has been available year-round, but environmental pressure is limiting its availability. A large and meaty fish, its taste is so mild you hardly know it's fish. Winter months bring red and yellowtail snapper to diners' plates. Warmer weather means pompano, cobia, shark, and dolphinfish (also known as mahi mahi). Tuna and flounder are caught sporadically, but year-round. Some restaurants serve less well known species, such as triggerfish and catfish, to offset spiraling costs caused by dwindling supplies of the more popular varieties. Fish-farming also addresses these shortages. Catfish and a Brazilian fish called tilapia (which tastes similar to snapper) are cultivated most commonly. Fresh fish from around the nation also land on local tables to supplement the bounty.

The best Gulf Coast restaurants buy their seafood directly from the docks of local commercial fishermen to ensure the utmost freshness. The traditional style of cooking seafood in Florida is deep frying. Although this constitutes a mortal sin in this day and age of gourmet standards and cholesterol awareness, it is a true art when properly executed. There's a vast difference between what you find in the frozen food department at the supermarket and what comes hand-breaded, crunchy, and flavor-sealed on your plate at the local fish house.

New Florida style, at the other extreme, has evolved from so-called California, New American, and eclectic styles of cuisine. It also depends upon freshness — of all its ingredients. For this reason, it uses local produce, prepared in global culinary styles. Regional cookery, sometimes termed Gulfshore or Floribbean cuisine, prefers tropical food ways and ingredients. Its influences come from New Orleans, Santa Fe, Mexico, Cuba, the Bahamas, Jamaica, and Trinidad. Pacific Rim styles often intrude, given today's obsession for lightness and, depending upon the cook, Deep South traditions take their place at the table, too. The outcome at its tamest merely twists the familiar, and, at its most adventurous, can treat your taste buds to a veritable bungee jump.

Between the two extremes of old and new Florida styles, continental cuisine survives in both classic and reinvented forms. Along with restaurants that serve the finest in French and Italian haute cuisine, you will find others that represent the Gulf Coast's melting pot with authentic renditions or interpretations of a wide variety of cuisines — Native American, Thai, Vietnamese, East Indian, German, Irish, Greek, Cuban, Jamaican, Amish, Jewish, Mexican, and Puerto Rican.

The following listings cover all of these versions of Gulf Coast feasting in the following price categories:

Inexpensive	Up to $15
Moderate	$15 to 25
Expensive	$25 to 35
Very Expensive	$35 or more

Cost is figured on a typical meal that would include an appetizer, salad (extra when the menu is à la carte), entree, dessert, and coffee. Many restaurants offer early dining discounts, usually called "early bird specials." These are rarely listed on the regular menu and generally are not publicized by tip-conscious servers. I have noted restaurants that offer them. Certain restrictions apply, such as time constraints, a specific menu, or number of people first in the door. Call the restaurant to learn its policy.

Given the many waterfronts, dining without a view is practically an exception. Nothing says Gulf Coast dining more plainly than a window from which you can watch swooping pelicans or anchored yachts. The listings note exceptional locations under the *Special Features* heading.

The following abbreviations are used for credit card information:

AE - American Express	DC - Diners Card
CB - Carte Blanche	MC - MasterCard
D - Discover Card	V - Visa

Meals served are indicated with B for breakfast, L for lunch, and D for dinner.

Unpretentious dining reflects the overall attitude of Everglades City.

RESTAURANTS — SARASOTA BAY COAST

"Imagine, without traveling outside Sarasota and Manatee Counties that it is possible to have lunch and dinner out every day for a year and never dine in the same place twice."

—*Events Magazine*, December, 1992

Eating out, for Sarasotans, is as much a cultural event as attending the opera. It is often an inextricable part of an evening at the theater or a gallery opening. Sarasotans take dining out quite seriously and keep restaurants full, even off-season. Their enthusiasm for newness makes kitchens more innovative than those of their neighbors to the south. Sarasota slides along the cutting edge of New Florida cuisine, while maintaining classic favorites that range from rickety oyster bars to French *auberges*.

Anna Maria

ROTTEN RALPH'S
778-3953
902 Bay Boulevard, S.
Price: Moderate
Early Dining Menu: Yes
Cuisine: Old Florida
Serving: L, D
Credit Cards: MC, V
Handicapped Access: Yes
Reservations: No

Atmosphere here is due entirely to the setting. It's a place that locals frequent, full of character and characters. The laminated placemat menu describes many finger food selections (steamed shellfish, chili, chicken wings, nachos), Old Florida fried seafood standards, a couple of British specialties (meat pies, fish 'n' chips), steamed seafood pots, and some more esoteric concessions, such as blackened chicken Caesar salad. Everything tasted

The consummate flavor of Anna Maria Island

Special Features: Porch
seating over the water,
marina-side

SANDBAR
778-0444
100 Spring Ave.
Price: Moderate
Early Dining Menu: Yes
Cuisine: Seafood
Serving: L, D
Credit Cards: AE, CB, D,
DC, MC, V
Handicapped Access:Yes
Reservations: Preferred
seating available
Special Features: Outdoor
deck seating

good, although the frozen fries were a disappointment. We enjoyed the view more than we did the food.

At the Sandbar, you can dine al fresco or within a porch-like, wood-ensconced dining room. Either way, you enjoy a close-up view of the Gulf and sea-oats-fringed beach. The view makes it a popular spot. It's one of those places where you can sit outdoors on patio furniture and order a good sandwich, and perhaps the Sandbar should stick to that. Instead, it tries, without much success, to provide a gourmet flair. Lunch offerings include conch fritters, Caesar salad, tuna tropic salad, cold pasta with shrimp remoulade, Cajun grouper sandwich, steakburger, smoked salmon, and caviar. Dinner adds dishes such as shrimp scampi provencale, soft shell crabs, and filet mignon. Service tends to lag and dishes seem to lack forethought. Go there for the view and ambiance; order a sandwich or a salad.

Bradenton

THE PIER
748-8087
Memorial Pier, 1200 First
Ave. W., downtown
Price: Moderate

A bank of windows peers out upon waters once traveled by mail boats from Tampa arriving to the old pier. Built in the 1940s, it knew many lives, which its namesake restaurant recalls with historic memorabilia. The Pier's many rooms sport a mod-

Waterfront dining views without peer, at Bradenton's downtown Pier.

Cuisine: American/Continental
Serving: L, D, Sunday Brunch
Credit Cards: AE, DC, MC, V
Handicapped Access:Yes
Reservations: Accepted
Special Features: River view, luncheon buffet

ern, nautical look of dark wood and ships' lanterns. At lunch, it caters to downtown's mixed bag of retirees and business folk with a wide-ranging menu and a buffet. From pot roast to grouper Lafayette (broiled with crabmeat and hollandaise), lunches are prepared with care and flavor. I especially enjoyed the alligator appetizer, fired Caribbean style with hot and sweet peppers, onions, and mushrooms, and served in a cast-iron skillet. The lunch buffet includes soup, hot dishes, cold cuts, salads, and fruit. The dinner menu specializes in baby back ribs, chicken cordon bleu, and roast Long Island duckling, with beef, and seafood, and various light choices besides.

Longboat Key

THE COLONY RESTAURANT
383-5558
Colony Beach and Tennis Resort, 1620 Gulf of Mexico Dr.
Price: Very Expensive
Cuisine: Continental
Serving: B, L, D, Sunday Brunch
Credit Cards: AE, CB, D, DC, MC, V
Handicapped Access: Yes
Reservations: Required for dinner
Special Features: Gulf view and spectacular wine list

The Colony Restaurant set standards for the region when it opened in the 1970s. Since then, it's stolen just about every award the food and wine world has to offer. The restaurant exudes perfection without being overly pretentious — children's menus come with stickers, for instance. Tuxedoed servers are attentive, but not snobbish or overbearing. The dining room is designed with touches of neoclassicism and a beach-play focus. The menu relies on traditional continental style sprinkled with nouvelle wizardry. *Escargots feuillete*, for example, involves black mushrooms and a bed of spinach. For salad, try chilled angel hair pasta and grilled vegetables or a melange of sweet and bitter greens, both served with balsamic vinegar. The chilled, grilled gazpacho thrills with a cooling tang, color, and Parmesan lacings. The extensive selection of entrees includes several seafood items — *pailliard* of grouper with pecan crust, Suncoast bouillabaisse, char-grilled brochette of Gulf Coast seafood — as well as meat selections — phyllo-wrapped roast pork tenderloin, filet mignon, and scallopine of veal Colony (with shrimp, asparagus, wild mushrooms, and bearnaise). The pasta-seafood dish changes daily, and results in such tasty marriages as linguine with lobster and halibut in a dill cream sauce.

L'AUBERGE DU BON VIVANT
383-2421
7003 Gulf of Mexico Dr.
Closed: Sunday
Price: Very Expensive
Cuisine: French
Serving: D
Credit Cards: AE, DC, MC, V
Handicapped Access: Yes
Reservations: Required

"The inn of good living," says the name in literal translation and succinct assessment of the pleasures in store here. A landmark of Longboat Key dining and French cookery, it resists temptation to stray from classic haute cuisine into trendier modes, but manages, nonetheless, to maintain an ageless appeal with perky touches and strict attention to detail. The experience at first feels quite provincial, set in a country cottage ambiance with dried flower arrangements, dark wood accenting stucco, French cookware adorning walls, and cut carnations freshening tables. The à la carte menu offers several entrees for two, such as chateaubriand, *carré d'agneau grillé*, and young roast duck. These selections, along with the setting, a great wine list, and the beach just a stroll away, stir romance. Service is impeccable, the food full-flavored (but a bit salty), the management just a bit stuffy: do wear a jacket and leave the children with a babysitter (neither of these are requisite, but you'll feel more comfortable). Other menu selections cover the realm of appetizers, salads (I recommend the hearts of palm or the roast pepper salad with garlic vinaigrette), soups, poultry, veal, meat, and seafood. I sampled one of the day's specials, grouper provencale, which spectacularly retained the flavor of the fish, and was served with a mini-popover and side dish of well-seasoned winter vegetables.

MAR-VISTA DOCKSIDE RESTAURANT & PUB
383-2391
The Village, 760 Broadway St.
Price: Moderate
Cuisine: Seafood
Serving: L, D
Credit Cards: MC, V
Handicapped Access: Yes
Reservations: Preferred seating

Locals refer to it simply as The Pub. Casual at its best, it has that lovely, lived-in, borderline ramshackle look on the outside, crowned by the appropriately rusting tin roof. Inside, tables don't match, mounted fish adorn the wall, boaters hoist beers at the bar, and a view of the harbor dominates the decorator's scheme. There's also seating on the patio, on plastic chairs. Seafood is fresh, and prepared with a tropical twist: oysters Longboat for an appetizer (topped with crabmeat, horseradish, and hazelnut dressing), grilled grouper reuben, Cajun-fried oysters, and blackened catfish sandwich for

*Mar-Vista means sea view —
one of the greatest assets at
this so-named Longboat Key
classic.*

lunch; garlic-fried shrimp and changing pasta selections for dinner. Steamer
pots in two sizes are brimming with shellfish and vegetables, large enough to
be shared by two.

**MOORE'S STONE CRAB
RESTAURANT**
383-1748
The Village, 800 Broadway
St.
Price: Moderate
Cuisine: Seafood
Serving: L, D
Credit Cards: MC, V
Handicapped Access: Yes
Reservations: No

Exemplifying an era of Florida dining marked by
rough, wood paneling, cafeteria-style openness,
and a magnificent view of the bay, Moore's has
been a Longboat tradition since the 1960s. Its reputation is built upon fresh crab, brought in by the
restaurant's own fleet during stone crab season.
The owners claim they serve approximately 50,000
pounds of claws each season. They only comprise
one item on the extensive seafood menu, however,
which touts everything from calamari, to Florida
lobster, to frogs' legs. The fresh fish of the day, be it
grouper, mullet, freshwater catfish, or Spanish mackerel, comes broiled, fried,
or almondine. With hush puppies, of course.

Nokomis

PELICAN ALLEY
485-1893
At the south bridge to
Casey Key, Nokomis
Price: Moderate
Cuisine: Seafood
Serving: L, D
Credit Cards: CD, DC,
MC, V
Handicapped Access: Yes
Reservations: No
Special Features: Water-
front view

"Simple food done well...Local and New England sea fare offered in usual and unusual
ways." So says Pelican Alley of itself, summing up
the menu with the mermaid motif. Grouper is prepared in nine different ways, from broiled to Baja
(topped with artichoke bottoms, asparagus, and
cheese sauce). Devoted grazer that I am, I especially appreciate the finger food selection of homemade onion rings with horseradish cream, escargot, raw or deep-fried veggies, and especially the
HMS — a combination of batter-fried artichoke bot-

toms, pepperoncini peppers, and mushrooms. Raw bar items, ceviche, sandwiches, salads, shrimp, and steak are all served waterside along the intracoastal route. Dine inside, in wood slat booths, or outdoors, with a view of boat traffic.

Sarasota

CARMICHAEL'S
951-1771
1213 No. Palm Ave.,
  downtown
Closed: Sunday for dinner,
  Saturday, Sunday and
  Monday for lunch
Price: Expensive to Very
  Expensive
Cuisine: New American
Serving: L, D
Credit Cards: MC, V
Handicapped Access: No
Reservations: Recommended
Special Features: Patio dining, after-theater menu

Individualized antique place-settings, cozy nooks, a perfect presentation, and fresh ingredients from the gardens and wilds across America, make Carmichael's one of my favorite Sarasota restaurants. Housed in an historically designated home, you can dine in a private room, before a roaring fire, or outside in the courtyard. The changing menu presents not only outstanding dishes, but also healthy ones: no preservatives, additives, dyes, butter, flour, or fats are used in the sauces. Its signature dinner special gives you a clue to Carmichael's style: wild baby mixed greens; choice of either filet of pan-fried High Sierra Buffalo with Alpine mushrooms, wild lingonberry, and herb crust; or Steelhead salmon grilled over pecan wood with roast baby vegetables; and homemade dessert. Other selections read like an atlas that collided with a cookbook: hand-picked baby Maine mussels served chilled with peach-Scotch Bonnet mojo juice; roasted four-onion soup with pepper jack cheese crust; duckling paté glazed with warm passion fruit, roast nuts, and baby greens; wild boar pizza with shiitake mushrooms, gorgonzola, and white truffle oil; grilled Yucatan sausage with white figs and pine nuts, finished in chili juice.

An historic home combined with brave new regional cuisine makes Carmichael's one of downtown Sarasota's most unique dining experiences.

CHOPHOUSE GRILLE
951-2467
214 Sarasota Quay, Tami-
    ami Tr. & Fruitville Rd.
Price: Expensive
Early Dining Menu: Yes
Cuisine: New American
Serving: D
Credit Cards: AE, CB, D,
    DC, MC, V
Handicapped Access: Lim-
    ited
Reservations: Recom-
    mended
Special Features: Jazz bar
    downstairs

Sometimes, in striving to be the talk of the town, Sarasota restaurants go overboard in an attempt to be ultra-creative. Sarasotans seem to thrive on innovation, sometimes at the cost of common sense. I found this to be true of the Chophouse which, nonetheless, has reigned as a clear local favorite, remaining popular even when its novelty wore off. Located in the Sarasota Quay, it draws a *cognescenti* crowd with an à la carte menu of oak-grilled meats and fish, and fresh pasta. Most things work. My shrimp stuffed with feta, dill, and cashews on roasted tomato coulis was not one of them. However, roasted whole garlic, sweet peppers, goat cheese, and sun-dried tomato tampenade presented a fun mix-and-match appetizer. The baked French onion soup was full flavored, and the house plum dressing a sure winner. The Caesar salad, however, lacked identity. Other entrees certainly have intrigue: pork tenderloin marinated in orange, ginger, and hoisin, with peanut sauce; potato-crusted, pan-seared snapper with whole grain mustard and chive cream; spinach fettucine and oak-seared chicken breast with various accoutrements. But if you're not daring, be safe and order the prime, aged steaks. The surroundings are chic, spacious, and bustling with the action of Sarasota nights.

**COASTERS SEAFOOD
    HOUSE**
923-4848
Sarasota Boatyard, 1500
    Stickney Point Rd.,
    before the bridge to
    Siesta Key
Price: Moderate
Cuisine: Seafood
Serving: L, D
Credit Cards: AE, D, DC,
    MC, V
Handicapped Access: Yes
Reservations: Accepted
Special Features: Outdoor
    seating, view of intra-
    coastal waterway

Part of a New England-style shopping complex, Coasters has a nautical personality with a modern twist. Among its many dining areas are two outdoor decks that overlook waterway traffic and contribute greatly to its popularity. But, surprise! The food is good, too. Seafood is the focus, with changing specials reflecting what's fresh at local docks. Inventive touches freshen standard fishhouse fare. A nice remoulade accompanies the crab cake appetizer, while iron-skillet beans, couscous, creamed spinach with artichokes, or salsa and nachos are available on the side. On the dinner menu, there's chicken and crawfish jambalaya, shrimp steamed in beer, mahi mahi teriyaki, linguini with shrimp *fra diavolo*, baked grouper with mustard topping, prime rib, and crispy duck honey with fennel and mango chutney. At lunchtime, the selection grows to 14 appetizers, a dozen salads, full dinners, sandwiches, pastas, and eggs benedict.

EMPHASIS COFFEE HOUSE CAFE & GALLERY
954-4085
1301 1st St.
Closed: Sunday
Price: Inexpensive
Early Dining Menu: No
Cuisine: New American
Serving: L, D, limited breakfast
Credit Cards: MC, V
Handicapped Access: Yes
Reservations: No
Special Features: Coffee shop and adjacent gallery

Black-and-white checkered flooring, a coffee-and-crossword wall mural, sleek black chairs, tables painted gaily with backgammon boards, oil paintings, and a bistro ambiance emphasize downtown's artistic temperament. We tried it brand-new, perhaps a bit too soon, as a long wait for food one weekend suggested. Luckily the food was worth it. Specialties — including crayfish lasagna and Norwegian salmon, pan-seared with roasted red pepper sauce — arrive on contemporary black plates. I tried the fajita pita pizza, a delight of pan-seared beef, sweet pepper, jack cheese, and guacamole. There are lots of veggie dishes: goat cheese pizza with roasted red pepper, garlic, and spinach; veggie sandwich; California Roll-Up (flat bread with guacamole, sprouts, tomato, and Jack cheese);

baked rigatoni primavera. In the sandwich department, try the pan-seared Thai chicken with pickled ginger mayonnaise. Follow up with reosa peach pie or Death by Chocolate Cake for dessert, with one of many possible espressos or cappuccinos.

GUADALAJARA
951-6394
1375 Main St., downtown
Closed: Sunday
Price: Moderate
Cuisine: Authentic Mexican
Serving: L, D
Credit Cards: AE, CB, DC, MC, V
Handicapped Access: Yes
Reservations: Suggested for dinner
Special Features: Congenial cantina with Mexican and American memorabilia (parts of vintage automobiles); live music upstairs weekends; porch dining

Forget all your preconceptions of Mexican restaurants. At Guadalajara, the dining room holds less than a dozen linen-covered tables. Seven entrees comprise the dinner menu, with not a taco in sight. Words such as "no cholesterol" and "vegetarian" appear on the menu. Dishes are prepared to order using organic produce, fresh seafood, and Angus beef. The food is authentically Mexican, the bartender stresses, made from her family's recipes. Her family, former circus trapeze artists, makes the restaurant what it is in many ways. *"Mi casa, su casa,"* one son greets everyone who walks in the door, even if he's way at the back of the cantina. Patrons yell greetings back to him with the familiarity of repeat customers. In the small dining room with deep red walls and silver-framed mirrors, they relish black bean soup; corn dough cakes called *sopes*, which are layered with refried beans, chorizos, cheese, and the trimmings; pan-fried

strips of herbed rib-eye called Jalisco Steak; fresh fish specials; and the house specialty, not to be missed, *pollo on mole poblano* — a crescendo of 23 spices and better-than-classic, chocolate-flavored *mole.* You can dine more casually at the bar, or in booths at the back of the cantina. You may have to wait a while, but the primo salsa and unusual selection of beers and tequilas eases hunger pangs and tension. I've heard there's outdoor dining, but I didn't witness that on the chilly night I visited.

**PHILLIPPI CREEK VIL-
LAGE OYSTER BAR**
925-4444
5353 S. Tamiami Tr.
Price: Inexpensive to Mod-
   erate
Cuisine: Seafood/Old
   Florida
Serving: L, D
Credit Cards: MC, V
Handicap Access: Yes
Reservations: No
Special Features: Patio and
   floating dock seating
   creekside

This is the kind of place locals like to keep a secret. But I know the weathervane for great seafood: like semis at a roadside stop, boats hitched up to a restaurant dock are a sure sign. Combo pots for two are the specialty of the house — unadorned pans full of steamed oysters, rock shrimp, gulf shrimp, corn on the cob, and a selection of specialty items (topneck clams, Maine lobster, snow crab, etc.), and toppings. I prefer the sandwiches because it's rare to get such flavor between a bun. My blackened grouper sandwich was the best I've ever tasted, and the oysters in my husband's sandwich were exceptionally sweet. Banana peppers topped the sandwiches, a serendipitous touch, along with a superior tartar sauce. The servers, with their "Meet Me Up The Creek" tees and aprons, were both pleasant and helpful. Southern hospitality and conviviality at its best.

SUGAR & SPICE
953-3340
1850 S. Tamiami Tr.
Closed: Sunday
Price: Inexpensive
Cuisine: Amish
Serving: L, D
Credit Cards: MC, V
Handicapped Access: Yes
Reservations: No
Special Features: Folk art
   — quilts, country-style
   wood items, etc. — decorate the restaurant and
   are for sale, along with
   books teaching the Men-
   nonite faith

A happy result of the Amish/Mennonite community on Sarasota's outskirts is the home cooking found in family restaurants throughout the area. These folks principally are farmers, so you can expect homegrown freshness at their table. Most of their eateries occupy large dining rooms with all the ambiance of a fast-food chain. This one displays some nice cut-stone touches, a wooden cathedral ceiling, and homey curtains. Daily specials showcase the typical old-fashioned goodness: baked chicken and dressing, beef and noodles, Swiss steak, turkey and dressing. I sampled the baked chicken, accompanied by mashed potatoes, full-flavored chicken gravy, and a well-spiced dressing — all the real thing. Under the "Just Downright Good Eat'n" heading, you can choose from meat loaf, fried ham, roast beef, breaded chopped veal, breaded shrimp — good old Midwestern comfort foods. There are also sandwiches and salads on the menu, which ends with a prayer. Don't dare forget to leave room for the Amish famous forte — pie. Sugar & Spice tempts you with close to a dozen desserts, including cakes. I reveled in my rhubarb pie, crusted with sugar and topped with rich, ivory-colored vanilla ice cream. The pie could have used some warming, but I don't suppose they use microwaves.

Siesta Key

THE OLD SALTY DOG
349-0158
5023 Ocean Blvd.
Price: Inexpensive
Cuisine: Seafood/American and English
Serving: L, D
Credit Cards: No
Handicapped Access: Yes
Reservations: No
Special Features: Outdoor seating

A bit of limey has been squeezed into this casual beach dining experience. You feel the English pub influence mostly inside around the bar. Aside from the traditional Fish & Chips and a dessert sherry trifle, the unpretentious menu sticks close to what Americans like to eat at the beach. Hot and cold sandwiches are served all day, as are main meal selections of Cajun shrimp and fresh catch, either beer-battered or Cajun-spiced. Try the filet of fresh Florida fish made the way you like it, or custom order a burger.

Venice

THE CROW'S NEST
484-9551
1968 Tarpon Center Dr. on the South Jetty
Price: Moderate
Cuisine: Seafood
Serving: L, D
Credit Cards: D, MC, V
Handicapped Access: Limited to downstairs pub, where full menu is available to persons unable to get to the upstairs restaurant
Reservations: No
Special Features: Marina view

Perched on a second story, over a marina, The Crow's Nest also earns its name from a tastefully seaworthy ambiance: no, not tons of dusty fish netting and tired trappings — this is yacht-class stuff. Tall windows look down upon spiring masts. Brass, birgies, and navy blue decorate soaring ceilings. The menu has sailor appeal — casual and uncomplicated. Appetizers, raw bar items, seafood, and other hot sandwiches are served in the tavern all day and upstairs at lunchtime: baked Brie, seafood bisque, smoked peppered mackerel (large and nicely presented), charbroiled mahi mahi sandwich, classic reuben, and hamburgers. Lunch features a changing pasta dish and seafood favorites such as crab cakes and scallops Venice. Dinner entrees concentrate on seafood and surf-and-turf combinations such as shrimp and tenderloin kabobs, seafood saute, or chicken and sesame shrimp.

SHARKY'S
488-1456
1600 S. Harbor Dr. on the Venice Fishing Pier at Casperson Beach
Price: Moderate
Cuisine: Seafood
Serving: L, D, Sunday Brunch

Named to associate with Venice Beach's reputation for shark-tooth collecting, Sharky's roosts upon the 750-foot-long Venice Pier, with a cabana bar outside sharing the structure. Its enviable location brings a frenzy of diners to its busy and buzzing dining rooms. Cartons of sea salt on the table and warm, homemade caraway rolls promise

Credit Cards: D, MC, V
Handicapped Access:
Ramp into smoking section, small step into non-smoking
Reservations: No
Special Features: Great Gulf views

an unique experience. But, alas, the food falls short of the excellence one might expect based upon the purple sunset view and menu descriptions of seafood nachos, shark skewers, steaks, catfish, Caribbean shrimp, sea pasta, and combo platters. During my in-season meal on a frantically busy night, I was disappointed by the canned quality of sauces and side dishes. Lunch and sundeck munchies include "konk" fritters, smoked mullet dip, burgers, sandwiches, salads, and entrees. Sunday brunch features a make-your-own Bloody (or Virgin) Mary bar.

SNOOK HAVEN
485-7221
5000 E. Venice Ave.
Price: Inexpensive
Cuisine: American/Barbecue
Serving: L, D
Credit Cards: AE, MC, V
Handicapped Access: Yes
Reservations: No
Special Features: Barbecue bashes Sundays; view of the river with canoeing available

For a poignant taste of rural Old Florida, visit Snook Haven on a Sunday for live bluegrass and hot-off-the-spit barbecue. Make a day of it and go for a boat or canoe ride. Hear the legend of the killer turtles. Or visit any day and enjoy ultra-casual dining — burgers, fried fish, etc. — on the banks of the Myakka River. It's truly a "y'all come" kind of place.

RESTAURANTS — CHARLOTTE HARBOR COAST

Punta Gorda

CAPTAIN'S TABLE
637-1177
Fishermen's Village, Maud St. and Marion Ave.
Price: Moderate
Early Dining Menu: Yes
Cuisine: American/Seafood
Serving: B, L, D
Credit Cards: AE, D, MC, V
Handicapped Access: Single steps to negotiate
Reservations: Accepted
Special Features: Riverfront and harbor view

Crusty, jaunty shrimper boats bob alongside sleek, luxury yachts in the harbor. Inside the contrasts continue. In a very plush and formal setting fraught with pewter and models of classic sailing ships, a casual mood is cast by a devil-may-care pirate's theme. Dishes such as Walk the Chicken Plank (chicken fingers), Blackbeard's teriyaki (steak or chicken breast), steak Gaspar (tenderloin au poivre), Useppa fried oysters, Captiva clam strips, and Calico Jack sandwich (chicken topped with provolone and honey mustard sauce) draw on the area's legendary swashbuckling past. Dishes are well-designed, nicely presented, and tasty. And you can't beat the stilted river view from either the dining room or Harpoon Harry's Lounge, which also serves lunch.

Boca Grande

LIGHTHOUSE HOLE
964-0511
Miller's Marina, Harbor Dr.
Price: Moderate
Cuisine: Seafood/Florida
Serving: L, D
Credit Cards: MC, V
Handicapped Access: No
Reservations: Suggested for dinner
Special Features: Screened porch with view of harbor

A perennial favorite among boaters, tarpon fishermen, and locals, it has a super-casual air despite the million-dollar masts that festoon its view. The attitude here perhaps is best described by the names of its neighborhood streets: Dam-If-I-No, Dam-If-I-Care, and Dam-If-I-Will. Rough-hewn wood beams are hung with baseball caps and Japanese glass floats. Grouper features prominently on the dinner menu, served Florentine (topped with spinach, crab sauce, and cheese), Gaspar (sauteed with garlic, lemon, and wine), and fresh fried. Other seafood entrees include five shrimp preparations and Cajun mahi mahi. Lunch sandwiches, burgers, salads, and specials make flavorful use of Boca's fishing reputation. We eat here often and have never been disappointed by the quality of the food.

CASUAL CLAM
964-2300
Uncle Henry's Marina Resort, Route 771; 5800 Gasparilla Rd.
Price: Inexpensive to Moderate
Cuisine: American
Serving: B, L, D
Credit Cards: AE, MC, V
Handicapped Access: To downstairs bar/breakfast room only
Reservations: No
Special Features: Harbor view

Stuffed croissant sandwiches, Tex-Mex specialties, burgers, seafood sandwiches, creative salads, and a few dinners, on a menu used for lunch and dinner, appeal to all sorts of appetites at this bright, fresh, resort marina eatery. Though highly varied, the menu holds together well to maintain excellence with every offering, particularly the homemade desserts. Some recommendations: Baked Casual Clams appetizer (seasoned with Parmesan and garlic on the half shell), fritter of the day, marinated chicken breast sandwich with spicy waffle fries, taco salad, fish of the day (broiled, baked, blackened, or fried), New York strip steak, baby back ribs, and the cheesecake of the day.

THEATRE RESTAURANT
964-0806
321 Park Ave.
Closed: Sunday
Price: Expensive
Cuisine: American
Serving: L, D
Credit Cards: MC, V

I asked a friend, a local chef, to take us to the area's finest dining spot. I have to admit I expected something fancier and more highly priced than the Theatre, but she assured me the chef's talents were locally acclaimed. I did like the location, set in an historic wood building-turned-mini-mall that housed the San Marco movie theater back in 1928. That's Boca for you, historic but unpreten-

The Theatre Restaurant remembers Boca Grade's big-screen heyday

Handicapped Access: Yes
Reservations: Suggested for dinner
Special Features: Historic building; live entertainment

tious. The menu builds on the house's former life, with headings such as Matinees, Sneak Previews, Seafood Adventures, and Wild, Wild Westerns (red-meat items). The fare, as described on the dinner menu, at first appeared less than stellar. Appetizer and entree specials better showcased the fresh fish for which the island is known, as well as the chef's inventiveness. The day's basil-tomato crab soup was sweet and well flavored, enriched with cream, but a bit shy with the basil. The menu's Jamaican jerk pork appetizer was done successfully, and the blue crab fritters well-liked by half of the party. Freshness was obvious in the two fish specials we ordered, one using yellowtail snapper, the other grouper. Off the menu, the creamy tortellini was pleasing, but the Szechuan pork and chicken too timid (after the server was assured we like it hot). Dark squaw bread — a sweet, coarse variety — adds interest, as do the various side dish options, which include cheese grits, black beans, and a fresh vegetable (that night asparagus done perfectly al dente.) The lunch menu features Florida specialties such as fried mullet, Cuban sandwich, and crab burger. The natural wood and lattice decor frame a huge aquarium. Romantic nooks set into bay casement windows, a screened porch, loft, and musician provide added atmosphere.

RESTAURANTS — ISLAND COAST

The Island Coast is home to two of the nation's shellfish capitals. Shrimp — that monarch of edible crustaceans — reigns in Fort Myers Beach, where more than 250 shrimp boats are headquartered, and an annual festival pays homage to America's favorite seafood. The sweet, pink, Gulf shrimp is the trademark culinary delight of the town and its environs.

The fish markets of Pine Island, an important commercial fishing and trans-shipment center, sell all sorts of fresh seafood — oysters, shrimp, scallops, mullet, snapper, catfish — but the signature seafood is the blue crab that comes from local bay waters.

Sizing Up a Shrimp

Gulf shrimp are graded by size, and assigned all sorts of vague measurements — jumbo, large, medium-sized, boat grade, etc. The surest way to know what size shrimp you are ordering is to ask for the count-per-pound designation. This will be something like 21-25s, meaning there are 21 to 25 shrimp per pound. *Boat grade* normally designates a mixture of sizes, usually on the small side.

Bonita Beach

BIG HICKORY FISHING NOOK RESTAURANT
992-0991
26107 Hickory Blvd. SW
Closed: Tuesdays in off-season
Price: Moderate
Cuisine: Seafood/Florida
Serving: B, L, D
Credit Cards: AE, D, MC, V
Handicapped Access: Yes
Reservations: Accepted in off-season
Special Features: Old Florida marina atmosphere; dining dockside and in a screened porch

I love old fish-shack-style restaurants just for themselves — their water view, often precarious stance, and no-nonsense seafood. Big Hickory gave me new reasons, besides. Its extensive menu goes beyond the standard fried-basket fare (which it does with great aplomb, I might add). Take, for instance, the Fin, Feather, Frog, and Fur dinner for two, which is composed of sauteed alligator, grilled frogs' legs, quail, and venison; or the buffalo burger, or Pinocchio sandwich (sardines on grilled rye with sliced egg, alfalfa sprouts, and tomato). Other selections cater to vegetarians, health-conscious diners, and gourmets. Tropical fruits abound in the Floribbean Shrimp Salad. Fresh spinach lines a fried tortilla shell bowl, heaped with small, fresh shrimp, melons, strawberries, oranges, and pineapple — all topped with a well-balanced mango dressing. The conch chowder is some of the best I've tried, and I've tried it throughout the Caribbean and Bahamas. It comes in a clamshell bowl with a fifth of sherry on the side. From atop a charter-boat stand, a blue heron eyed me greedily as I devoured my chocolate volcano — a wedge of brownie, cheesecake, and raspberry heaven. His name, according to the menu, is Ol' Blue, the mascot for the marina upon which three outdoor tables face. Indoors, the small dining room features a lovely wood sculpture and a saltillo-paved floor. There's also seating on the screened porch. The service staff is cheerfully accommodating.

Cape Coral

LAFAYETTE GOURMET SEAFOOD
540-1222
1428 Lafayette St.
Closed: Monday
Price: Expensive
Early Dining Menu: Yes
Cuisine: Continental
Serving: D
Credit Cards: AE, MC, V
Handicapped Access: Yes
Reservations: Recommended

Our favorite new discovery for fine dining on the Island Coast distinguishes itself with dishes that deliver all the perfection and polish the menu promises, and elegant touches that are, at the same time, not self-conscious. Like many of the region's eateries, the Lafayette specializes in seafood, but with a whole new concept. The changing menu gives you a selection of the night's seafood which you can coordinate with a multiple-choice list of sauces. For instance, with my chunky filet of baked grouper I selected (as recommended by the chef) a nicely balanced mustard sauce, a blend of Dijon and grainy types. We also sampled the superb mango-curry sauce with our crab cake appetizer, a stunning combination. Carefully crafted sauces plus the best of local catches: a formula that seems so simple, yet I've never seen it done with this degree of flair. As for the elegant touches, they were numerous enough to keep the experience a continuing carousel of surprises: champagne honey mustard dressing; kiwi and roquefort cheese on the house salad; sassy but glamorous bird-of-paradise china; twice-stuffed potato served in a pear half; white asparagus. We'd heard rumors of snobbishness that was somewhat in evidence, but felt Lafayette has a right to nose the air in pride. Fondue bouillabaise-style is also a specialty and is served in a separate room, *prix fixe*. Meat and pasta dishes receive detailed attention. We loved the linguine with shrimp and andouille sausage.

RESTAURANT TANNENGARTEN
549-1300
3724 Del Prado Blvd
Closed: Monday
Price: Moderate
Early Dining Menu: Yes
Cuisine: German
Serving: D
Credit Cards: MC, V
Handicapped Access: Yes
Reservations: Recommended

Cape Coral's German heritage culminates at Tannengarten. Hearty meals begin with tangy sliced bread, a bracing soup, and a three-in-one salad containing greens, potato salad, and cabbage salad. Hefty beers are delivered in earthenware mugs. Entrees come with various German side dishes. Order *spaetzle* and red cabbage on the side if they're not included with your selection. I invariably order the excellent *sauerbraten* — a classic soused beef dish. Different varieties of homemade sausages, and pork and veal cutlets, spell authenticity. A sampling: *Wienerschnitzel*, steak with sauteed onions, beef rolls, roast pork, liver dumplings. Desserts vary; apple streudel and cheesecake are standards. If they have cottage cheesecake on hand, try it no matter how sated you may be.

Captiva Island

MUCKY DUCK
472-3434
Andy Rosse Ln.
Price: Moderate
Cuisine: Seafood/Continental
Serving: L, D
Credit Cards: AE, D, MC, V
Handicapped Access: Yes
Reservations: No
Special Features: Gulf view, English pub atmosphere

Dining at "The Duck" is practically a requisite part of a visit to Captiva. (Some will say the same of the Bubble Room, but locals prefer the former.) Known for its sense of humor, panoramic sea view, and excellent seafood, lunch or dinner there often means a long wait to be seated. Luckily, the beach in front of the door provides ample diversion, especially at sunset, when there's standing room only. A take-off on the White Swan and other British pub names, the Duck copies their atmosphere and includes a few meat pies and fish 'n chips selections on the menu. Its barbecued, bacon-wrapped shrimp is the house signature entree, however, and the specials promise freshly and creatively prepared fish and shellfish. Whenever my brother visits, he goes there expressly for the mahi mahi with dill sauce. The kitchen freezes its key lime pie for a refreshing twist on a classic.

Fort Myers

PETER'S LA CUISINE
332-2228
2224 Bay St., downtown
Price: Very Expensive
Cuisine: Continental
Serving: D
Credit Cards: AE, MC, V
Handicapped Access: Yes
Reservations: Recommended

Peter's is the first name in fine dining, in downtown Fort Myers. It turns a refurbished, red brick warehouse into the warmest, coziest dining room you can imagine. Tables are dressed in linens and silver — but don't look for salt and pepper shakers. The rotating menu infuses nouvelle continental with inspiration. Fresh seafood and meat are cloaked royally in rich, heavy sauces such as *beurre blanc* or champagne basil cream. Everything is

Peter's transformed an old warehouse into Fort Myers' most chic downtown gathering spots.

Special Features: Blues'
   club upstairs

creamy and dreamy, from the escargot soup (topped with puff pastry), to the ragout of lobster and crawfish, to the indescribable dark and white Kouverture (fine Swiss chocolate) mousse.

RUNABOUTS ROAD-
   SIDE GRILLE
939-5247
4329 Cleveland Ave.
Price: Moderate
Cuisine: American
Serving: L, D
Credit Cards: AE, D, MC,
   V
Handicapped Access: Yes
Reservations: Accepted

I can't decide which I like best about Runabouts, the food or the atmosphere. Both are cutting-edge. The gleaming, high-tech decor is warmed by mahogany tables, ceiling, and trim. Etched glass between booths provides an extra measure of privacy. The kitchen is open, and dominated by pizza ovens and oak grills, which gives you a solid clue about the cuisine. Plates drizzled artistically with fruit glazes and sauces hold nicely designed surprises off the grill: Jamaican jerk swordfish skewers with black bean salsa and red pepper jelly; dolphin with pineapple salsa and minted couscous; filet mignon with Gorgonzola butter and smashed potatoes. Pizzas come in varieties such as wild mushroom or oak-grilled vegetable. Plus there are a few pasta items, sandwiches, and salads. The menu is à la carte, but entrees normally need no filler. Servers in black-and-white checkered aprons are exceptionally cheerful, edging on bothersome: everyone wants to know how your food is. Why not? It's great.

THROUGH THE
   LOOKING GLASS
275-9973
Royal Palm Square, 1400
   Colonial Blvd.
Price: Moderate to Expen-
   sive
Cuisine: American/Conti-
   nental
Closed: Sunday
Serving: L, D
Credit Cards: AE, MC, V
Handicapped Access: Yes
Reservations: Suggested
Special Features: Al fresco
   dining

The sheer cheeriness of this place will bring Cheshire Cat smiles. Chairs, tablecloths, place mats, and doors are painted in bright Easter egg colors and the theme is obviously Wonderland. Menu items are appropriately titled: The White Knight sandwich, Looking Glass burger, Mock Turtle soup (black turtle bean, that is), Jamaican Jabberwocky (jerked N.Y. Strip), March Hares Fare (a health-conscious dream of veggies and pasta), and Shrimply Nonsense (shrimp, jalapenos, tomatoes over red pepper linguine with feta cheese). I especially enjoy lunch here, on the back porch, overlooking bubbling fountains and goldfish. Sandwiches come on hefty planks of homemade bread aboard black Fiestaware, and the potato salad is extra creamy and dilly.

THE VERANDA
332-2065
2122 Second St.

Victorian trappings and Southern charm create an atmosphere of romance in an historic home setting. Occupying two turn-of-the century houses,

*Fort Myers shows its
Confederate roots at the
historic Veranda restaurant.*

Closed: Saturday for
lunch, Sunday for lunch
and dinner
Price: Expensive
Cuisine: Florida/Southern
Serving: L, D
Credit Cards: MC, V
Handicapped Access: Yes
Reservations: Recom-
mended
Special Features:
Garden/courtyard din-
ing

the Veranda is furnished with elegance. The dining room huddles around a two-sided, red brick fireplace, mounted with a moose head wearing a Panama hat. A white picket fence separates the cobblestone garden courtyard from downtown traffic. Wine cases line the dark-wood bar, displaying one of the largest selections in the area. Start with something unusual from Veranda's appetizer board — perhaps escargot in puff pastry with Stilton blue cheese (a sublime rendition), Vidalia onion soup, blue crab cakes with Dijon and roast red pepper sauce, or Southern grit cakes with pepper Jack cheese and grilled Andouille sausage. The house salad contains surprises: a dollop of marinated black beans and slices of hearts of palm, and is served with fresh baked bread, corn muffins, and the Veranda's signature Southern pepper jelly. Entrees wax traditional, but exceed the ordinary. Medallions of filet are dressed Southern style, in smoky sourmash whiskey sauce. Roast duckling is prepared with a raspberry sauce; rack of New Zealand lamb à Dijonaise. Marinated grilled prawns are treated to fresh tomatoes, basil, garlic and Parmesan, and served over linguini. Daily specials typically include fresh seafood catches. The night's winner at our table was the chef's grilled yellowfin tuna with *beurre blanc*. The roast duckling came in a close second, but the rack of lamb fell short of expectations. Diet-destroying desserts tend toward the Southern tradition with trademark twists, such as the chocolate paté, peanut butter fudge pie, and Southern fruit cobblers.

Fort Myers Beach

SNUG HARBOR
463-4343

 perennial favorite, Snug Harbor is balanced above the waters of Estero Pass. Exposed air-

645 San Carlos Blvd.
Price: Moderate to Expen-
  sive
Cuisine: Seafood/Ameri-
  can
Serving: L, D
Credit Cards:
Handicapped Access: To
  main-floor restaurant
  only
Reservations: No
Special Features: Water-
  side view, upstairs al
  fresco Shanty Bar

conditioning ductwork contrasts with immaculate linen and classy touches to embody the spirit of Fort Myers Beach dining. The cozy, L-shaped dining room is lined with windows that look out upon boat traffic, shrimpers, and mangroves. Snug's regular menu has remained much the same for over a decade, providing a banquet of fried and broiled seafood traditions, plus some meat-lover's conces-sions. Pay more attention to the changing specials. I recently enjoyed the day's conch cake appetizer, which was prepared in a pancake form and topped with a mild jalapeno sauce and Jack cheese. Out-standing! Besides appetizers, the changing menu offers a pasta of the day, a classic selection (mahi mahi Creole the evening we visited), and several catches, such as tuna *au poivre* (which we found weak in flavor) or snapper with fresh herbs, artichoke hearts, and cheese. At lunchtime, fish sandwiches, shrimp platters, salads, oysters, and starters compete for your appetite. Try the Buffalo-style shrimp appetizer (also offered at dinner), a local version of spicy chicken wings.

North Captiva

BARNACLE PHIL'S
472-6394
Safety Harbor, 4401 Point
  House Tr.
Price: Inexpensive
Cuisine: Seafood/Ameri-
  can
Serving: L
Credit Cards: MC, V
Handicapped Access: Not
  to porch or dining room,
  but easy availability to
  front yard tables
Reservations: No
Special Features: Outdoor
  dining, view of the har-
  bor

Unpretentious, salt-assaulted, and laid back Phil's, one of our favorite hideaways, is becom-ing all too well known for its secret recipe — black beans 'n yellow rice — the rave of celebrities who come to hide out on North Captiva. (Henry Winkler once had some flown to Hollywood.) Besides this favorite, you can bite into a grouper sandwich, ham-burger, fried shrimp, clam strips, steamed shrimp, seafood sampler, pizza, key lime tarts, and brownie pie. Dine casually in the tiny dining room, on the porch, or on picnic tables in the yard.

North Fort Myers

GUANTANAMERA
656-3505
4400 Hancock Bridge
  Pkwy.
Closed: Weekends for
  lunch
Price: Inexpensive

Splashy pink and green umbrellas flag your approach to this heart of local Hispanic culture. Inside, the cotton-candy color scheme is repeated. The Cuban menu, with English translations, por-trays all of the island's culinary trademarks: Cuban bread, black bean soup, *mojo* (garlic, lime, and oil)

Cuisine: Country-style Cuban
Serving: L, D
Credit Cards: AE, CB, D, DC, MC, V
Handicapped Access: Yes
Reservations: Not necessary
Special Features: Outdoor dining

sauced pork, *vaca frita* (fried, shredded flank beef), Cuban sandwiches, fried cassava and green plaintains, *arroz con pollo, paella, lechon asado* (roast suckling pig), flan, and Cuban coffee. All is prepared with authentic goodness. A soup and salad bar can be enjoyed either alone or with your meal, but looked considerably less interesting than the menu.

Pine Island

ALICE'S FLAMINGO
283-4919
4195 Pine Island Rd., Matlacha
Price: Inexpensive to Moderate
Cuisine: Florida
Serving: L, D
Credit Cards: No
Handicapped Access: Yes
Reservations: No
Special Features: View of two waterfronts

First, drive through the town to get yourself into the Matlacha state of mind. It's a miniature fishdom, where seafood purveyors once precariously perched their enterprises on shallow-strutting stilts. Many of today's shops and restaurants played a role in history, and Alice's is no exception. It demonstrates exactly how the town has reinvented its present by artistically restoring its past. The back of the menu tells Alice's story. Inside, Old Florida meets new with hot buckets of shellfish prepared clambake-style, fried oysters or grouper, grilled yellowfin tuna, jerk pork tenderloin sandwich, hot or cold stone crab claws, and variations on chicken wings and Caesar salad. The small dining room holds only seven tables, and eight bar stools. Rolls of paper towels are pegged to plain wood, shellacked tables. French doors and some Haitian art decorate bare wood walls, topped with a tin ceiling. Straddling a narrow strip of fill in Matlacha Pass, it allows views of water out of both the front and back doors.

Sanibel Island

BANGKOK HOUSE
472-4622
1547 Periwinkle Way
Closed: For lunch off-season
Price: Moderate to Expensive
Cuisine: Thai
Serving: L (in season only), D
Handicapped Access: Yes
Reservations: No
Special Features: Thai import shop in same complex

The first Thai restaurant on the Island Coast, Bangkok House continues to set new standards for the genre. Tantalizing specialties on its latest à la carte menu — fish tamarind, chicken on fire (flamed with whiskey on a bed of sauteed bok choy), beef in peanut curry sauce — extend options for regulars such as ourselves. My all-time favorites: *satay* appetizer, the hot/sour shrimp soup, grilled beef salad, *mussamun* curry, noodles in curry. You choose the degree of burn: from mild to native Thai. The cook's thermometer, however, is not consistent. Decor relies on the principal of Oriental beauty and minimalism.

BUD'S ANY FISH YOU WISH
472-5700
1473 Periwinkle Way
Price: Moderate to Expensive
Cuisine: Seafood
Serving: B, L, D
Credit Cards: AE, MC, V
Handicapped Access: Yes
Reservations: For clambakes only
Special Features: Sea life art decor, in-house bakery, ice creamery and fish market

In the front room, a sculptured hammerhead shark, rays, and a baby dolphin lurk in true-to-life imagery. The back room looks more like the Little Mermaid on bad drugs, featuring imaginative creatures in the "Octopus's Garden." All in all, the decor and menu speak loudly of seafood — if the restaurant's name itself didn't clue you in. Bud's is unusual, in that it allows customers to design their "fish wish." The menu is rather confusing, but the service staff is helpful in putting together the best combinations. Our favorites include grilled teriyaki-ginger tuna, pompano or snapper with lemon sauce, and Cajun-fried soft shell crab. Side dishes include beans 'n rice (a meal in itself), and homemade pasta with a choice of sauce. With a day's notice, you can enjoy a lobster clambake, steamed at your table. The homemade baked goods and ice cream put a perfect spin on the whole experience.

THE GREENHOUSE
492-9200
Casa Ybel Resort, Casa Ybel Rd.
Price: Very Expensive
Cuisine: New American/Eclectic
Serving: D
Credit Cards: D, MC, V
Handicapped Access: Yes
Reservations: Recommended
Special Features: Extensive list of specialty and boutique wines; Gulf view

Recently moved from its popular spot on Captiva Island, the Greenhouse still excels in eclectic eats. Some of the dishes and ingredients sound scary, but the staff is very gracious, and willing to explain everything. I still rave to friends about the salad I had there. Composed of arugula, pancetta, edible flowers, bruschetta, and warm goat cheese dressing, it is presented in the guise of a tropical flower. It's too pretty to eat and too delicious not to. Menu selections change regularly. Rack of lamb remains constant, by popular demand. Shipped from Colorado, it is encrusted in goat cheese and roasted with garlic. Seared tuna sashimi, red hot Caribbean fish stew, lobster and goat cheese calzone, four-by-four vegetarian lasagna, southern pan-roasted venison, and grilled Florida grouper demonstrate chef and owner Danny Mellman's global virtuosity. Atmosphere at the two-room Greenhouse, named for its many-paned wall of windows, depends on minutia: fresh flowers on the table, crisp linens, hand-lettered bills, antique buffets. Both rooms offer Gulf views, with an open kitchen center stage in one.

TARWINKLES SEAFOOD EMPORIUM
472-1366
Periwinkle Way and Tarpon Bay Rd.

If I were to choose a perfect prototype for Gulfshore cuisine, Tarwinkles' menu would be it. It concentrates on seafood — with a fish nutritional chart on the back, no less. Sample the regular menu

Price: Moderate to Expensive
Early Dining Menu: Yes
Cuisine: New Florida/American
Serving: L, D
Credit Cards: AE, CB, D, DC, MC, V
Handicapped Access: Yes
Reservations: No

preparations: snapper ceviche, Ragin' Cajun fish cakes, grouper New Orleans, Jamaican jerked chicken, Jamaican curried snapper and prawns, *puerco asada*, and baked shrimp Creole. We usually select off the extensive nightly special menus, where fresh fish, inventiveness, and pasta interact — grilled swordfish with fresh key lime thyme *beurre blanc*, or broiled mahi with tropical fruit salsa, for example. Cascading waters and an aquarium soothe an otherwise bustling, nautical ambiance.

RESTAURANTS — SOUTH COAST

Goodland

STAN'S IDLE HOUR SEAFOOD RESTAURANT
394-3041
221 W. Goodland Dr. (left off Route 92 after the Goodland bridge)
Closed: Monday, and the month of August
Price: Moderate
Cuisine: Seafood/Old Florida
Serving: L, D
Credit Cards: AE, MC, V
Handicapped Access: Yes
Reservations: Accepted
Special Features: Sunday afternoon entertainment — home of the "Buzzard Lope" dance; outdoor seating on the boat docks

Goodland is a town where tourism, or lack thereof, has allowed folks to remain hometown and proud of it. In other words, do not expect the staff here to be ingratiating. Stan's, named for the colorful owner, embodies the town's spirit with fresh — really fresh — seafood, done mostly old-Florida style, i.e. fried. But fried so that it's not a bad word: hand-battered, not dripping in grease, accompanied with a tasty tartar sauce, and just plain good. The house features a daring all-you-can-eat stone crab feast, and will prepare your catch after a day's fishing with Stan's son. Pies are homemade, gooey, and delicious. You can dine outdoors on cracking laminated or plastic tables by the tiki bar, or indoors with real tableware in a modern setting of light wood. I opted for the dock and, despite the rude smell caused by a chef who poured bleach right beside my table, enjoyed watching the local, colorful pageant of crabbers unloading their catch, pelicans awaiting handouts, and the catch-all decor of the bar.

Marco Island

OLDE MARCO INN
394-3131
100 Palm St.
Price: Expensive
Cuisine: Continental

This Marco Island tradition was built in 1883 by pioneer Captain William D. Collier as a home, and later became his rustic inn. Restored to its original gracious Southern style, it boasts a collection of Audubon originals and a beautiful cranberry glass

Serving: D
Credit Cards: AE, D, DC, MC, V
Handicapped Access: Yes
Reservations: Accepted
Special Features: Historical structure

chandelier, within its six rooms of varying motif — from fully formal to airy veranda. The international/seafood menu has a German accent, with such selections as *wienerschnitzel, sauerbraten* with red cabbage and potato pancake, and German farmers soup. *Escargot à la bourguignonne*, Florida grouper *à la meunière*, filet mignon *au poivre vert*, pork chops Dijon, Hawaiian Toast (chicken breast on toast with pineapple and sweet sauce), and veal Madagascar tour the culinary globe. Eleven coffee drinks provide various international flavors.

Naples

Fashionable feasting on Naples' Third Street South.

THE CHEF'S GARDEN
262-5500
1300 Third St. S., Old Naples
Closed: Lunch in off-season
Price: Very Expensive
Cuisine: Continental
Serving: L, D
Credit Cards: AE, D, DC, MC, V
Handicapped Access: Yes
Reservations: Recommended

Chef's Garden is the old guard of Naples gastronomy; the standard to which all new restaurants aspire. It sits prettily among the gold-paved streets of downtown Naples, yet manages to remain unpretentious. Lots of French doors, fresh roses on the table, and green-and-blue plaid cloth napkins spell casual class, as only Naples can. The award-winning à la carte menu combines New American's predilection for fresh produce with Continental's classic techniques. To start, try the shrimp bisque with tarragon and peppered-seared shrimp; grilled scallops with roasted three pepper and chive sauce; a baby greens salad with slices of fresh mozzarella, basil, and balsamic vinaigrette; or a classic Caesar about which my husband — who believes a restaurant's Caesar salad is a measure of its excellence — raved. My filet mignon with brandy and green peppercorn sauce came with the sweetest onion I have ever tasted, slow roasted and stuffed with duxelle. The grilled veal chop is filled with prosciutto, fontina, and spinach — a flavorful and juicy combination. Pasta, seafood, and vegetarian dishes round out the menu. Dessert is a must, either here or upstairs at Truffles.

Naples' Crayton Cove — one of the Gulf Coast's many dock-and-dine options.

DOCK AT CRAYTON COVE
263-9940
12th Ave. S.
Price: Moderate
Cuisine: Florida
Serving: L, D
Credit Cards: AE, D, MC, V
Handicapped Access: Yes
Reservations: No
Special Features: Open dining on Naples Bay

The Dock has all the right ingredients: location over the water; open-air dining; rustic, Old Florida decor; tropical cuisine; signature "rhum" drinks; and a fun attitude. It's my kind of place. The menu shows great promise, spanning the traditional to the inventive of Florida gastronomy: fish and chips, broiled Brie escargot mushroom caps, Caribbean crab fritters, chicken chili, blackened shrimp tacos, grilled tuna and rotini salad, smokey basil snapper with Jamaican rice, Floribbean fish stew, grilled Florida swordfish, shrimp Alfredo, and baked grouper Martinique. This place has been a favorite since it opened, almost 20 years ago. In the old days it did mostly its traditional menu of fried foods, and did it well. I like the direction its taken in theory, but in practice, I think it may need more practice. My selections, anyway — a crab quesadilla special and the fish stew — lacked character.

FERNANDEZ DE BULL
263-2996
4951 N. Tamiami Tr.
Price: Inexpensive to Moderate
Cuisine: Cuban
Serving: L, D
Credit Cards: MC, V
Handicapped Access: Yes
Reservations: Accepted for dinner

Selected by readers of a local magazine as Southwest Florida's best Cuban cuisine, Fernandez failed to live up to such high expectations. It outfits its small dining room in raw leather, Mexican tiles, and fresh flowers — festive enough, except that the flowers on my table had died long ago. The food was flavorful, and authentic enough. I especially appreciated the bowl of homemade pepper sauce which graced each table. The cook does a proper *lechon asado.* This version of the classic roast pig uses lemons and sour oranges with the garlic, for a nice tang. I found the black bean soup hearty but uneventful, and the Cuban bread crusty as it should be. My pork was a bit on the tough side, however, and the service suffered from a lackadaisical attitude. Other lunch and dinner offerings: Cuban sandwich, Spanish sausage sandwich, *palomilla* steak, *escabeche* salad, *ropa vieja*, shrimp with garlic and wine, filet mignon, *pollo a la Cubana*, and a vegetarian plate.

LAFITE
597-3232
The Registry Resort, 475
  Seagate Dr.
Closed: May operate limited schedule in off- season
Price: Very Expensive
Cuisine: New
  American/Continental
Serving: D
Credit Cards: AE, CB, D,
  DC, MC, V
Handicapped Access: Yes
Reservations: Recommended

Superlatives are commonly used to describe this uncommon bastion of epicurean delight. Housed within the swanky, spectacular lobby of the Registry Hotel, it provides diners with an atmosphere of rich wood, polished metal, and elegant furnishings. Fresh orchids delicately adorn the spotless linen on the tables. Hot dishes arrive under polished metal warmers. Bottles of mineral water stay chilled in wine buckets to fill crystal goblets. Fresh kiwi sorbet is served between courses, in an iced glass flower. The menu is inspired by regional specialties and creative ingenuity, mixing and matching contrasting flavors with careful thought. For an appetizer, I tried the twice-seared fresh goose liver with dried sour cherries on crisp sourdough pudding in *gewurtztraminer* glaze. A taste bud revolution! Escargot, nestled in a Vidalia onion, waded in a cream sauce which was a bit too rich for my taste. But richness is what Lafite is about. The cappuccino of oxtail soup with tortellini was superb, but a bit too salty, as was my sauteed salmon entree, rolled with arugula and served with tomato linguini in garlic balsamic vinegar butter. The sauce, nonetheless, excelled. My companion's choice was better — ahi tuna loin in Japanese mustard with hot and sour shredded cucumbers and sesame seed oil. Never had I tarried so over selecting from a menu. We wanted to try the New Zealand venison chops with lingonberries in port wine and Michigan sour cherries, or the hickory smoked Colorado rack of lamb with tamarind barbecue crust — but alas, there was the dessert cart for which to leave room. And we were glad we did sacrifice for the wonderfully decadent, flourless chocolate cake, strawberry torte, and cappuccino served with a rock-candy stirring stick. Elegance all the way. Had we been there on a different night, we'd have been entertained by a harpist.

NICK'S ON THE WATER
649-7770
Coconut Grove Marketplace, 1001 10th Ave. S.

Discriminating selection of product and a lively, picturesque setting elevates Nick's in the highly competitive field of Italian dining. Red brick

Price: Expensive
Early Dining Menu: Yes
Cuisine: Italian
Serving: L, D, Sunday
     Brunch
Credit Cards: AE, D, MC,
     V
Handicapped Access: Yes
Reservations: Recom-
     mended
Special Features: View of
     bay and city dock

archways, the intimate Wine Room, and two-level seating with a view of Naples Bay and the yachts at City Dock, set the mood for classics with an innovative flair, from north and south Italy. Nick's angel hair pasta in tomato cream basil sauce with peas and proscuitto; rigatoni à la vodka (featuring pureed ham and a vodka marinara sauce); fettuccini carbonara; and veal canneloni can be ordered as an appetizer, at both lunch and dinner. They all constitute "items that made us famous," and you won't wonder why. Salads, pasta, seafood, poultry, and specialty veal from the à la carte menu are treated with good taste and imagination. Sauces reflect the freshness of Nick's ingredients, perfect seasoning, and careful reduction. The atmosphere downstairs is more casual, with tables huddled around a red-brick bar dominated by a spit-shined cappuccino steamer.

**RIVERWALK FISH &
     ALE HOUSE**
263-2734
Olde Marine Market Place,
     1200 5th Avenue S.
Price: Moderate
Cuisine: Seafood
Serving: L, D
Credit Cards: AE, D, MC,
     V
Handicapped Access: Yes,
     but some manipulation
     required
Reservations: No
Special Features: View of
     bay

This is Naples' spirited side, where things can get a little noisy and everything isn't always polished. I like it. The ambiance is provided by splintered wood, with only plastic sheets separating you from the sea air in inclement weather. Seafood preparations transcend the standard. Shrimp and Andouille pasta with a Cajun flair is a filling and pleasantly spicy lunch or dinner option. Other interesting choices: grilled shrimp and scallops appetizer served with red pineapple salsa; grilled seafood salad; English shrimp and crab melt sandwich; seared sea scallops; lager steamed shrimp; red snapper teriyaki.

FOOD PURVEYORS

BAKERIES

Sarasota Bay Coast

Caribbean Pie Co. (925-9069; 5773 Beneva at Clark, Sarasota) Freshly baked desserts. Key lime and Caribbean cream pies, whole or by the slice, and ice cream.

French Hearth (351-4304; 5230 N. Tamiami Tr., Sarasota) Freshly baked breads, croissants, pastries, light meals, and wines.

Strudels 'n Cream (955-6167; 246 Sarasota Quay, Sarasota) The specialty, of course, baked strudel. Also: breads, croissants, cookies, desserts, coffee, and cappuccino.

Charlotte Harbor Coast

Belgian Bakery (625-1252; 4040 N. Tamiami Tr., Port Charlotte) Belgian breads from Old World recipes using no sugar, preservatives, milk, or eggs; Belgian–French pastries, Belgian cookies, meringues.

Island Coast

Andre's French Bakery (482-2011; 12901 McGregor Blvd., Fort Myers) Small but chockful of treats *français*: baguettes, great olive bread, cookies, sublime tortes, and custard-filled pastries.

Bud & Deb's Island Bakery (472-5700; 1473 Periwinkle Way, Sanibel Island) From-scratch key lime pies, cakes, breads, and ice cream.

South Coast

Hardcrust Bakery (598-1400; Imperial Square; 975 Imperial Golf Course Blvd. #101, Bonita Springs) Hardcrust breads, pastries, bagels, and filled croissants.

Island Bakery (394-4508; 287 N. Collier Blvd., Marco Island) Specializes in cakes. Also: key lime pie, tortes, croissants, Danish, breads.

Naples Cheesecake Co. (598-9070; 8050 Trail Blvd., Naples) Eight to 12 different flavors, including key lime, amaretto, and peanut butter.

CANDY & ICE CREAM

Sarasota Bay Coast

Caffe Classico (925-2644; 4256 Tamiami Tr. S., Sarasota) Homemade *gelato*, ice cream, and yogurt.

Martha's Candy & Clutter (485-4904; 237 W. Venice Ave., Venice) Homemade bonbons, chocolates in all shapes and foils, old-fashioned hard candies.

Charlotte Harbor Coast

The Loose Caboose (964-0440; Railroad Plaza, Boca Grande) Katharine Hepburn, among others, left her compliments on the bulletin board at this restaurant known for its homemade ice cream.

Island Coast

The Fudgery (472-1552; Jerry's Shopping Center, 1700 Periwinkle Way, Sanibel Island) Fresh fudge made as you watch.

The Loose Caboose in Boca Grande's Railroad Plaza carries a cargo of highly acclaimed homemade ice cream.

South Coast

Breakfast & Cream (591-4060; 881–103rd Ave. No., Naples) Homemade ice cream and yogurt.

Olde Marco Fudge Factory (642-5200; Port of Marco Shopping Village, 212 Royal Palm Dr., Marco Island) Homemade fudge in key lime, rum raisin, and other flavors, plus gourmet jelly beans, chocolate-covered pretzels, and gourmet preserves.

COFFEE

Sarasota Bay Coast

Boston Bean 'N Tea (923-4022; Gulf Gate Mall, Stickney Point Rd., Sarasota) More than 50 varieties of freshly roasted coffee, plus teas and brewing accessories.

Venice Wine & Coffee (484-3667; 121 Venice Ave. W., Venice) Buy gourmet coffee by the bag or cup at the espresso bar. Also wine, international beers, chocolates, and cookies.

Island Coast

Cafe and Coffee Exchange (433-5233; Bell Tower Mall, Fort Myers) Gourmet beans and blends, tasting tables, and a sandwich and dessert menu.

The Daily Grind (472-1516; Bailey's General Store, Sanibel Island) Espresso bar.

DELI & SPECIALTY FOODS

Sarasota Bay Coast

Alexander's Gourmet Market (925-1498; 5252 S. Tamiami Tr., Sarasota) Fine take-out, fresh seafood, patés, desserts, cheeses, smoked fish.

Centre Market (383-2887; Centre Shops, 5370 Gulf of Mexico Dr., Longboat Key) European-style market with fresh produce, seafood, meats, and specialty grocery items.

Geier's Sausage Kitchen (923-3004; 7447 Tamiami Tr., Sarasota) European-style sausage and smoked meats, prime fresh meats.

The Polished Piglet (485-5226; 137 W. Venice Ave., Venice) Gourmet pastas, cookies, candy, herbs, and canned goods for gift baskets or individual purchase.

Charlotte Harbor Coast

Hudson's Grocery (964-2621; Park Ave., Boca Grande) Look for the hot pink (non-functional) gas pump out front. Cheeses, wines, deli products, and meat cut to order. Free delivery to boats, homes, and condos, with a minimum $25 order.

Island Coast

Barney's Incredible Edibles (472-2555; 2330 Palm Ridge Rd., Sanibel Island) Bakery and deli specializing in croissants, stuffed croissants, and croissantwiches. Also: muffins, cookies, cakes, pizza, and gourmet groceries.

Hungry I (936-4823, Edison Mall, 4125 Cleveland Ave., Fort Myers) German gourmet items, candies, and deli; take-out or eat-in sandwiches.

Oriental & Tai Grocery (936-0916; 3258 Cleveland Ave., Fort Myers) Fresh and packaged ingredients.

South Coast

Artichoke & Company (263-6979; The Village at Venetian Bay, Naples) Gourmet take-out, soups, breads, cheeses, pastries, and wines, with related tropical juice bar and cafeteria.

Crayton Cove Gourmet (262-4362; 800 12th Ave. S., Naples) Citrus and fresh-squeezed juice, novelty dressings, "tipsy" vegetables, local fruit jams, fine imported cakes and candies.

Sharon's Gourmet Pantry (394-7883; 715 Bald Eagle Dr., Marco Island) Specialty sandwiches, homemade soups, salads, croissants, muffins, cheesecake, and cookies.

FAST FOOD & PIZZA

Sarasota Bay Coast

Crusty Louie's Stuffed Pizza (366-3100; Crossroads Shopping Center, 3800 Tamiami Tr. S., Sarasota) Stuffed, pan, or thin-crust pizza made with whole wheat crust and low-fat, low-salt cheeses.

Luigi's Pizza & Eatza (371-7060; 5114 Fruitville Rd., Sarasota) Ribs, chicken wings, gyros, burgers, subs, Chicago-style and stuffed pizza, sausage rolls, spinach pie, *baklava.*

Charlotte Harbor Coast

Barnacle Bill's (474-9703; 1975 Beach Rd., Englewood) Dagwood-sized sandwiches and other beach eats.

Island Coast

Hickory Bar-B-Q (481-2626; 15400 McGregor Blvd., Fort Myers) Hickory smoking, a secret sauce, creamy cole slaw, and fresh coconut cream pie make this my favorite barbecue around.

Juicy Lucy's (454-0319; 17260 San Carlos Blvd., Fort Myers Beach) One of a local chain of burger joints.

Plaka (463-4707; 1001 Estero Blvd., Fort Myers Beach) Gyros, spinach pie, *moussaka*, and *baklava* in a screened-in dining room near the beach.

Taste of New York (278-3222; 2215-B Winkler Ave., Fort Myers) Take-out or eat-in pizza — regular, vegetarian, and white — and other New York-Italian specialties.

South Coast

Cracker's Grill (643-7400; 493 Airport Rd. N., Naples) Burgers and oversized sandwiches, eat-in or take-out; breakfast and lunch.

Lindburgers (598-2176, Pavilion Shopping Center, 847 Vanderbilt Beach Rd., Naples) Gourmet hamburgers, salads, sandwiches, wings.

Pizza Factory (263-6016; 6631 Dudley Dr., Naples) Family fun — games, big screen TVs, to go along with pizza.

FRUIT & VEGETABLE STANDS

For the freshest produce, visit the plentiful roadside stands along the Coast. Some feature U-Pick options, especially for tomatoes and strawberries, sometimes for oranges.

Sarasota Bay Coast

Mixon Fruit Farms (748-5829; 2712 26th Ave. E., Bradenton) Large, old family-owned business specializing in citrus; tours of the grove and processing plant, free sampling, shipping, and a gift shop.

Island Coast

Iona Farm Market (433-2028; 8591 Gladiolus Dr., Fort Myers) Located in the middle of a tomato field, you can't help but trust the freshness of its products. The open-air stand sells fruit and vegetables.

Sunburst Tropical Fruit Company (283-1200; 7113 Howard Rd., Bokeelia, Pine Island) One of the oldest island groves, it specializes in mangoes, but also grows carambola, lychee, and other exotics, and sells fruit products and its own cookbook. There are also paid tours, via a converted mango-picking trailer.

Sun Harvest Citrus (800-743-1480 or 768-2686; 14810 Metro Pkwy. S. at Six Mile Cypress, Fort Myers) Part tourist attraction, part citrus stand, it offers free samples, tours, demonstrations, a playground, and a gift shop.

Fruitful Island

For those in the know, Pine Island is synonymous with exotic fruit. Guavas once grew wild all over the island, brought to this semitropical land from the tropical Caribbean. Later, mangoes flourished. The only other place in Florida where such tropical fruits grow in such abundance is Homestead, on the East Coast, at a latitude some 90 miles south of Pine Island.

What makes Pine Island so nearly tropical? The warm waters of Charlotte Harbor run wide at the island's north end, around Bokeelia. They insulate the land, warming cold air before it reaches fragile fruit groves. Longans, sapodillas, carambolas, lychees, and other rare treats thrive as a result of this pocket of climate. Fructose freaks from miles around make a pilgrimage to roadside stands along Pine Island and Pineland roads, throughout the summer and fall.

South Coast

Stallings Farm (263-1028; 2600 Pine Ridge Rd., Naples) U-Pick, We-Pick, and shipping.

NATURAL FOODS

Sarasota Bay Coast

Granary (366-7906; 1451 Main St., downtown Sarasota) Fresh produce, natural foods, grains, deli, and cafe.

Island Coast

Island Health Foods (472-3666; 1640 Periwinkle Way, Sanibel Island) Complete line of food and beauty products, plus sandwiches, frozen yogurt, and carrot juice.

South Coast

Fletcher's Natural Foods (394-8361; Marco Towne Center, Marco Island) Full service health food grocery store with juice bar and fresh bakery goods.

Martha's Natural Food Market (992-5838; Sunshine Plaza, 9118 Bonita Beach Rd. E., Bonita Springs) Natural baby food and diapers, pet care products, sports nutrition, Cambridge diet, organic produce, no-cholesterol cheese.

SEAFOOD

Sarasota Bay Coast

Siesta Fish Market (349-2602; 221 Garden Ln., Siesta Key) A long-standing family operation whose fresh and prepared products have become an island institution.

Island Coast

Beach Seafood Market (463-8777; 1100 Shrimp Boat Ln., San Carlos Island, Fort Myers Beach) Fresh seafood at its source, specializing in shrimp — fresh, steamed, and dinners.

Pine Bay Seafood Market (283-7100; 4330 Pine Island Rd., Matlacha, Pine Island) Fresh and smoked fish and shellfish from the area's major trans-shipment center.

Skip One Seafood (482-0433; 15820 S. Tamiami Tr., San Carlos Park) Fresh catches and sandwiches, seafood, and clambakes for eat-in, take-out, or delivery.

South Coast

Crab Factory (262-7323; 338 Ninth St. N., Carvel Plaza, Naples) Specializes in blue crab.

Doxsee Seafood (394-6999, 1165 Bald Eagle Dr., Marco Island) Major wholesaler and retailer of local seafood.

FOOD FESTIVALS

Sarasota Bay Coast

Florida Winefest and Auction (351-8497; Charles Ringling Mansion on the USF/New College bay-front campus) A prestigious event featuring food and wine seminars, tastes from the area's finest restaurants, top entertainment, black-tie dinner, fine wine auction, and public Funfest. Three days in April.

Stone Crab & Seafood Festival (383-6464, Colony Beach & Tennis Resort, Longboat Key) Benefits Mote Marine research facility. October.

Island Coast

Fort Myers Beach Shrimp Festival (463-3221; Lynn Hall Park, Fort Myers Beach) Blessing of the fleet, 5K run, parade, and shrimp boil. One week in late February.

Southwest Florida Wine Fair (1-800-237-3102 or 472-5111; South Seas Plantation, Captiva) Participation by leading California wineries. Early June.

Taste of the Cape (574-0372; German–American Club, Cape Coral) Tastes from local restaurants, live entertainment. One day in late September.

Taste of the Islands (472-3355; Dunes Golf and Tennis Club, Sanibel Island) Twenty Captiva and Sanibel restaurants participate, with live music and competitions to benefit wildlife. One day in late April.

Taste of the Town (482-7377; Centennial Park, downtown Fort Myers) Fifty restaurants sell their wares; live entertainment and children's games. One day in early November.

South Coast

Bonita Tomato Seafood Festival (992-2943; Bonita Recreational Center, Lee Blvd., Bonita Springs) Honors the town's two culinary trademarks. Two days in March.

Tropicool Food Festivals — Naples' May-time celebration brings along with it a variety of food fairs:

> **Caribbean Sunsplash** (643-0001; Naples Beach Hotel, Naples) West Indian cuisine, dancing, and music.

> **Everglades Seafood Festival** (695-3941; Everglades City) Local catches, music, and artisan fair.

> **Olde Naples Italian Food Fest** (649-6707; Third St. S., Old Naples) Pasta, children's Italian costume contest, antique Italian cars, Italian artisans, and discounts on Italian imports in the shops.

> **Taste of Marco** (394-4441, Marco Town Center, Marco Island) Samples from 30 restaurants, live entertainment. May.

Watermelon Festival (992-5001; Bonita Springs) Summertime celebration of a juicy crop.

CHAPTER SIX
Fun in the Sun
RECREATION

Angler's silver: a hooked tarpon fights for freedom in Boca Grande Pass.

Lee County Visitor & Convention Center

Outdoor recreation — 365 days a year — makes the Gulf Coast a sport-lover's mecca. From lazing on beaches, to cheering on professional base-ball teams, to less sedentary activities such as tennis, fishing, golf, and scuba diving — the Gulf Coast offers it all year-round.

BEACHES

After climate, visitors list beaches as the primary magnet that draws them to Gulf Coast Florida. The area's best fringe benefits, the beaches form a large part of our identity, dictating our dress code and inspiring our arts.

Miles of beach stretch from Bradenton to Marco Island. Each beach has its own personality and unique appeal. Since beach connoisseurs regularly select

Beach potatoing at its best.

Gulf Coast beaches as among the world's best, their listing deserves description as critical as a restaurant or hotel review. Following are the best in my book.

<u>Note:</u> Many Gulf Coast beaches forbid pets or require leashes.

Sarasota Bay Coast

ANNA MARIA BAYFRONT PARK
Northeast end of Anna Maria Island
Facilities: Picnic areas, rest rooms, showers, playground, recreational facilities

One of the region's more secluded beaches, this one boasts frontage on both the bay and Gulf. Narrower than the rest of the island's beaches, it is bounded by boulders. You get a magnificent view of St. Petersburg's Sunshine Skyway Bridge from the bay. An historical marker tells tales of Timucuan Indians, the island's naming, and legendary Spanish explorers. (It claims Ponce de Leon stopped here first, contrary to Punta Gorda's claim.) Heed danger signs that mark where heavy tidal currents make swimming perilous.

CASPERSEN BEACH
Harbor Dr. and Center Rd., Venice
Facilities: Picnic areas, rest rooms, fitness trail, fishing pier, restaurant

This narrow, dark-sand beach threads under the Venice Fishing Pier and around picnic tables. For secluded sunning, head south where the sands widen. On and round the pier, folks fish, hang out at the tiki bar, and hunt for shark's teeth.

COQUINA BEACH
Southern end of Gulf Blvd., Bradenton Beach, Anna Maria Island
Facilities: Picnic areas, rest rooms, showers, lifeguard, concessions, boat ramps

Recently renourished, this large and popular park boasts plump, wide sands, edged in Australian pines. Waters at the south end of the pier provide good snorkeling. The park continues on the bay, where swimming should be avoided because of currents and boat traffic.

A hard day at Venice's Caspersen Beach.

CORTEZ BEACH
North end Gulf Dr.,
  Bradenton Beach, Anna
  Maria Island

Here's a long stretch of revamped beach that meets up with Coquina, its more popular cousin. Surfers like it here. It's convenient for the heavily laden visitor because you park right along the sands' edge.

CRESCENT BEACH
South of Siesta Public
  Beach near Midnight
  Pass Rd. and Stickney
  Point Rd. intersection

Here is found the same luxurious sand as at Siesta's public beach, but without the facilities and ease of parking. Named for its half-moon configuration, it appeals to sports-minded beachers because of catamaran and water bike rentals, nearby. Divers and snorkelers head to Point of Rocks at the south end of the beach, where marine life and coral formations abound.

GREER ISLAND
North Shore Rd., north
  Longboat Key

Locals call this Beer Can Island, but I believe that nickname is based upon past reputation. It seems clean and tame enough to me. The walk over the dunes needs repair and is blocked off for the time being, but you can still get to the beach via a path beside it. Lack of facilities keeps all of Longboat's beaches relatively unpopulated. Avoid swimming in the pass, where danger signs warn of brisk currents.

LIDO BEACH
700 block of Benjamin
  Franklin Dr., Lido Key.
Facilities: Picnic areas,
  playground, rest rooms,
  showers, lockers, life-
  guards, swimming pool,
  snack bar, volleyball

This is the main beach on the island, heavily developed around a pavilion built by John Ringling. Canvas-shaded lounge chairs may be rented along this stretch of sparkling sand. It's a great beach for tiki-bar hopping along the hotel strip. South of the pavilion, you'll find watersports equipment rentals.

LONGBOAT KEY
Public accesses at north
  end of island, next to
  L'Auberge du Bon
  Vivant restaurant, and
  about a mile south

These accesses are marked subtly and have no facilities or lifeguards. With renourishment from a recent program, the beach now stretches wide as well as long, with fluffy, white sand and dramatic sunset views.

**MANATEE COUNTY
  PARK**
Gulf Blvd., Holmes Beach
Facilities: Picnic area, rest
  rooms, showers, life-
  guard, playground,
  restaurant

The hot spot of Anna Maria Island beaching, this park appeals to families because of all the available facilities. The beach is now wide enough to accommodate rows and rows of beach towels. Beach renourishers predict a 50 percent reduction in beach width within the first few months, however.

**NOKOMIS
  BEACH/NORTH
  JETTY**
South end Casey Key Rd.,
  Casey Key
Facilities: Picnic area, rest
  rooms, lifeguards, con-
  cessions

Remote and exclusive Casey Key gives way to beachy abandon at its south end. The town of Nokomis Beach is a fisherman's haven, and North Jetty, to its south, draws anglers. Its wide sands are well-loved by serious local beachers, too.

NORTH LIDO BEACH
North end of John Rin-
  gling Blvd., Lido Key.

The beach less traveled on Lido, this one extends from the main beach up to New Pass. Lack of facilities and limited parking keep the throngs away. Wide with fine, spic-and-span sand.

**PALMA SOLA CAUSE-
  WAY BEACH**
Anna Maria Bridge, Route
  64
Facilities: Picnic area, rest
  rooms

Fairly narrow sands edge the causeway between the mainland and Anna Maria Island. They gain some character from Australian pines. Popular with windsurfers and jetskiers, most beachers congregate around the bar-and-grill at the causeway's west end.

SIESTA KEY PUBLIC BEACH
Midnight Pass Rd. at Beach Way Dr., Siesta Key
Facilities: Picnic areas, rest rooms, showers, lifeguard, snack bar, tennis courts, ball fields, soccer field, fitness trail, sundecks

Siesta Key sand was judged "the finest, whitest beach in the world" by the Woods Hole Oceanographic Institute. The blinding whiteness comes from its quartz origins; the fineness, from Mother Nature's efficient pulverizer, the sea. Unfortunately, these facts have not been kept secret. The park averages nearly 20,000 visitors a day. Arrive early to find a parking space. Condos and motels line the edge of the wide beach. Swimming is wonderful, with gradually sloping sands and usually clear waters. I prefer the public accesses along Beach Road to this center of beach activity.

SOUTH LIDO BEACH
South end of Benjamin Franklin Dr., Lido Key
Facilities: Picnic areas, playground, volleyball, rest rooms, ball fields, soccer field, fitness trail, sundecks

A wide, sugar beach wraps around the Gulf to the bay, facing south, on Siesta Key. Picnic areas are overhung with Australian pines and carpeted by their needles. Within its 130 acres, several brands of Florida ecology thrive on different waterfronts. Hiking trails lead you through woodsy parts into the swampland of Brushy Bayou, a good place to canoe.

TURTLE BEACH
South end Blind Pass Rd., Siesta Key
Facilities: Picnic areas, rest rooms, playground, volleyball, boat ramps, horseshoes

The sands become coarser and more shell-studded at Siesta's lower extremes, and the highrise buildings fewer. Both along here and Midnight Pass Road reside the island's upper echelon and more exclusive resorts. Less crowded than the other Siesta beaches, it's family-oriented, but without lifeguards.

VENICE BEACH
Tarpon Center Dr., Venice
Facilities: Picnic area, rest rooms, showers, concessions, lifeguards

Known for its prehistoric sharks'-tooth fossils, you can even rent a professional sand-sifter here. You are bound to find some specimens because of the area's ancient offshore "shark graveyard." This beach feels cramped to me.

Charlotte Harbor Coast

BLIND PASS BEACH
Route 775, mid-island on Manasota Key
Facilities: Rest rooms

Narrow and minimally developed beach characterizes this uncommercialized stretch of sands. Finding shells is no problem; finding a parking spot is.

Sea oat sentinels and a guiding light on Boca Grande's beach.

**BOCA GRANDE LIGHT-
HOUSE PARK**
South end of Gulf Blvd.,
Boca Grande, Gasparilla
Island

Marked by the historic lighthouse, this park ledges the deepwater tarpon grounds of Boca Grande Pass. The plush, deep beach encompasses 135 acres. The view of oil tanks tends to intrude upon the otherwise uninterrupted ambiance. Swimming is not recommended because of strong currents through the pass.

**BOCA GRANDE PUBLIC
BEACH**
Along Gulf Blvd., Boca
Grande, Gasparilla
Island
Facilities: Picnic area, rest
rooms
Admission: $1 per car on
the honor system

The beach is narrow here, and the sand is coarse with an abundance of shells. It's a fine spot for family picnicking, beach-walking, and swimming.

**DON PEDRO ISLAND
STATE RECREATION
AREA**
North of Palm Island,
accessible only by boat
Facilities: Picnic area, rest
rooms

Newly completed facilities provide more comfort for those who have always reveled in the secluded beaching at this 129-acre island getaway.

ENGLEWOOD BEACH
Route 775, south end of
Manasota Key
Facilities: Picnic areas, rest
rooms, showers, conces-
sions

A popular hangout for the local youth, this is, nonetheless, a well maintained and policed area — no alcohol, dogs, glass, surfboards, or motor vehicles are allowed. You can rent inner tubes, snorkel masks, volleyball nets, and other beach toys. Several resorts, shops, and restaurants huddle around the area, which keeps activity levels high.

MANASOTA BEACH
North end of Route 775,
Manasota Key
Facilities: Picnic area, rest
rooms, lifeguard, boat
ramps

Relatively peaceful sunning and shelling venue across Stump Pass from Venice. Swift currents at the island's tip preclude safe swimming.

PORT CHARLOTTE BEACH
Southeast end of Harbor
Blvd., Port Charlotte
Facilities: Picnic areas, rest
rooms, showers, conces-
sions, volleyball, basketball, tennis courts, playground, horseshoes,
boat ramps, fishing pier,
swimming pool

A highly developed recreational center that sits on Charlotte Harbor along a man-made beach, this is a good place to go if you (or the children) like to keep busy at the beach. The sands are fine, but too many cigarette butts are there for my taste.

Island Coast

BAREFOOT BEACH
South end Bonita Beach
Rd., Little Hickory
Island
Facilities: Nearby restau-
rant for rest rooms and
refreshment

The only real public area on Bonita Beach, Barefoot Beach becomes lively during high season and on weekends. Watersports and volleyball, plus a hamburger and bar joint reflect a youthful spirit. Vegetation is sparse; there's nothing hidden about this beach.

BONITA BEACH
Public access every 300
feet or so, along Bonita
Beach Rd., Little Hick-
ory Island

People from Bonita Beach will tell you that the shelling here is as good, possibly better, than on fabled Sanibel. Though it lacks Sanibel's east–west heading, it benefits from less traffic, especially along the north end. The sand is also coarser.

BOWMAN'S BEACH
Bowman's Beach Rd. off
Sanibel–Captiva Rd.,
Sanibel Island
Facilities: Picnic area
Admission: $2 per car for
parking

Once known to naturalists as Sanibel's nude beach, that reputation has been redressed by strict enforcement. Because it is county-owned, it's the only Sanibel beach that forbids alcohol. It is also Sanibel's most natural beach, stretching long, edged by an Australian pine forest, on a sort of island all its own. It can be reached by footbridges from the parking lot (a rather long walk, so go light on the beach paraphernalia). Shells are plentiful here — in some places a foot or more deep along the high-tide mark.

Sanibel: serenity at sunset.

CAPTIVA BEACH
North end Captiva Rd.,
Captiva Island

Only early arrivals get the parking spots for this prime spread of deep, shelly sand. It's a good place to watch a sunset.

Fort Myers Beach: playground of the Island Coast.

Lee County Visitor and
Convention Bureau

CARL E. JOHNSON PARK/LOVERS KEY
Route 865 between Fort Myers Beach and Bonita Beach
Facilities: Picnic area, rest rooms, showers, concessions in season
Admission: $1.50 adults, $.75 children at Carl E. Johnson; $2 per car at Lovers Key

Ride a tram through the natural mangrove environment to a beach very few visitors find. Or you can walk to it. The area between Estero and Little Hickory Island consists of natural island habitat, much of it protected by the state. You can park on state property at a low-impact entrance point, or to the south, at the county-owned Johnson Park and tram.

CAYO COSTA ISLAND STATE PARK
La Costa Island, accessible only by boat
Facilities: Picnic ground, rest rooms, showers

The Island Coast is blessed with some true getaway beaches, untamed by mainland connection. On these, one can actually realize that romantic fantasy common to beach connoisseurs — sands all your own. Cayo Costa stretches seven miles long and is most secluded at its southern extremes. A larger population of beachers occurs at the north end, where docks and a picnic and camping ground attract those who seek creature comforts with their sun and sand. Shelling is wonderful in these parts. If you can't find your private beach on Cayo Costa, look on boat charts for Chino Island, or keep your eyes open for sand among the many mangrove islands.

LAKES PARK
7330 Gladiolus Dr., Fort Myers
Facilities: Picnic areas, rest rooms, showers, playgrounds, concessions
Admission: $1 adults; $.50 children 6–17

This land of freshwater lakes features a small sand beach with a roped-off swimming area. A great place for the family to spend the day, it offers canoeing, paddle-boating, fishing, nature trails, an exercise course, an observation tower, and terrific playground facilities within 277 heavily vegetated acres. The quality of the water is questionable, since the lakes — erstwhile quarries — are stagnant.

LIGHTHOUSE BEACH
South end of Periwinkle Way, Sanibel Island
Facilities: Picnic area, rest rooms, nature trail

Skirting Sanibel's historic lighthouse is an arc of natural beach fronting both the Gulf and San Carlos Bay. One of Sanibel's most populated beaches, its highlights include a nature trail and a fishing pier. Strong currents forbid swimming off the point. The wide beach gives way to sea oats, sea grapes, and Australian pine edging. I like the neighborhood around it — more laid-back than other parts of the island.

LYNN HALL MEMORIAL PARK
Times Square vicinity
Facilities: Picnic areas, rest rooms, showers and playground
Admission: Fee for parking. (**Warning:** Park in designated areas or your car will be towed at great expense)

Most locals know this simply as Fort Myers Beach or "The Beach." Billed as a family destination, it attracts a youthful crowd, especially during spring break. A rocking, rollicking place, it appeals to beach bar-hoppers, crowd-watchers, and those interested in watersports — with loud music, volleyball, a fishing pier, beachside drinks, parties, parasailing, jet-skiing — and action, action, action. The sand lends itself perfectly to sculpting and inspires an annual competition (see *Seasonal Events*).

NORTH CAPTIVA
Across Redfish Pass from South Seas Plantation and Captiva Island; accessible only by boat

Like Cayo Costa, here's a place to look for private beaching. The sands are like gold dust, though narrow at the north end. Most of the island is state protected. You'll find no facilities unless you venture across the island to the bay, where restaurants and civilization abide.

SANIBEL CAUSEWAY BEACH
Sanibel Causeway Rd.
Facilities: Picnic area, rest rooms

Windsurfers especially favor this packed-sand, roadside beach. It's been dressed up with palms and pines, but it's still noisy, and typically jammed. RVs and campers often pull up here to picnic and spend the day in the sun.

SANIBEL'S "STICKER" BEACHES
Along the Gulf drives

You will see signs at beach accesses, designating parking only with A or B stickers. Anyone can get a B sticker by paying $30 (good November to November) at the police department, located in City Hall at 800 Dunlop Rd. Island property owners can buy the same sticker for $1. Full-time residents can obtain a $1 sticker for the prime parking spots along secluded beaches in the most affluent neighborhoods. Cyclists and walk-ins, however, can take advantage of these accesses without stickers.

TARPON BEACH
Middle Gulf Dr. at Tarpon Bay Rd., Sanibel Island
Facilities: Rest rooms

Another popular beach, this one is characterized by sugar sand and a nice spread of shells. It's a bit of a hike from the parking lot to the beach, and the area gets congested on busy days.

TURNER BEACH
South end Captiva Rd., Captiva Island
Facilities: Rest rooms

It's a pretty beach with wide, powdery sands, but it tends to get crowded and parking is limited. The entrance is on a blind curve, which can be dangerous. More bad news: rip tides coming through the pass make this taboo for swimming. Park your beach towel north of the pass for calmer, swimmable waters. We like to come here in the evening, to watch the sunset and walk the beach. Surfers like the area to the north in certain weather. It's also a hot spot for fishermen, who line bayside shores and the bridge between Sanibel and Captiva.

South Coast

**CLAM PASS RECRE-
ATION AREA**
Registry Hotel, North
  Naples
Facilities: Rest rooms,
  showers, concessions
Admission: $1 per car for
  parking

Open to the public, but not widely known, this beach is reached by a tram that follows a boardwalk over a tidal bay and through estuarine mangroves. Boat and cabana rentals are available. Here you will find some of Naples' best shelling.

**DELNOR-WIGGINS
PASS STATE RECRE-
ATION AREA**
597-6196
11100 Gulf Shore Dr. N.,
  Naples
Facilities: Picnic areas,
  pavilion, rest rooms,
  showers, boat ramp, lifeguard
Admission: $3.25 per car;
  $1 walk-ins

This is a highly natural, low-key beach that extends for one mile from the mouth of the Cocohatchee River. The lush white sands are protected during loggerhead nesting season (summer) and support stands of natural vegetation such as cactus, sea grapes, knickerbean, and yucca. A nature trail leads to an observation tower at the beach's north end. Restrict your swimming to south of the pass's fast-moving waters.

LOWDERMILK PARK
Gulf Shore Blvd. at Banyan
  Blvd., Naples
Facilities: Picnic areas, rest
  rooms, showers

Beach headquarters for the South Coast, lots of special activities go on at this gulfside party spot.

**OLD NAPLES MUNICI-
PAL BEACHES**
Gulf Shore Blvd. south of
  Doctors Pass, Naples
Facilities: Rest rooms,
  shower, concessions,
  fishing pier

Stretches of natural beach are anchored by the historic pier, where facilities and a parking lot are located.

TIGERTAIL BEACH
Hernando Dr., south end
  of Marco Island
Facilities: Picnic area, rest
  rooms, showers, conces-
  sions, volleyball

The only public beach on Marco, this is a good place for shelling and sunning. Arrive early in season if you want a parking spot. Wooden ramps cross dunes to 31 acres of marvelous beach.

VANDERBILT BEACH
End of Vanderbilt Dr.,
  Vanderbilt Beach, north
  of Naples

Lack of facilities keep these fine sands fairly untrammeled. If you want refreshment, head south to where the Ritz-Carlton operates a stand.

BICYCLING

County officials from Sarasota to Collier are recognizing the potential of bicycle transportation in their cities of the future. In response to a growing, vocal segment of bike riders and environmentalists, they are looking at bikeways as possible solutions to pollution and congestion.

These bikeways come in two varieties. Bicycle paths are those which are separated from traffic by distance and, ideally, a vegetation buffer. Lanes are a part of the roadway designated for bike traffic.

Where bicyclists share the road with other vehicles, they must follow all the rules of the road, according to Florida law.

BEST BIKING

Sarasota Bay Coast

Oscar Scherer Park offers a bike path with a view. Longboat Key's 12 miles of path parallel Gulf of Mexico Drive's vista of good taste and wealth.

Charlotte Harbor Coast

In Port Charlotte, lightly traveled city roads are designated as bike routes. Englewood draws the line for bike lanes along major routes. About a mile after Gasparilla Island's causeway (which can be crossed by bicycle for $1), the Boca Grande bike path starts. Here, you pedal along old railroad routes. Seven miles

Boca Grande's bike path follows the trail the railroad once took to deepwater port.

of pathway travel the island from tip to tip along Railroad Avenue and Gulf Boulevard.

Highway 776 through beachy Manasota Key is shouldered with a bike lane that begins in Englewood and ends at the Sarasota County line.

Island Coast

Lee County's bicycle–pedestrian program is working toward a system by which mass transit buses would install bike racks, and water shuttles carry bikes from one path's termination point to another's beginning. The newest stretch of path along Daniels Parkway reaches from Summerlin Road to the airport. The Summerlin path leads to the Sanibel Causeway (bikers cross for $1), to connect with island paths, which the county plans to extend someday through Captiva Island.

Sanibel's 30-mile path covers most of the island, and occasionally leaves the roadside, to plunge you into serene backwoods scenery.

Pine Island has imminent plans for connecting existing paths at island's extremes.

Over 30 miles of paved paths accommodate bike riders on Sanibel Island.

Lee County Visitor & Convention Bureau

South Coast

Naples lays out a sporadic system of metropolitan bike paths. A favorite route of local cyclists loops through ten miles of pathway in the north-end Pelican Bay development. Within it, a 580-acre nature preserve provides a pristine change of scenery from upscale suburbia.

Bike paths traverse Everglades City and cross the causeway to Chokoloskee Island.

RENTALS/SHOPS

Sarasota Bay Coast

Bicycle Center (377-4505; 4084 Bee Ridge Rd., Sarasota) Offers pick-up and delivery.

Charlotte Harbor Coast

Island Bike 'N Beach (964-0711; 333 Park Ave., Boca Grande)

Island Coast

Beach Cycle & Repair (463-8844; 1901 Estero Blvd., Fort Myers Beach)
Bike Route (472-1955; 2330 Palm Ridge Rd., Sanibel Island)
Walter's Bicycle Center (542-4474; 1401 SW 47th Terrace, Cape Coral)

South Coast

Bicycle Shoppe of Naples (455-3646; 813 Vanderbilt Beach Rd., Naples)
Ride My Bike (695-2111; Everglades City)
Scootertown (394-8400; 855 Bald Eagle Dr., Marco Island)

CANOEING AND KAYAKING

Sarasota Bay Coast

Intracoastal Kayaks (485-8598; 127 E. Tampa Ave. #8, Venice) Rentals, tours, sales, and instructions.
Oscar Scherer State Recreation Area (483-5956; 1843 S. Tamiami Tr., Osprey) Canoe rentals and tidal creek canoeing along scrubby and pine flatwoods. River otters and alligators inhabit the waters; scrub jays, bobcats, and bald eagles the land.
Ocean Blvd. Sailboarding (346-9463; 1233 Gulf Stream Ave. N., Siesta Key) Rents kayaks.
Snook Haven (485-7221; 5000 E. Venice Ave., Venice) Canoe rentals and trips on the Myakka River.

Island Coast

Gulf Coast Kayak Company (283-1125; Matlacha, Pine Island) Day or overnight trips in the Matlacha Aquatic Preserve and other local natural areas; full moon and new moon astronomy ventures.
Island Kayak Tours (549-1631; Sanibel Island) From north Sanibel and South Seas Plantation on Captiva, half- and full-day tours.
Island Outfitters (472-0123; 1554 Periwinkle Way, Sanibel Island) Kayak rentals.

Lakes Park (7330 Gladiolus Dr., Fort Myers) Canoe rentals for paddling on freshwater lakes.

Sanibel Sea Kayak Adventures (472-9484; Sanibel) Instruction in kayak operation and guided tours in local waters.

Tarpon Bay Recreation (472-8900; 900 Tarpon Bay Rd. Sanibel) Rents canoes and kayaks for use in the bay and through Ding Darling Refuge's Commodore Creek Canoe Trail. Avoid doing the refuge trail at low tide, or you will do a lot of shallow-water portaging. Also, guided canoe and tram tours.

South Coast

Estero River Tackle and Canoe Outfitters (992-4050; opposite Koreshan Park, Tamiami Trail, Estero) Rents and outfits canoes for a four-mile adventure down the natural Estero River, to Estero Bay.

Everglades National Park Boat Tours (695-2591; Everglades Ranger Station, Everglades City) Canoe rentals.

North American Canoe Tours (695-4666; Glades Haven RV Park, Everglades City) Rentals, outfitting, and guided tours into the Everglades.

ESPECIALLY FOR KIDS

Sarasota Bay Coast

301 Raceway (355-5588; 4050 N. Washington Blvd., Sarasota) Go-carts and video arcade.

Mote Marine Summer Science Program (388-2451; 1600 Ken Thompson Pkwy., City Island, Sarasota) Future scientists of America gather along Sarasota Bay for classroom, lab, and field work under the supervision of renowned scientists and other certified teachers. They travel on-location to barrier islands, the Florida Keys, and secluded spots along the Gulf, studying ecology and biology.

Rinky Dink Adventure Golf (756-0043; 2000 Cortez Rd. W., Bradenton) Eighteen holes with an island motif.

Charlotte Harbor Coast

Babcock Wilderness Adventures (639-3958; Route 31, Punta Gorda) A 90-minute swamp-buggy ride delves into old Florida wildlife, including deer, relocated bison, panthers, turkeys, and alligators. Reservations required.

Island Coast

Aqua Trek and Sealife Learning Center (472-8680; 2353 Periwinkle Way, Sanibel Island) Children especially benefit from the 100-gallon touch tank, 15 aquariums, and other sea animal displays that introduce nature enthusiasts to life in the Gulf. The center serves as a marine laboratory, classroom, and departure point for informative beach walks on Sanibel Island's beach-combers' mecca.

Fort Adventure (936-3233; 1915 Colonial Blvd., Fort Myers) Miniature golf, batting cages, bumper boats, and a video arcade with 70 games.

Greenwell's Bat-A-Ball and Family Fun Park (574-4386; 35 NE Pine Island Rd., Cape Coral) Named after the city's favorite sports son, Red Sox Mike Greenwell, it contains batting cages, miniature golf, a video arcade, and go-carts.

Periwinkle Park (472-1433; Periwinkle Way, Sanibel Island) The owner of this trailer park raises and breeds exotic birds and waterfowl. He daddies roughly 600 birds of 133 species, specializing in African and Asian hornbills, and the country's largest collection of the rare African touraco. Flamingos, parakeets, cockatiels, cockatoos, and others occupy the park and 15 aviaries. During the off season, visitors can drive through; in season, biking is recommended. A few of the birds raised here can be seen more easily at *Jerry's Shopping Center* (1700 Periwinkle Way). Take the children in the evening, when the birds are most talkative.

Sun Splash Family Waterpark (574-0557; 400 Santa Barbara Blvd, Cape Coral) This spot offers wet fun in a dozen varieties, with pools, slides, a log roll, cable drops, a river ride, volleyball, and special events. Admission is charged: $7.95 for guests over 53 inches tall; $5.95 for children.

South Coast

Golf Safari (947-1377; 3775 Bonita Beach Rd., Bonita Springs) Jungle-themed mini-golf.

Naples Go-Cart Center (774-7776; 11402 Tamiami Tr. E., Naples)

FISHING

Non-residents age 16 and over must obtain a license unless fishing from a vessel or pier covered by its own license. You can buy inexpensive, temporary non-resident licenses at most bait shops, or at the county tax collector's office.

Snook and tarpon are the prized catch of local anglers. Snook, which is a game fish and cannot be sold commercially, is valued for its sweet taste. Most tarpon (also known as Silver King) are released in these days of environmental consciousness.

Redfish is another sought-after food fish. More common catches in back bays and waters close to shore include mangrove snapper, spotted seatrout,

Fishing Casey Pass between Venice and Nokomis Beach.

shark, sheepshead, pompano, and ladyfish. Deeper waters offshore yield grouper, tuna, red snapper, marlin, amberjack, mackerel, and dolphinfish. Check local regulations for season, size, and limit restrictions.

DEEP-SEA PARTY BOATS

Sarasota Bay Coast

Blue Seas (484-5788; Venice) Trips lasting a few hours to a few days.
Flying Fish Fleet (366-3373; Marina Jack, Island Park, Sarasota) Half-day, six-hour, and all-day trips.
Miss Cortez Fleet (794-1223; 12507 Cortez Rd., Cortez) Charters out of the area's fishing core, lasting four hours to a day.

Island Coast

Class Act Deep Sea Fishing (463-7800; 416 Crescent St., Fort Myers Beach) Daily deep-sea charters aboard a 48-foot vessel.
Getaway Deep Sea Fishing (466-3600; Getaway Marina, 18400 San Carlos Blvd., Fort Myers Beach) The most recognized name in party-boat fishing in these parts, its excursions are aboard a 90-foot craft.

South Coast

Dalis (262-4545, Tin City, Naples) Half-day excursions into the Gulf aboard Naples' largest, air-conditioned head boat, with full bar.

FISHING CHARTERS

Sarasota Bay Coast

Gypsy Guide Service (923-6095, Sarasota) Light tackle and fly fishing, bay and backwater fishing, half- or full day trips, and summer night fishing.

Charlotte Harbor Coast

King Fisher Fleet (639-0969; Fishermen's Village Marina, Punta Gorda) Back bay and deep sea.
Tarpon Hunter II (743-6622; Port Charlotte) Charters in Charlotte Harbor and backwaters.
The Boca Grande Fishing Guides Association (964-2266; Boca Grande) Organization of qualified charter guides especially knowledgeable about tarpon.

Island Coast

Sanibel Marina (472-2723; 634 North Yachtsman Dr., Sanibel Island) Several experienced fishing guides operate out of the marina.
She-Mar Charters (283-5836; Bokeelia, Pine Island) Fishing and specialty excursions.

South Coast

A&B Charters (775-4394; Naples City Dock, Naples) Trips that last anywhere from a half-day to three days; groups of six to 20.

A forest of masts at the Naples City Dock.

FISHING PIERS

Sarasota Bay Coast

Anna Maria City Pier (Anna Maria Island) Unrailed and low to the water, it juts 700 feet into Anna Maria Sound at the northeast end of Bayshore Park.
Bradenton City Pier (Bridge St., Bradenton)
Rod & Reel Pier (875 North Shore Dr., Anna Maria) A privately owned fisherman's complex with cafe, bait shop, and motel. Admission $.50.
Bradenton Beach City Pier (Cortez Rd., Bradenton Beach) Juts into intracoastal waters; contains restaurant and bait concession. It was part of the first bridge from the island to the mainland.

Braving a winter's day cold blast to fish the pier on Anna Maria Island

Tony Saprito Fishing Pier (Hart's Landing, Ringling Causeway Park on way to St. Armands Key) Bait store across the road.

Nokomis Beach Jetty (South end Casey Key Rd., Nokomis Beach) Man-made rock projection into the Gulf, with beach and picnic area.

Venice's South Jetty (Tarpon Center Drive) A stretch of boulder buffer with a paved walkway at Venice's north end.

Venice Fishing Pier (Casperson Beach, Harbor Dr., South Venice) 750 feet long, complete with rest rooms, showers, bait shop, and restaurant. Admission costs $1 for adults, $.50 for children.

Bait-net casting off Venice Pier.

Charlotte Harbor Coast

Charlotte Harbor Pier (Bayshore Dr., Charlotte Harbor)

Gasparilla Island (Two piers on the north and south end of Route 776)

Port Charlotte Beach (Southeast end of Harbor Blvd., Port Charlotte) Pier with bait and tackle concession, part of a beach and pool recreational center.

Don't Kill With Kindness

Gray, white, and endangered brown pelicans live and vacation on local shores and shoals, and are somewhat emblematic of Gulf Coast life. Graceful in flight and awkward in pursuit, they can become downright pesky when pursuing the fish that's on your hook.

No matter how endearing they appear and how cruel it may seem, remember to ignore their relentless begging. Throwing pelicans unwanted fish can result in painful and fatal bone-puncture injuries.

If you happen to snag the pelican's hard-to-miss bill with a fish hook, experts advise that you gently reel in the bird, then cover its head with a towel or shirt while carefully backing the hook out. Then snip the barb. Be sure to hold the bird's beak closed and keep your face clear.

To further protect the pelicans, throw discarded fish line and plastic loop beverage can-holders into the garbage, not the water.

"His bill will hold more than his belican", as one poet put it, but the brown pelican's narrow gullet cannot withstand the punctures of bony fish.

Island Coast

Cape Coral Yacht Club (549-4926; End of Driftwood Pkwy., Cape Coral) A 620-foot lighted fishing pier is part of a boating/recreational complex.

Centennial Park (near the Yacht Basin downtown Fort Myers)

Fort Myers Beach Pier (at Lynn Hall Memorial Park, Times Square) Recently rebuilt after a tumble into the sea, it holds a bait shop and a lot of casting room.

Matlacha Park (Matlacha, Pine Island) Playground and boat ramps.

Sanibel Lighthouse Beach (southeast end of Periwinkle Way, Sanibel) A T-dock into San Carlos Bay.

South Coast

Naples Fishing Pier (12th Ave. So., Naples) Extends into the Gulf 1,000 feet, with bait shop, snack bar, rest rooms, and showers.

GOLF

"Depending upon where you play, the area's average cost for 18 holes of golf and a single seat on a two-player golf cart is about $30.... You can play for more and you can play for less, but anything much less than $30 per player is apt to be somewhat 'cow-pasture-y.'"

—Bill Kilpatrick in the *Fort Myers News-Press Visitors Guide*

Home of such golfing greats as Patty Berg, Chi Chi Rodriguez, and the late Herb Graffis, Southwest Florida golf is as much fun to watch as it is to play.

PUBLIC GOLF COURSES

Sarasota Bay Coast

Here, in the birthplace of Floridian golf, there are more courses than you can swing a club at, the majority of which are private or semi-private. Most resorts have their own greens or arrange golf-around programs at local links.

Bobby Jones Golf Club (955-8097; 1000 Azinger Way, Sarasota) Sarasota's only public course, it has 36 holes plus a nine-hole executive course.

Heather Hills Club (755-8888; 101 Cortez Rd. W., Bradenton) Public executive course with 18 holes, par 61.

Palma Sola Golf Club (792-7476; 3807 75th St. W., Bradenton) 18 holes, par 72.

Charlotte Harbor Coast

Deep Creek (625-6911; 1260 San Cristobal Ave., Port Charlotte) 18 holes, par 70.

Island Coast

Alden Pines (283-2179; 14261 Clubhouse Dr., Pineland) Semi-private, 18 holes, par 71.

Bay Beach Golf Club (463-2064; 7401 Estero Blvd., Fort Myers Beach) 18 holes, par 61.

Cape Coral Golf and Tennis (542-7879; 4003 Palm Tree Blvd., Cape Coral) 18 holes, par 72.

Dunes Golf & Tennis Club (472-2535; 949 Sandcastle Rd., Sanibel Island) Semi-private 18-hole, par-70 course.

Fort Myers Country Club (936-2457; Fort Myers) Fort Myers' oldest and most distinguished greens; 18 holes, par 71.

South Coast

Naples earns its title as Golf Capital of the World with more golf holes per capita than any other statistically tracked metropolitan area.

Marco Shores Country Club (394-2581; Route 951 before Marco Island bridge) Semi-private, 18 holes, par 72.

Naples Beach Golf Club (434-7007; 851 Gulf Shore Blvd. N., Naples) 18-hole, par-72 resort course.

Pelican's Nest Golf Club (1-800-952-6378 or 947-4600; 4450 Bay Creek Dr. SW, Bonita Springs) 18-hole course, par 72; and 9-hole course, par 36.

GOLF CENTERS

Sarasota Bay Coast

Eagle Golf Center (371-1776; 4735 Bee Ridge Rd., Sarasota) Practice sand traps, chipping and putting greens, PGA pros.

Sara Bay View Golf Range (753-0177; 1414 Bay Dr., Sarasota) Lighted range, practice sand trap, lessons.

Island Coast

Rick's Family Golf Center (481-3400; 15825 S. Tamiami Tr., South Fort Myers) Driving range with 40 hitting stations, 18-hole miniature golf, lessons.

Summerlin Driving Range (454-5777; 17105 San Carlos Blvd., Fort Myers) Lighted driving range, pro shop, lessons, and clinics. Comes highly recommended from friends of mine.

South Coast

Gulf Coast Golf (597-8868; 6700 N. Airport Rd., Naples) Full-service driving range with chipping and putting greens, and lessons.

Naples Golf Center (775-3337; 7700 E. Davis Blvd., Naples) Video, single, series, and group lessons.

FITNESS & HEALTH CLUBS

Sarasota Bay Coast

Aerobics and Iron of Longboat Key (383-3938; 29 Avenue of Flowers, Longboat Key) Weight training, stairs trainers, aerobic classes, massage therapy.

Olympian Gym (758-7579; 6731 15th St. E., Sarasota) 8,000 square feet of equipment, kick boxing, wrestling, cardiovascular training, free weights, sauna.

Wilbanks Family Fitness Center (921-4400; 8383 S. Tamiami Tr., Sarasota) Exercise equipment, sauna, steam, whirlpool, lap pool, suntanning, child care.

Charlotte Harbor Coast

Charlotte County Family YMCA (629-2220; 22425 Edgewater, Charlotte Harbor) Aerobics, trimnastics, bodyshaping, yoga, volleyball, basketball, golf tournaments, youth sports competition, and kiddy facilities.

Charlotte Racquet & Health & Fitness (629-2223, 3250 Loveland Blvd., Port Charlotte) Racquetball, squash, tennis, stairclimbers, bikes, treadmill, universal weights, ballet, karate, jazzercize.

Island Coast

Club Sanibel (395-2639; 975 Rabbit Rd., Sanibel Island) Aerobics, free weights, cardiovascular and personal training, massage therapy, hair salon.

New Life Fitness (337-1981; 2531 Cleveland Ave., Fort Myers) Racquetball courts, indoor pool, running track, tae kwon do, tanning, free weights, aerobics, child care.

The Workout (549-3354; 1013 Cape Coral Pkwy, Cape Coral) Jazzercize, step aerobics, slimnastics, sauna/steam, indoor pool, nutritional guidance, child care.

South Coast

Body Quest (643-7546; 2975 S. Horseshoe Dr., Naples) Complete fitness center, aerobics, karate, heart-healthy cafe, nursery.

Fit For You (591-3443; 644 98th Ave., Naples) Personal training in your home, condo, or club, specializing in aqua-aerobics.

Marco Fitness Club (394-3705; 871 Elkcam Circle, Marco Island) Full-service gym, step aerobics, Nautilus, sauna, workout machines.

HUNTING

G iven the region's heightened environmental consciousness, most shooting of wildlife is done with a camera.

To hunt in Florida preserves, you must obtain a state license plus a Wildlife Management Area stamp. Early season hunters need a quota permit, which is awarded randomly by a drawing in June from applications submitted to the Game and Fresh Water Fish Commission. Special stamps are also required for muzzleloading guns, archery, turkey, or waterfowl hunting.

For more information, pick up a copy of the *Florida Hunter's Handbook* when you buy your license. It will tell you when seasons begin and end, and bag limits. Most popular game includes deer, doves, snipe, quail, turkey, duck, and coot.

Big Cypress National Preserve 564,320 acres, adjacent to the Everglades.
Cecil M. Webb Wildlife Management Area (639-1531; 29200 Tucker Grade, Port Charlotte) 65,000 acres, on one of Florida's 62 designated hunting preserves. Advance permission required.

ICE SKATING

Sarasota Bay Coast

Ice Chateau (484-0080; 1097 N. Tamiami Tr., Nokomis) Yes, ice skating in Florida. For those suffering frostbite nostalgia, don blades and get over it. Rentals available. Admission is $4.55 for adults and $3.75 for children.

ON THE WATER

DINING CRUISES

Sarasota Bay Coast

Marina Jack II (455-9488; Marina Jack Restaurant, Island Park, Sarasota) Lunch and dinner cruises; closed in September.

Island Coast

Black Whale Cruises (765-5550, Fort Myers Beach.) Dinner, luncheon, and champagne buffet excursions into the Gulf.

Everglades Jungle Cruises (334-7474; Fort Myers Yacht Basin, downtown Fort Myers) Dinner, buffet, and theme cruises along the Caloosahatchee River.

South Coast

Rosie (775-6776; 1484 5th Ave. S., Naples) Breakfast, lunch, and dinner cruises aboard a sternwheel paddleboat, into Gulf and bay waters. Acclaimed for its casual "Keys" cuisine.

MARINE SUPPLIES

Sarasota Bay Coast

Venice Marine Center (485-3388; 1485 Tamiami Tr. S., Venice)

Charlotte Harbor Coast

Millers Marina (964-2283; Harbor Dr., Boca Grande) Tackle and marine supplies, bait, groceries.

Island Coast

Boat/US (481-7447; 12901 McGregor Blvd., Fort Myers) All boating, yachting, and fishing needs. Memberships available for discounts and emergency service.

Ships Store (466-3633; 1548 San Carlos Blvd., Fort Myers Beach) Discount supplies, riggings, charts, electronics, gifts, and paints.

POWERBOAT RENTALS

Sarasota Bay Coast

Cannons Marina (383-1311; 6040 Gulf of Mexico Dr., Longboat Key) Rentals by half-day, day, and week; runabouts, pontoons, and open skiffs.

Don & Mike's Boat & Ski Rental (966-4000, Casey Key Marina, (Osprey) Nokomis Beach) Power and sailboats.

Charlotte Harbor Coast

Whidden's Marina (964-0708; 1st and Harbor, Boca Grande)

Island Coast

Bonita Beach Resort Motel (992-2137; 26395 Hickory Boulevard, Bonita Beach)

Four Winds Marina (283-0250; Bokeelia, Pine Island) Open fishermen and pontoons.

Palm Grove Marina (463-7333; 2500 Main St. Fort Myers Beach) Runabouts and pontoons.

Sanibel Marina (472-2723; 634 North Yachtsman Dr., Sanibel Island) Power-boats for trips into intracoastal waters only.

South Coast

Fish Head Bait & Tackle (597-2063; 179 Commerce St., Naples)

Marco Island Powerboats (394-1006; 1135 Bald Eagle Dr., Marco Island) Pontoons, cabin cruisers, wave runners.

Park Shore Marina (434-6964; 4310 Gulf Shore Blvd. N., Naples) Pontoons, cabin cruisers, water-ski equipment.

PUBLIC BOAT RAMPS

Sarasota Bay Coast

City Island (New Pass south of Longboat Key) Three ramps.

Coquina Beach Bayside Park (Gulf Blvd., Bradenton Beach) Picnic and recreational facilities; rest rooms nearby.

Higel Park (Tarpon Center Dr., Venice Beach, Venice Inlet)

King Fish Ramp (On Hwy. 64 on intracoastal at Holmes Beach) Picnic facilities.

Nokomis Beach (Venice Inlet)

Palma Sola Causeway (Palma Sola Bay and Route 64)

Turtle Beach (Blind Pass Rd., Siesta Key) Two ramps.

Charlotte Harbor Coast

Manasota Beach (Manasota Beach Rd., Manasota Key)

Ponce de Leon Park (Punta Gorda)

Port Charlotte Beach (Harbor Blvd., Port Charlotte) Beach recreational area, access to Charlotte Harbor.

Indian Mounds Park (951-5572; Englewood) On Lemon Bay. Access to Stump Pass, picnic pavilion, rest rooms, Indian trails.

Island Coast

Lake Kennedy Park (Santa Barbara Blvd., Cape Coral) Ramp into freshwater lake with playground, fishing, and rest rooms.

Lover's Key Recreation Area (Route 865 between Fort Myers Beach and Bonita Beach)

Matlacha Park (Matlacha, Pine Island) Playground and fishing pier.

Punta Rassa (Summerlin Rd., Fort Myers, before the Sanibel Causeway) Picnic facilities and rest rooms.

Sanibel (Causeway Rd.) Two ramps directly across the Sanibel Causeway.

South Coast

Delnor-Wiggins Pass State Recreation Area (11100 Gulf Shore Dr. N., Naples) Admission.

Rookery Bay Reserve (775-8569; Shell Road off Route 951 on the way to Marco Island) Shell ramp into estuarine preserve.

SAILBOAT CHARTERS

Sarasota Bay Coast

Clancy Sail Charters (778-1816; Galati Yacht Basin, 900 Bay Blvd., Anna Maria Island) Half-day, full-day, sunset, weekend, and five-day Boca Grande cruises aboard the 30-foot *Sea Wench*.

The Enterprise Sailing Charters (951-1833; Marina Jack Marina, Island Park, Sarasota) Morning, afternoon, sunset, and full moon sails on a Morgan 41-footer.

Sailing Adventures (776-2104; Seafood Shack Marina, Cortez) Half- and full-day voyages aboard a 40-foot yacht.

Charlotte Harbor Coast

Casey J (964-0708; Whidden's Marina, 1st and Harbor, Boca Grande) 46-foot ocean cruiser.

Island Coast

Island Tall Ship Cruises (765-7447; Snug Harbor, Fort Myers Beach) Sunset cruise aboard the red-sailed *Island Rover*.

New Moon (395-1782; 'Tween Waters Marina, Captiva Island) Up to six passengers aboard a 35-foot sloop.

Quest (334-0670; Fort Myers City Yacht Basin, Fort Myers) Sightseeing, champagne, sunset, and moonlit sails.

South Coast

Captain Quinn's (394-2511, ext. 6740; Marco Island Marriott, 400 S. Collier Blvd., Marco Island) Shelling and sightseeing in Ten Thousand Islands.

Gulf Wind Yachting (FL 1-800-329-4884 or 775-7435; Naples City Dock #70, Naples) Sail charters and instruction; half-day trips to extended sails; Gulf Coast islands, Keys, or Dry Tortugas.

SAILBOAT RENTALS & INSTRUCTION

Sarasota Bay Coast

O'Leary's Sarasota Sailing School (953-7505; Island Park, Sarasota, next to Marina Jack) Rents sailing crafts from 14 to 50 feet; rates for two hours, half days, full days, and weekly. Instruction available.

Island Coast

Offshore Sailing School (1-800-221-4326 or 454-1700; South Seas Plantation Marina, Captiva) Instruction available, from beginning sailing courses to advanced racing and bareboat cruising preparation; operated by an Olympic and America's Cup veteran.

South Coast

Naples Beach Hotel (261-2222; 851 Gulf Shore Blvd. N., Naples) Sailboat rentals, rides, and lessons.

SIGHTSEEING & ENTERTAINMENT CRUISES

Sarasota Bay Coast

Sarasota Water Taxi (359-1167) Stops at Anna Maria Island, Siesta Key, Sarasota Quay, and City Island Park.
Sunset Blues Cruise (794-1223; 12507 Cortez Rd., Cortez) Evening musical cruises some Saturdays aboard a double-decker.

Charlotte Harbor Coast

King Fisher Cruise Lines (639-0969; Fisherman's Village, Punta Gorda) Excursions to Cayo Costa, Cabbage Key, and Useppa (a private island where only owners, registered guests, and special cruise guests may come ashore).

Island Coast

The Capt. J.P. (334-7474 or 334-2743; Fort Myers Yacht Basin, Fort Myers) A 600-passenger paddlewheeler takes sightseeing and dinner boat tours into Lake Okeechobee, the Gulf, and the Caloosahatchee River. Excursions last anywhere from three hours to a day.
Captiva Cruises (472-7549; South Seas Plantation, Captiva) A complete menu of sightseeing and luncheon trips aboard the 150-passenger *Jean Nicolet*. One of the few ways, as a non-guest, to see private Useppa Island, where you can enjoy lunch at the Barron Collier Inn restaurant.
Catfisher's Funtoon Excursions (574-2524; Marinatown, North Fort Myers) Sightseeing tours, ecology excursions, and sunset and moonlight cruises aboard a 36-foot pontoon catamaran.
Europa FunKruz (1-800-688-PLAY; Palm Grove Marina, Fort Myers Beach) Day and evening cruises include table-side meal, casino gambling, live entertainment, and dancing.
Island Water Tours (463-6181, ext. 246; Pink Shell Resort, Fort Myers Beach) Ride aboard the *Pelican Queen*, a 40-foot pontoon, to Big Hickory Island, Mound Key, and other islands.
Sanibel Marina (472-2723; 634 North Yachtsman Dr., Sanibel Island) Half-day

charters depart to the upper islands of Cayo Costa and Cabbage Key, and southern islands of Estero, Lover's Key, and Big Hickory Island.

Tropic Star Cruises (283-0015; Four Winds Marina, Bokeelia, Pine Island) Island-hopping cruises to Cayo Costa and Cabbage Key for lunch or dinner.

<u>South Coast</u>

Fish Head Bait & Tackle (591-0990; 179 Commerce St., Naples) Sightseeing and shelling tours.

Marco Island Sea Excursions (642-6400; 601 Elkcam Circle, Marco Island) Represents 50-plus vessels selling all varieties of charters, especially deserted island beach parties.

Naples Water Taxi (774-7277) Electric boats run routes along commercial and residential areas in the north Naples Bay area. Hail the taxi from a dock, or call for pickup.

Tiki Islander (262-7577, Tin City, Naples) Sightseeing tours of Naples mansions and natural sights aboard a Polynesian-style, thatched vessel.

Wooten's Everglades Tours (1-800-282-2781; Tamiami Tr., Ochopee, 35 miles south of Naples) Follow ancient Native American trails through the mysterious "River of Grass" via airboat or swamp buggy, the trademark vessels of the Everglades. The loud airboat is designed for the area's shallow waters; the swamp buggy is an all-terrain bus. Touristy, but an easy introduction to this complex wilderness.

PARASAILING & WATERSKIING

Winged flight in Gulf Coast Waters.

Lee County Visitor and Convention Bureau

Sarasota Bay Coast

Don & Mike's Boat & Ski Rental (966-4000, Casey Key Marina, Nokomis Beach) Ski rides and lessons.

Island Coast

Days Inn at Lover's Key (463-3334; 8701 Estero Blvd., Fort Myers Beach) Skiing pulls and lessons.
Holiday Ski School (472-5111, ext. 3459; South Seas Plantation, Captiva Island) Waterskiing, parasailing, and jet-skiing.
Skyrider Parasailing (463-3351; Island Sailboat and Jet Ski Rental; 1010 Estero Blvd., Fort Myers Beach)

South Coast

Marco Island Ski Water Sports (394-6589; Marriott's March Beach Resort) Parasailing, waterskiing, and watersport rentals.

RACQUET SPORTS

Sarasota Bay Coast

Anna Maria Youth Center (Magnolia Ave., Anna Maria) Two lighted courses.
Glazier Gates Park (Manatee Ave. E., Bradenton) Two unlighted, cement, public tennis courts.
G.T. Bray Recreation Center (5502 33rd Ave., Dr. W., Bradenton) Eight each of cement, clay, and racquetball courts.
Holmes Beach Courts (near City Hall, Holmes Beach) Three lighted courts.
Jessie P. Miller (9th Ave. & 43rd St. W., Bradenton) Four lighted cement courts and one handball court.
Nick Bolletieri Tennis Academy (1-800-872-6425 or 755-1000; 5500 34th St. W., Bradenton) Training camp for adults and juniors, with state-of-the-art tennis and sports facilities. Andre Agassi and other pros have trained here.

Charlotte Harbor Coast

Boca Grande Community Center (964-2564; 131 First St. W., Boca Grande) Two lighted courts.
McGuire Park (Elkcam Blvd., Port Charlotte) Four lighted, hard-surface courts.
Port Charlotte Junior High (625-5554; 23000 Midway Blvd., Port Charlotte) Three hard courts and two racquetball courts.
Punta Gorda Junior High (639-5188; 825 Carmalita St., Punta Gorda) Three hard courts and two racquetball courts.

Island Coast

Beach and Tennis Health Club (992-1121; 5800 Bonita Beach Rd., Bonita Beach) Public club with 10 Har-Tru courts, three lighted, plus health club and instruction.

Fort Myers Racquet Club (278-7277; 4900 DeLeon St., Fort Myers) Eight clay courts, two hard courts, lessons, and tournaments.

Sanibel Recreation Complex (472-0345; Sanibel Elementary School, 3840 Sanibel–Captiva Rd., Sanibel Island) Five lighted tennis courts.

Signal Inn Resort (472-4690; 1811 Olde Middle Gulf Dr., Sanibel Island) Two racquetball courts for hire.

South Coast

Collier County Racquet Club (394-5454; 1275 San Marco Rd., Marco Island) County facility with five deco-turf courts, two racquetball courts, pro shop, and lessons.

Naples Park Elementary (111th Ave. N., Naples) Two lighted courts.

Tommie Barfield Elementary (Goodland, Marco Island) Two lighted courts.

SAILBOARDING & SURFING

Gulf Coast waters generally are too tame to inspire awe in wave-riders, except in inclement weather. Sailboarders, however, find perfect conditions all along the Coast. Look in the *Beaches* section to discover favorable surfing and windsurfing venues.

Sarasota Bay Coast

Surfing World (794-1233; 11904 Cortez Rd. W., Bradenton) Sells and rents surfboards and sailboards; lessons available.

Charlotte Harbor Coast

Bikes & Boards (474-2019; 1249 Beach Rd., Englewood) Rents, sells, and services surfboards, sailboards, skimboards, and bodyboards.

Island Coast

Island Outfitters (472-0123; 1554 Periwinkle Way, Sanibel Island) Rents boards and offers lessons.

South Coast

Fred'z Surf Shop (591-3733; 103 Ave N., Naples) Surfboards, beach, and swimwear.

SHELLING

HOT SHELLING SPOTS

Sarasota Bay Coast

Venice Beach is known for its sharks' teeth, which come in all sizes and various shades, from black to rare white. Sharks continually shed teeth and grow new ones. Most of what you find is prehistoric. The white ones are recent sheddings. Teeth range in size from one-eighth of an inch to a rare three inches. For an easy guide to what's valuable and what's not, pick up a place mat from Sharky's restaurant, on the pier at Caspersen Beach. You can rent official sifters at Venice Beach. Or bring a colander. Digging for specimens is taboo.

Island Coast

Big Hickory Island (Northwest of Little Hickory Island, accessible only by boat) An unhitched crook of beach favored by local boaters and shellers.
Bonita Beach (Little Hickory Island) Look north of the public beach.
La Costa Island (Between North Captiva and Boca Grande, accessible only by boat) Because it takes a boat ride to get there, these sands hold caches of shells merely by virtue of their remoteness. Nearby Johnson Shoals provides a thin strip of sandbar for good low-tide pickings.
Sanibel Island Known as the Shelling Capital of the Western Hemisphere, the island even has its own name for the particular stance of the beach collector:

A great blue heron stands aloof from shellers on Sanibel Island.

Lee County Visitor and Convention Bureau

Shellaceous Treasures

"Little by little one's holiday vision tends to fade. I must remember to see with island eyes. The shells will remind me; they must be my island eyes."

—Anne Morrow Lindbergh, *Gift From the Sea*

Stormy weather and low tides bring out the best in Gulf Coast shelling. Typical finds include lightning whelks, conchs, cockles, coquinas, pens, olives, cones, tulips, worm shells, top shells, and scallops. The rare junonia is the trademark prize of Sanibel Island. Shellers who find one, get their picture in the paper. Devoted searchers, often known as conchologists or malacologists, uncover other precious finds, such as the fragile sand dollar, the porcelain-like wentletrap, or the intricate lace murex. Most shells found on the beach in fair weather have been abandoned by their mollusk inhabitants, and have suffered the assault of wind, sun, and waves. Collectors and dealers search for the more colorful and intact live specimens. For them, shelling requires detective work. Perhaps that's why Raymond Burr, television's *Perry Mason* and *Ironsides*, has become such an avid Sanibel collector. As a frequent visitor, he lent his celebrity toward the realization of a shell museum on the island.

Professional shellers take only specimens they plan to keep, so as not to deplete populations. Sanibel restricts the taking of live shells to two per species, per person. Live shelling is forbidden in Ding Darling Refuge. Non-resident live shellers must obtain a fishing license.

Laws aside, the less-than-glamorous chore of cleaning live shells makes the most convincing argument for limiting one's take. There are as many methods for cleaning shells as there are shellers; boiling, freezing, bleaching, or burying them for the ants to eat out being the most favored. Just make sure the entire animal has been removed before packing it away. The best advice for an aspiring conchologist is to buy a good book that will help you to identify and clean shells. You will find an abundance of these in local shell shops and bookstores.

Sanibel Stoop. Unlike the other Gulf Coast barrier islands, Sanibel takes an east-west heading. Its perpendicular position and lack of offshore reefs allow it to intercept shells that arrive from the South Seas. Its fame as the third best shelling area in the world has made Sanibel a prime destination for shell collectors for decades. With shell-named streets, store shelves awash in shells and shellcrafts, an annual Shell Fair, and a shell museum, one risks suffering shell shock by just visiting there. Best Gulfside shelling spot: Bowman's Beach, mid-island, but away from the paths leading to the parking lot. For a different selection of shells and less competition, try bayside areas at the end of Bailey or Dixie Beach roads, or the sandflats east of the causeway at low tide.

South Coast

Keewaydin Island (South of Naples, accessible only by boat) A private, unbridged island. It holds a great many shell prizes that are not as picked over as on beaches that are accessible by car.

SHELLING CHARTERS

Most charter boat services will take you shelling. Some know more about it than others; a few specialize in finding shells. Many maintain a no-live-shells standard.

Island Coast

Alice Anders' Tours (472-6797; Sanibel Island) The queen of Sanibel shelling, Alice is known internationally for her expertise and has been featured in major publications. Her tours scan the best shelling beaches of Sanibel and Captiva.

Capt. Mike Fuery's Shelling Charters (472-1015; Captiva Island) A local shelling expert, who authors how-to columns for local papers, takes you to Cayo Costa, Johnson Shoals, and other shell habitats.

South Coast

Tiki Too (262-7577, Tin City, Naples) Half-day shelling trips to Keewaydin Island.

SNORKELING AND SCUBA

Gulf Coast waters generally are murkier than those along Florida's East Coast and in the Keys. They clear up on the way north, but lack the interest natural reefs provide. Experienced divers normally head to deep waters for wreck diving and sightseeing along man-made reefs.

DIVE SHOPS & CHARTERS

Sarasota Bay Coast

Gypsy Guide Service (923-6095, Sarasota) Summer snorkeling charters with gear included.

The Hunter (778-2446, Anna Maria Island) PADI divemaster offers instruction, rentals, and dives to reefs and wrecks; lobster diving, spearfishing, and night dives.

Scuba Quest (497-5985; 4197 Tamiami Tr. So., Venice)

Island Coast

Pieces of Eight Dive Center (472-9424, South Seas Plantation, Captiva Island) Full line of scuba gear, plus rentals, video equipment, instruction, and daily dive and snorkel trips.

Redfish Dive Center (472-3483; 2330 Palm Ridge Place, Sanibel Island) NAUI and PADI instruction, sales, and rentals; dive and snorkel trips.

South Coast

Aqua Adventures (394-3483; Factory Bay Marina, 1079 Bald Eagle Dr., Marco Island) Full-service shop with charters and lessons.

Naples Diving Center (775-6220; 1949 Davis Blvd., Naples) Scuba instruction, complete dive shop, dive boat.

SHORE SNORKELING AND DIVING

Sarasota Bay Coast

Bradenton Beach (Anna Maria Island) An old sugar barge sank here many years ago and houses various forms of marine life.

Point of Rocks (Siesta Key) South of Crescent Beach at the island's central zone; rocks, underwater caves, and coral formations make good underwater sightseeing.

Island Coast

Cayo Costa State Park Nice ledges in two to five feet of water, teeming with fish, sponges, and shells.

Florida Power & Light Plant Snorkelers may be able to see manatees in the warm discharge waters of the plant. **Warning:** Look but do not touch; it's against the law.

SPAS

Sarasota Bay Coast

Warm Mineral Springs (426-1692; San Servando Rd., Warm Mineral Springs, south of Venice) Water of a rare quality attracts health-seekers to a 2.5-acre lake. If you know your spas, you will appreciate the spring's chemical analysis of 17,439 parts per million, way above the content of the world's most renowned mineral waters. The lake, which maintains a year-round temperature of 87 degrees, has soothing and, some believe, healing powers. Folks bathe at a roped-off beach area. Opened in 1940, the facilities show their age with a less-than-modern look and attitude. The snack bar, for example, carries bakery goods and sandwiches — nothing remotely healthy. Organic mud, laxative water, whirlpools, saunas, massage therapy, and staff doctors comprise the available services. Historic significance adds to the allure. Archaeologists have discovered artifacts suggesting that Native Americans came here for a bit of mineral-washed R & R 10,000 years ago. Plus, an on-property cyclorama shows the history of the area, with dioramas and Lowell Thomas narration. There are apartments for rent, for the real enthusiasts. For the casual attendee, I suggest staying in one of the area's resorts instead. The odor of sulphur water would get to me after a while. Admission is $6 for adults, $4 for students, and $2 for children under 12. Beachwear, chairs, and towels can be rented.

Island Coast

Sanibel Harbour Resort & Spa (466-4000; 17260 Harbour Pointe Dr., Fort Myers) Directly before the Sanibel Causeway, Sanibel Harbour was a spa years before it became a resort. It began as Jimmy Connors' namesake tennis center, complete with state-of-the-art fitness and spa facilities. Today, there's a 300-plus unit resort (see *Lodging*). Guests, members, and day visitors can take advantage of the swimming pool, whirlpools, training room, aerobics classes, saunas, hot steam, and racquetball courts. Special services include herbal wraps, aromatherapy massage, Swiss shower, spa luncheon, counseling, training, facials, and other salon treatments.

SPECTATOR SPORTS

CRAB RACES

Island Coast

'Tween Waters Inn (472-5161; Captiva Rd., Captiva Island) Held every Monday night, 7:00–10:00. Participate or watch.

PRO BASEBALL

The so-called Grapefruit League plays its spring exhibition season in many Florida locales, through March and into April. Five major league teams call the Gulf Coast their training home.

Sarasota Bay Coast

Ed Smith Stadium (954-SOXX; 2700 12th St., Sarasota) Spring training home of the Chicago *White Sox*.

McKechnie Field (747-3031; 9th St. and 17th Ave. W., Bradenton) Site of the Pittsburgh *Pirates'* exhibition games.

Pirate City (747-3031; 1701 27th St. E., Bradenton) Spring practice field for the Pittsburgh *Pirates*. Catch them during season, working out from 10:00 a.m. to 1:30 p.m..

Charlotte Harbor Coast

Charlotte County Stadium (625-9500; Route 776, Port Charlotte) Spring training grounds of the Texas *Rangers*.

Bradenton's McKechnie Field, where the Pittsburgh Pirates warm up every spring.

Island Coast

Lee County Sport Complex (768-4270; Six Mile Cypress Road, Fort Myers) Hosts the Minnesota *Twins* for spring training. From April through August, the Miracle Professional Baseball team, member of the Florida State League, competes here (768-4210).

A bit of classic Florida design went into the building of Lee County Sports Complex, the Minnesota Twins' spring training camp

City of Palms Park (334-4700; Edison Avenue, downtown Fort Myers) Home of the Boston *Red Sox*'s spring exhibition games.

RACING

Sarasota Bay Coast

Sarasota Kennel Club (355-7744; 5400 Bradenton Rd., Sarasota) Greyhound racing, pari-mutuel betting, matinee and evening shows. Also simulcasts thoroughbred horse racing from Miami.

South Coast

Naples–Fort Myers Greyhound Track (992-2411; 10601 Bonita Beach Rd. SE; Bonita Springs) Matinees, night races, and trackside dining.

WATERSKIING

Sarasota Bay Coast

Sarasota Ski-A-Rees Show (City Island, behind Mote Marine, Sarasota) Free performances in the bay every Sunday at 2:00 p.m.

WILDERNESS CAMPING

Sarasota Bay Coast

Oscar Scherer State Recreation Area (483-5956; 1843 S. Tamiami Tr., Osprey) Close to 1,400 acres in size, this natural oasis provides full facilities for the camper, in a wooded setting of palmettos, pines, and venerable, moss-draped oaks. The threatened Florida scrub jay seeks refuge here, along with bald eagles, bobcats, river otters, gopher tortoises, and alligators. There's swimming in a freshwater lake, plus a bird-walk, nature and canoe trails, picnicking, and fishing.

Island Coast

Cayo Costa State Island Preserve (964-0375, LaCosta Island) You'll need boat transportation to reach this unbridged island, home to wild pigs and myriad birds. Bring your own fresh water and lots of bug spray. And don't expect to plug in the camcorder. There's running water for showers, picnic grounds, boat docks, a tram that runs cross-island, tent sites, and some very primitive cabins. Call ahead to reserve the latter. Camping was once allowed any-where on the 2,225-acre island, but today it's restricted to certain areas.

South Coast

Collier Seminole State Park (642-8898; Tamiami Trail, 17 miles south of Naples) Providing the least roughing-it way to camp in Everglades Country, this 6,470-acre park straddles Big Cypress Swamp and Ten Thousand Islands Mangrove Wilderness. There are RV hookups and tent sites. The park is full of possibilities for exploring nature and history, but no swim-ming.

Everglades National Park (695-2591) Backcountry camping along the Ever-glades canoe trails requires a permit, available from the Everglades City Ranger Station on Route 29. Most sites provide chickee huts on pilings, with

The Everglades' "River of Grass" deceptively appears as solid prairieland.

chemical toilets, many of which have been newly rebuilt since Hurricane Andrew in 1992. Take mosquito repellent.

Koreshan State Historic Site (992-2184; Tamiami Tr., Estero) There's a lot to do within these 130 acres, for tenters and RVers. Historic buildings remember the property's past as a cult settlement. Canoeing, playgrounds, trails, boating, and fishing are available.

WILDLIFE SPOTTING

More endangered and threatened species of wildlife survive in Florida than in any other state. Florida golden panthers, bobcats, manatees, scrub jays, brown pelicans, wood storks, black skimmers, and loggerhead turtles thrive here. Some, such as the panther and bobcat, are rarely seen out of captivity. Others, especially the brown pelican, live side by side with residents.

ALLIGATORS

Once endangered, the alligator population has sprung back in recent years, thanks to organizations and laws that fought to protect the prehistoric reptiles. Sanibel Island paved the way, by pioneering a no-feeding regulation that later became State law. (Hand-fed alligators lose their fear of man.)

Innate homebodies, alligators leave their home ponds only during spring and summer mating, when spotting them is easiest. You will often hear the bellow of the bull 'gator in the night, and see both males and females roaming from pond to pond in search of a midsummer night's romance. They can do serious damage to a car, so be alert. And never approach one on foot.

When it's cold, alligators stay submerged to keep warm. On sunny days throughout the year, you can spot them catching rays on the banks of freshwater rivers and streams. In the water, you first spot their snout, then their prickly profile. Once your eye becomes trained to distinguish them from logs and background, you'll start noticing them more.

Serious searchers should try nature preserves such as Sanibel's Ding Darling, Naples' Corkscrew Swamp, and along the Tamiami Trail through the Everglades.

BIRDS

Oystercatchers working a bed of barnacles.

Southwest Florida is a bird-watcher's haven, especially in winter when migrating species add to the vast variety of the Coast's residential avifauna. Rare visitors and locals include the roseate spoonbill, blackwing skimmer, yellow-crowned night heron, wood stork, and bald eagle. More commonly seen are frigates, ospreys, Louisiana herons, great blue herons, ibises, snowy egrets, pelicans, anhingas, cormorants, terns, seagulls, plovers, oystercatchers, sandhill cranes, doves, owls, and hawks.

Best birdwatching: Passage Key sanctuary north of Anna Maria Island (bring binoculars — landing ashore is forbidden), Oscar Scherer Park in Osprey, Sanibel Island's Ding Darling, Pine Island National Wildlife Refuge's Big Bird Rookery, Naples' Rookery Bay Sanctuary, and Ten Thousand Islands. Look for the wild peacocks that roam the streets of the village on Longboat Key. Marco Island is a proclaimed sanctuary for bald eagles. Barfield Bay in Goodland is one of their favorite locales.

PORPOISES

The playful porpoise cruises the sea, performing impromptu acrobatic shows that it's hard to believe weren't staged. When the next performance will be is anybody's guess, but if you learn their feeding schedules you have a better chance of catching their act. They often like to leap out of the wake of large boats. I've been out in the Gulf, surrounded by their antics to the point where I got a sore neck from spinning around to keep track of them all. Don't expect them to get too close — take some binoculars — and forget seeing them

---

Holy Sea Cows!

We know them today as Florida manatees: 2,000-pound blimps with skin like burlap and a face only an environmentalist could love. They also go by the name sea cow, although they are more closely related to the elephant. In days of yore, many a sea-weary sailor mistook them for mermaids.

Well, Ariel they're not, but bewitching they can be. Gentle and herbivorous — consuming up to 100 pounds of seaweed daily — they make no enemies and have only one stumbling-block to survival: man. As mammals, manatees must surface for air, just like whales and porpoises. Their girth makes them a prime target for boaters speeding through their habitat. Warning signs designate popular manatee areas. Instead of zipping through these waters and further threatening the seriously endangered manatee population, boaters can better benefit by trying to spot the reclusive creatures as they take a breath. It requires a sharp eye, patience, and experience. Watch channels during low tides, when the manatees take to deeper water. Concentric circles, known as "manatee footprints," signal surfacing animals. They usually travel in a line, and appear as drifting coconuts, or fronds.

If you happen to spot an injured sea cow, please report it to the Manatee Hot Line at 1-800-342-1821.

Manatees eat up to 100 pounds of vegetables and seaweed a day to maintain their 2,000-pound figure.

Manatee County Convention & Visitors Bureau

in captivity around here. Locals staged a protest in Pine Island Sound recently, when collectors tried to take some of their porpoises. More protests finally freed penned animals at Moore's Stone Crab Restaurant on Longboat Key.

MANATEES

The warm waters discharged from Florida Power and Light Company in North Fort Myers attract the warm-blooded manatees in the winter months. They congregate behind the plant, at the confluence of the Caloosahatchee and Orange Rivers, and can often be spotted upstream in the wild and natural Orange.

Pine Island's backwaters offer a good venue for manatee spotting. Check out the bay behind Island Shell & Gifts, a popular sea-watch site, just before the Matlacha bridge.

NATURE PRESERVES

Sarasota Bay Coast

Mote Marine Laboratory and Aquarium (388-2451; 1600 Ken Thompson Pkwy., City Island, northeast of Lido Key) Begun by members of the Vanderbilt family as a research facility at today's Cape Haze aquatic preserve in Charlotte Harbor, Mote is known around the world for its research on sharks and environmental pollutants. Its visitors' center educates the public on projects and marine life. A 135,000-gallon shark tank centerpieces the attraction and is kept stocked with sharks and fish typical of the area: grouper, snook, jewfish, pompano, and snapper. Twenty-two smaller aquariums and two touch tanks hold more than 200 varieties of common and unusual species: starfish, octopus, seahorses, skates, and scorpion fish. Displays and a video explain Mote's mission. Open daily, 10–5. Admission is $5 for adults, $3 for children 6–17.

Oscar Scherer State Recreation Area (483-5956; 1843 S. Tamiami Tr., Osprey) Home of the threatened Florida scrub jay, plus bald eagles, bobcats, river otters, gopher tortoises, and alligators. Admission is $3.25 per car.

Sarasota Bay Walk (361-6133; 1550 Ken Thompson Pkwy., City Island, next to Mote Marine) Take a quiet, self-guided walk along the bay, estuaries, lagoons, and upland to learn more about coastland ecology. Boardwalk and shell paths take you past mangroves, old fishing boats bobbing on the bay, egrets, and illustrated signs detailing nature's wonders.

Pelican Man's Bird Sanctuary (388-4444; 1550 Ken Thompson Pkwy., City Island, next to Mote Marine) The work of one man, Dale Shields, precursed this refuge for injured pelicans and other birds. It's a must if you're visiting Mote Marine, and also for nature lovers. Don't expect exotic birds, just on-the-mend, local varieties.

Charlotte Harbor Coast

Peace River Wildlife Center (637-3830; Ponce de Leon Park, Punta Gorda) A rescue and rehabilitation facility that conducts tours among cages of baby possums, taped-together gopher tortoises, and other rescued and recovering animals.

Island Coast

Cayo Costa State Island Preserve (964-0375; LaCosta Island, accessible only by boat) Refuge land occupies about 90 percent of this 2,225-acre island. Cayo Costa preserves the Florida that the Native Americans tried to protect against European invasion. Besides the wild hogs that survive on the island, egrets, white pelicans, raccoons, osprey, and black skimmers frequent the area. The path across the island's northern end features a side trip to a pioneer cemetery. Blooming cacti and other flora festoon the walk, which is sometimes a run when weather turns warm and uncontrolled mosquito populations remind us of the hardships of eras gone by.

C.R.O.W. (Care and Rehabilitation of Wildlife) (472-3644; Sanibel–Captiva Rd., Sanibel Island) This hospital complex duplicates natural habitat and attends to sick and injured wildlife: birds, bobcats, raccoons, rabbits, and otters. Visit by appointment or on open-house day, the last Sunday of every month, 12:30 to 3:00. A wildlife library and audio visual room are open to the public.

Sanibel–Captiva Nature Conservation Center (472-2329; 3333 Sanibel–Captiva Road, Sanibel Island) This research and preservation facility encompasses 1,192 acres. A guided or self-guided tour introduces you to indigenous fauna and natural bird habitat. Indoor displays further educate, and include a touch tank. Guest lecturers, seminars, and workshops address environmental issues during the winter season. Native plant nursery.

J.N. "Ding" Darling Wildlife Refuge (472-1100; Sanibel–Captiva Rd., Sanibel Island) More than 5,000 acres of pristine wetlands and wildlife is protected by the United States, thanks to the efforts of Pulitzer Prize- winning cartoonist and politically active conservationist, Ding Darling, a regular Captiva visitor in the 1930s. A five-mile drive takes you through the refuge, but to really experience it, get out of the car. At the very least, follow the easy trails into mangrove, bird, and alligator territory. The visitor's center holds wildlife displays and peeks into the world of the refuge's namesake. The refuge is open sunrise to sunset; visitor's center 9:00-4:00, every day but Friday. Admission is $3 per car; $1 per cyclist or walk-in.

Lee County Nature Center and Planetarium (275-3435; Ortiz Blvd., Fort Myers) Native birds inhabit the Audubon Aviary. A 1.5-mile boardwalk twists through a Miccosukee (Seminole) village, natural swampland, and indoor exhibits such as a live beehive and a sealife tank. Snake and alligator demonstrations are scheduled daily. The planetarium shows presentations day and night, with laser lights and lectures. Open 9:00-4:00, Monday through Saturday; 11:00–4:30 Sunday. Admission is $3 for adults and $2 for children under 12.

South Coast

The Conservancy (263-0119; Merrihue Dr. at 14th Ave. No., one block east of Goodlette Rd., Naples) This tucked-away nature complex on the Gordon River was built to educate the public about the environment. It encompasses, within its 13.5 acres, a natural science museum with serpentarium, a nature store, trail walks, boat tours of the wetlands, a rehabilitation aviary, and a lecture hall. Open 9:30-4:30 except Sunday, limited facilities May through October. Museum admission is $3 for adults, $1 for children 7–18.

Corkscrew Swamp Sanctuary (657-3771; off Naples–Immokalee Road, 21 miles east of N. Tamiami Tr., Naples) The 11,000-acre Corkscrew Swamp Sanctuary, operated by the National Audubon Society, protects one of the largest stands of mature bald cypress trees in the country. Some of the towering specimens date back nearly 500 years. The threatened wood stork once came to nest in great numbers. Diminished populations still do so, at which time the nesting area is roped off to protect them. A boardwalk 1.75 miles long takes you over swampland inhabited by rich plant and marine life. You can usually spot an alligator or two. Open 9:00–5:00. Admission: $5 for adults, $4 for college students, $2.50 for children age 5 to grade 12.

Delnor-Wiggins Pass State Recreation Area (597-6196; 11100 Gulf Shore Dr. N., Naples) Prehistoric loggerhead turtles lumber ashore to lay and bury their eggs every summer — away from the lights and crowds of other area beaches. Fifty-six days later the baby turtles emerge and scurry to the sea before birds can snatch them up. Guided night walks are available during the loggerhead season. Nearby Keewaydin Island is another major nesting area for the 300-pound mama turtle and her 60 to 180 eggs. Admission: $3.25 per car; $1 for bikers or walk-ins.

Everglades National Park (695-2591; Tamiami Trail south of Naples, Welcome Center at intersection of Route 29 or Ranger Station on Route 29, Everglades City) This massive wetlands — home to the endangered Florida panther and Everglades kite — covers 2,100 square miles and shelters more than 600 types of fish and 300 bird species. It also contains the largest mangrove forest in the world. So what's the best way to see this seemingly overwhelming expanse of wildlife? Take your pick. Driving through is quickest, but least satisfying. Make sure to veer off the Tamiami Trail on at least one side road, to the park's interior. Closest to Naples is Route 29 to Everglades City. Canoe trips from eight to 99 miles long put you in closer range to birds, manatees, sea turtles, and alligators. There's also a variety of other options: pontoon boating (if you're good at reading charts), sightseeing cruises, tram rides, bike rentals, and foot trails. Get advice at the Welcome Center or Ranger Station.

Rookery Bay Estuarine Reserve & Briggs Nature Center (775- 8569; Shell Road off Route 951 on way to Marco Island) The Gulf Coast's largest and most pristine wildlife sanctuary occupies more than 8,000 acres at the gateway to Ten Thousand Islands. It's Ding Darling without the crowds. A favorite for fishermen and bird-watchers, visitors can enjoy the mysteries of mangrove ecology from a 2,500-foot boardwalk (admission $2 for adults; $1 for children). You can walk Monument Trail around the bay for free. An exhibit hall introduces you to the estuarine world. I recommend taking one of the center's boat, canoe, or birding trips if you want to get close up and personal with nature. Manatees and alligators populate bay waters. Boat ramp. Open 9:00–5:00; closed Sunday.

WILDLIFE TOURS & CHARTERS

Island Coast

Canoe Adventures (472-6080; Sanibel Island) Guided tours with a noted island naturalist, in the Ding Darling Refuge, Sanibel River, and other natural areas.

Manatee & Eco Tours (693-1434; Coastal Marine Mart, Route 80 at I–75 exit 25, East Fort Myers) Specializes in tours up the Orange River to spot manatees.

Pine Island Nature Tours (283-1636; Pine Island Chamber of Commerce, Pine Island Road, before the Matlacha bridge) Local naturalists conduct tours on Tuesday, Thursday, and Saturday mornings, in search of active eagles' nests, mangrove habitat, and aquatic birds.

Tarpon Bay Recreation (472-8900; 900 Tarpon Bay Rd. Sanibel) Guided canoe and tram tours through Ding Darling Refuge.

South Coast

Estero Bay Boat Tours (992-2200; Weeks Fish Camp, Coconut Road, Bonita Springs) The best sightseeing tour of Mound Key's Caloosan history, and Big Hickory Island's wildlife, is conducted by a local native and his staff, who know these islands and waters like family.

Everglades National Park Boat Tours (1-800-445-7724 or 695-2591; at Ranger Station in Everglades City) Narrated tours through the maze of Ten Thousand Islands and its teeming bird and water life.

Majestic Tours (695-2777; Everglades City) Excursions designed specifically for the eco-tourist into Ten Thousand Islands.

SEASONAL EVENTS

Sarasota Bay Coast

Suncoast Offshore Grand Prix (955-9009, Sarasota's islands) A national attraction, with powerboat racers from around the world. Fourth of July weekend.

Charlotte Harbor Coast

Charlotte Harbor Fishing Tournament (627-2222) Thousands of dollars in prizes, includes a Kid's Day and barbecue. Five weeks, March and April.

Florida Invitational Windsurfing Regatta (Port Charlotte Beach, Port Charlotte) Races, entertainment, and food.

Tarpon Tide Tournaments (964-2232: Miller's Marina, Boca Grande) Mid-May through June.

World's Richest Tarpon Tournament (Boca Grande) $100,000 top prize. Entry fee: $3,500 a boat. Two days in July.

Island Coast

Blizzard (338-3300; Lee County Sports Complex, Fort Myers) Two tons of snow bring back wintery memories: ice skating, entertainment, ice carving contest. One day in late January.

Caloosa Catch & Release Fishing Tournament (1-800-282-4236; 'Tween Waters Inn, Captiva Island) Celebrity and amateur divisions. Four days in late May.

Caloosahatchee River Basin Festival (275-3435; Nature Center of Lee County, 3450 Ortiz Ave., Fort Myers) Planetarium shows, guided tours, and folk demonstrations. Two days in late March.

Christmas Boat-a-Long (574-0811; Four Freedoms Park, Cape Coral) Decorated boat parade with live entertainment, Santa, and other events.

Onshore Sports Festivals (574-0811, Lake Kennedy Recreation Complex, Cape Coral) Competitions in running, in-line skating, and biking. One week in May.

Sandsculpting Contest (463-6451; Fort Myers Beach) Amateur and masters divisions. One week in early November.

Summerfest Canoe Race (463-7776; Fort Myers Beach) One day in early June.

South Coast

Challenge Senior PGA Tour Event (1-800-457-7767 or 353-7767; Vineyards Golf and Country Club, Naples) Late February.

Swamp Buggy Races (774-2701; Naples) Nationally televised event; sort of the Everglades' equivalent to tractor pulls or monster truck racing. March and October.

CHAPTER SEVEN

Gifts from the Sea

SHOPPING

These days, no one laughs when you bring home a can of "Florida sunshine". Tiny bags of sand, labeled "Beachfront Property," show only slightly more imagination. Although popular mementos may still include sacks of oranges, pink flamingo yard decorations, coconut monkeys' heads, shell-wreathed mirrors, and alligator T-shirts, you will find a number of more sophisticated options on the Gulf Coast.

Florida souvenirs are still exotic, if more tasteful: a soothing seascape watercolor or a cotton playsuit, for example, or a shell-filled ginger-jar lamp. All manner and variety of possibilities exist: a gold dolphin

Naples is known for its gallery shopping and street sculptures.

pendant, seafood cookbook, Seminole blanket, or a sand-dollar Christmas tree ornament, to name just a few.

The business of buying and selling has become more refined since the days when "Panther Key John" Gomez duped unsuspecting tourists with maps to Gasparilla's pirate treasure. The ambiance of Gulf Coast shopping makes it an experience barely related to indoor malling, or outdoor excursions in the cold and rain. Lushly landscaped fresh air emporiums make contact with nature and the past. Babbling brooks, jabbering parrots, Mediterranean storefronts, palm-lined esplanades, waterfront views, and sultry breezes bring a new joy to the process of emptying your pockets.

The Gulf Coast does have its weatherproof malls and conglomerations of outlets. Even these, however, tend to instill a sense of place, with tropical touches and merchandise that reflects Florida's lifestyles. Manatee sculptures grace the new Port Charlotte Town Center, while palms and fountains decorate Fort Myers' Edison Mall. Nowhere do you find such a mix of influences, from Caribbean art, to South Seas rattan furnishings, to European fashions, to sculpture by local artists.

Two meccas of pocketbook depletion exist on the Gulf Coast, which provide world-class shopping that competes with the finest in the nation. Sarasota's St. Armands Circle is known far and wide for its arena of posh shops, galleries, and restaurants. At Southwest Florida's other extreme, Naples has been aligned for decades with chic boutiques and gala galleries.

My list of favorites, and friends' favorites, tends to lead to places steeped in Florida ways and styles. I include the unusual, the brave, and the sublime. The Gulf Coast is a natural source of unusual imports, due to its proximity to international ports. This is the stuff I search for — especially imports from the tropic belt: the Southwest, the Caribbean, Latin America, the Mediterranean, and the South Pacific.

In season, you may well be tempted, like everyone else, to save shopping and sightseeing for rainy, cold, off-beach days. Don't. You'll lose your diligently attained good beach attitude by the time you've found your first parking spot. Go in the morning, for best results and the most relaxing experience. Otherwise, you may find that the wear-and-tear outweighs the pleasure of window-shopping, or the joys associated with discovery of the perfect, one-of-a-kind gift or souvenir.

ANTIQUES & COLLECTIBLES

Sarasota Bay Coast

Antiques des Provinces (955-6255; 1505 Main St., downtown Sarasota) European antiques of all varieties, from hay forks to armoires.

Apple & Carpenter Antique Gallery (951-2314; 60–64 S. Palm Ave., downtown Sarasota) American and European paintings of the 19th and 20th centuries, as well as bronze and marble sculptures, fine furniture, French cameo glass, silver, bronze, porcelain, art glass.

August Antiques Emporium (351-6666; 5333 N. Tamiami Tr., Sarasota, near Ringling Museum) This is a large facility, housing several dealers of select antique furniture, decorative accessories, quilts, toys, dolls, art glass, and dishes.

Curiosity Shop (749-0179; 312 Main St., downtown Bradenton) For the best prices on antiques, leave Sarasota and venture to this Bradenton find. It has a large and broad selection of furniture, china, glass, and wedding gowns.

The Yellow Bird of St. Armands (388-1823; 35 S. Blvd. of Presidents, St. Armands Circle, upstairs in the Mettler Bldg.) An "antique boutique" specializing in decorative items.

Charlotte Harbor Coast

Deja Vu Antiques (627-5575; 1231 #48 Kings Hwy., Port Charlotte) Fine art, Orientalia, toys, political and military items, precious metal pieces.

Island Coast

Albert Meadow Antiques (472-8442; 15000 Captiva Dr., Captiva Island) Turn-of-the-century decorative arts by Tiffany, Gorham, and Steuben; antique jewelry, Navajo weavings, and art deco and nouveau.

Dynasty Antiques (656-6233; 1621 N. Tamiami Tr., North Fort Myers) Estate liquidators carrying art glass, figurines, porcelain, art, and fine furniture.

Fort Myers Antique Mall (693-0500; 924 Ortiz Ave., Fort Myers) Emporium of 15 dealers.

South Coast

Antiques & Uniques (394-0353; 10 Marco Lake Dr., Marco Island) Period furniture, tableware, military memorabilia, tools, and paintings.

Glenna Moore (263-4121; 465 Fifth Ave. So., Naples) Jewelry, furniture, majolica pottery, quilts, Oriental folk art, and other fine antiques.

Granny's Attic (775-5477; 2300 Linwood Ave., Naples) Cut glass, Depression glass, furniture, sterling, clocks, and china.

Renaissance Gallery (495-6033; 24181 Tamiami Tr. S., Bonita Springs) Artistic and antique decorative pieces, specializing in rare fireplace mantels.

BOOKS

Sarasota Bay Coast

Charlie's News (953-4688; 1341 Main St., downtown Sarasota) Books and periodicals that cater both to specific audiences (arts, gay life, etc.) and to the mainstream, in an uncramped environment. Large greeting card selection.

Kingsley's Book Emporium (388-5045; 24 N. Blvd. of the Presidents, St. Armands Circle) This is a huge facility full of wonderful things, including games, unusual children's toys, arty T-shirts, and cards. Also, an extensive selection of travel and children's books.

Read All Over Newsstand (923-1340; 2245 Bee Ridge Rd., Sarasota) Specializes in art, film, literary magazines, and foreign titles.

Charlotte Harbor Coast

The Paper Pad (627-0440; LaPlaya Plaza, 2811-K Tamiami Tr., Port Charlotte) New and used books for sale or trade.

Island Coast

The Bookshop (936-2539; 4456 Cleveland Ave., Fort Myers) A unique bookery with attractive decor, old and rare books, and a cappuccino bar.

Gilded Quill Bookshoppe (334-0448; 2219 Main St., downtown Fort Myers) Books, greeting cards, tapes, and stamp and coin supplies.

The Island Book Nook (472-6777; Palm Ridge Place, 2330 Palm Ridge Rd., Sanibel Island) Paperback exchange, hardbacks for sale and rent, complete collection of local books.

MacIntosh Books (472-1447; 2365 Periwinkle Way, Sanibel Island) A tiny shop packed full of books of local and general interest. A special room stocks children's books and provides toys to help out shopping parents. There's also a music store in back.

Shakespeare Beethoven and Co. (939-1720; Royal Palm Square, 1400 Colonial Blvd., Fort Myers) Provides one of the area's best selections of magazines and periodicals. It also carries tapes, CDs, and a full line of books.

South Coast

Song & Story Shop (261-7151; 659 Fifth Ave. S., Naples) Hardcovers, paperbacks, and books on tape.

Village Bookstore (592-1011; 11196 N. Tamiami Tr., Naples) Specializes in books on travel, cooking, interior design. and business.

Your Local Bookie (261-3608; Park Shore Plaza, 4139 N. Tamiami Tr., Naples) Large selection of local books, mainstream books, magazines, newspapers, and greeting cards.

CLOTHING

Sarasota Bay Coast

Dream Weaver (388-1974; 364 St. Armands Circle) Fine woven wear that crosses the line to fabric art, in silk, suede, and other extravagant materials.

Kepp's (388-5041; 301 John Ringling Blvd., St. Armands Circle) Carries distinctive designer labels and British name-brand men's clothing.

Tropical Peddler (485-7463; Nokomis Ave. N. between Venice Ave. W. and Tampa Ave., Venice) T-shirts, cotton wear, and fun-and-sun fashions for, and from, Florida and the Caribbean.

Young Islanders Children's Shop (388-2887; 320 John Ringling Blvd., St. Armands Circle) Carries lines by well-known children's designers, for infants through grade schoolers.

Charlotte Harbor Coast

Captain's Shoppe (637-6000; Fishermen's Village, Punta Gorda) Men's casual clothing with a nautical flair.

Giuditta del Porto (639-8701; Fishermen's Village, Punta Gorda) Exotic patterns and finely tailored styles for the sophisticated woman; mostly formal and dressy fashions.

The Island Bummer (964-2636; Railroad Plaza, Boca Grande) Casual, cotton, loose-fitting sportswear perfect for Florida climes.

Island Coast

Bonhomme Menswear (433-3440; Bell Tower Shops, Fort Myers) American and European fashions suited to Florida lifestyles.

Chico's Other Place (472-3773; Palm Ridge Shopping Center, Palm Ridge Rd., Sanibel Island) I prefer this Chico's store to the original (See page 196) because it's more low-key, with less hustle and bustle.

K.C. Smith (472-8487; Periwinkle Place, 2075 Periwinkle Way, Sanibel Island) My favorite shop for outstanding women's clothing in import patterns, raw silk, and cotton.

Stanley & Livingston's (472-8485; The Village, 2340 Periwinkle Way, Sanibel Island) Travel clothes, books, and paraphernalia à la Banana Republic.

Wildflower (275-5788; Royal Palm Square, 1400 Colonial Blvd., Fort Myers) The sign outside sums it up best: "Delightfully different fashions." From evening gowns to jumpsuits, each piece is unique and elegant; for the woman looking to define a style of her own. There are lots of great shoes, too.

Wings Wildlife T-Shirts & Boutique (472-2251; Jerry's Shopping Center, 1700 Periwinkle Way, Sanibel Island) Nature-themed T-shirts — many designed locally — plus Jimmy Buffett's line, and casual, warm-weather clothes.

South Coast

Earth Outfitters (261-5567; The Village on Venetian Bay, Naples) Casual and rugged designer clothes and accessories made "to explore the planet."

Images (262-7266, Coconut Grove Marketplace, Naples) One-of-a-kind men's and women's styles, suited to Florida.

Island Woman (642-6116; 1 Harbor Pl., Goodland) Imported batik fashions and handcrafted jewelry, Indonesian art, and handcrafts.

Kangaroo Klub (649-7066; 1170 Third St. S., Old Naples) Precious children's clothes, tennis outfits, toys, and other Florida-style wear.

Marissa Collections (263-4333; 1167 Third St. S., Old Naples) Top designer fashions for women.

Mondo Uomo (434-9484; The Village on Venetian Bay, Naples) Fine fashion and European styles for men; tropical wool and linen for Gulf Coast climes.

Mettler's (434-2700; 1258 Third St. S., Old Naples) Active men's and women's wear for boating, golfing, and Florida living.

Chico's Success Sanibel-born

Chico's was born in 1982 as a fledgling Sanibel Island boutique that carried Mexican folk art, as well as a few items of imported clothing. Today, the Fort Myers-based company nets $25 million a year by specializing in women's apparel and accessories. More than 75 corporate-owned and franchise outlets across the United States carry the stenciled Chico's logo.

When their imported clothing began to outsell their other stock, Chico's owners, Helene and Marvin Gralnick, decided to concentrate exclusively on fashion. Unwilling to carry the same products as other stores, they created their own line. As the first Chico's began to prosper, the Gralnicks reinvested in another Sanibel store, and then two on Captiva Island. Store number five was opened on Palm Beach's legendary Worth Avenue. From there, the Gralniks selected for expansion other affluent neighborhoods and resort communities. Although the Chico's line is described as medium-priced and casual, it has sold consistently to the high-end market.

The Gralnicks say their clothes reflect their own lifestyle: comfortable, natural, simple, easy to service, and highly transportable. They design mix-and-match clothes with a blend of peasant comfort and European sophistication, influenced by the Santa Fe look and Central American handiwork.

Chico's stores — where even the mannequins and clothes hangers are custom-made — have sprung up in places like Naples' Third Street Plaza, Sarasota's St. Armands Circle, New Mexico, New Orleans, Seattle, and Palm Desert, California.

Turkish cotton and factories once produced most of Chico's clothes, until the corporation bought a factory in Cape Coral and established its headquarters in south Fort Myers. Within one decade, the firm grew from a family store to a trendsetter in the world of casual fashion. It has turned lowly cotton and uncomplicated tailoring (some might even call it baggy) into haute couture.

CONSIGNMENT

It's not the embarrassment it is in some places, to buy second-hand on the Gulf Coast. Because of the wealthy and transient nature of its residents, the area offers the possibility of great discoveries in its consignment shops. In Sarasota especially, recycled apparel is the "in" thing among the young and artistic.

Sarasota Bay Coast

Laura Jean's Consignments (957-1357; 80 Northeast Plaza, 17th and Lockwood Ridge Rd.) Clothes for women and children.

Women's Exchange (955-7859; 539 S. Orange Ave., Sarasota) Furniture, family clothing, antiques, housewares, and china. Profits go to support local arts.

Charlotte Harbor Coast

Boca Bargains (at the Community House on Banyan St., Boca Grande) Second-hand merchandise, sold by a local woman's club.

Island Coast

Coming Around Again (549-2922; 4635 Coronado Pkwy., Cape Coral) Specializes in wedding gowns, plus other women's clothing.

Kid's Closet (275-5433; 1930 Park Meadow Dr., Fort Myers) Children's clothing, toys, books, furniture, and accessories.

Second Hand Rose (574-6919; 1532 SE 14th St., Del Prado Mall, Cape Coral) Clothes, furniture, and home items.

South Coast

Classy Collections (649-0344; 888 First Ave. S., Naples) Quality ladies' clothing and accessories, from casual to designer wear.

Timely Treasures (992-5852; 3962 Bonita Beach Rd., Bonita Springs) Furniture, antiques, collectibles, women's clothing, dinnerware, small appliances, and other housewares.

FACTORY OUTLET CENTERS

Sarasota Bay Coast

Sarasota Outlet Center (359-2020; 8203 Cooper Creek Blvd., I–75 Exit 40 at University Parkway, University Park) The largest and best factory outlet mall on the Gulf Coast, the Sarasota Outlet Center contains over 40 stores, including Jordache, American Tourister, Van Heusen, and Corning–Revere.

Island Coast

Metro Mall (939-3132; 2855 Colonial Blvd., Fort Myers) Indoor mall with factory outlets for specialty manufacturers of clothing, shoes, kitchenware, and books.

Sanibel Factory Stores (McGregor Blvd. and Summerlin Rd., Fort Myers) The newest addition to the Gulf Coast's growing fascination with factory outlet shopping, this one, which sits at Sanibel's doorstep, is still expanding. Phase One includes Corning–Revere, Maidenform, Van Heusen, Guess, and American Tourister.

South Coast

Coral Isle Factory Stores (775-8083; Route 951 on the way to Marco Island) Factory outlets for Capezio shoes, Dansk kitchenware, Anne Klein women's wear, Polly Flinders girls' clothing, and other name brands.

FLEA MARKETS & BAZAARS

Sarasota Bay Coast

Farmers Market (748-5862; 500 15th St. W., City Hall parking lot, downtown Bradenton) Fresh fruits, vegetables, baked goods, plants, arts and crafts. 8:00–12:00 Saturday, mid-October through April.

International Flea and Marketplace (365-5083; 1999 Main St., downtown Sarasota) A new weekend event with live entertainment, a farmer's market, an antiques center, food, and games.

Charlotte Harbor Coast

Charlotte Regional Flea Market (743-3576; Capricorn St., Port Charlotte) Open Friday through Sunday, 9:00–4:00.

Island Coast

Fleamasters Fleamarket (334-7001; Route 82, 1.25 miles west of I–75 exit 23, Fort Myers) Open Friday through Sunday, with 300,000 indoor square feet of produce, souvenirs, and novelties.

McGregor Boulevard Garage Sales (Fort Myers) Drive the boulevard early — the earlier you go, the better the pickings — every Saturday morning and watch for the forest of garage sale signs directing you to private sales.

Ortiz Flea Market (694-5019; 1501 Ortiz Ave., Fort Myers) Every Friday, Saturday, and Sunday.

South Coast

Naples Drive-In Flea Market (774-2900; 7700 Davis Blvd., Naples) Open Friday through Sunday.

GALLERIES

Sarasota Bay Coast

Empires Remembered (366-6868; 18 S. Palm Ave., downtown Sarasota) With the theme "history as an art," Empires features famous signatures, documents, golfing memorabilia, cartography, and military paintings and artifacts.

Four Winds Gallery (388-2510; 17 Fillmore Dr., St. Armands Circle) Contemporary, historic, and prehistoric Southwest Native American art, including pottery, weavings, and jewelry of the Pueblo, Hopi, Navajo, and Zuni tribes.

Hang-Up Gallery (953-5757; 45 S. Palm Ave., downtown Sarasota) One that doesn't take itself so seriously — art with a sense of humor: modern pop

Downtown Sarasota's gallery district.

sculptures using unusual media, and bright paintings in ever-changing exhibitions. Also offers framing, lectures, and art consultations.

Modern Art Gallery (366-3494; 49 S. Palm Ave., downtown Sarasota) Devoted to late 20th century paintings, sculpture, and tapestry, especially American artists whose work reflects modernism, abstract expressionism, and European romanticism.

Oehlschlaeger Galleries (388-3312; 28 S. Blvd. of the Arts, St. Armands Circle) Showcases paintings and meche dolls by known contemporary American, European, and South American artists.

Private Collections (346-3322; 5125 Ocean Blvd., Siesta Key) Features the limited edition Mother Goose and Grimm comic cells of resident Mike Peter, plus art, antique tableware and furniture, fine collectibles, and jewelry.

Charlotte Harbor Coast

Cabbage Court Gallery (964-0501; 333 Park Ave., Boca Grande) Sells local paintings and jewelry.

Sea Grape Artists Co-op Gallery (575-1718; 117 W. Marion Ave., Suite 111, Punta Gorda) Displays and sells work of members in many media.

Serendipity Gallery — art takes a turn toward the whimsical in downtown Boca Grande.

Crossed Palms Gallery in Bokeelia samples Pine Island's funky artistic nature.

Serendipity Gallery (964-2166; Old Theatre Mall, Park Ave., Boca Grande) Local works in fiber, glass, sculpture, paint, and prints.

Smart Studio & Art Gallery (964-0519; 383 Park Ave., Boca Grande) Shows and sells works of local artists.

Island Coast

Crossed Palms Gallery (283-2283; 8315 Main St., Bokeelia, Pine Island) Original works by local artists.

The Galleria (395-0348; 2353 Periwinkle Way, Sanibel Island) A gallery-in-the-round. Seven galleries in one, including Mermaid's Treasures and Rare Earth Creations.

Griffin Gallery (1-800-528-2685 or 283-0680; 4303 Pine Island Road, Matlacha) New wave Haitian art and showings of local and New York emerging artists.

Jungle Drums (395-2266; 11532 Andy Rosse Rd., Captiva Island) On the outside, dolphins and birds are carved into the stair rail and floor studs. Inside, local and national artists depict wildlife themes in various media.

Matsumoto Gallery (472-6686; 751 Tarpon Bay Rd., Sanibel Island) With its shocking blue and lavender restored beach-house exterior, the Matsumoto set new island standards by introducing Caribbean and Mexican style. The gallery features the work of co-owner Ikki Matsumoto, a Japanese graphics artist, as well as other island, national, and international artists.

Schoolhouse Gallery (472-1193; 520 Tarpon Bay Rd., Sanibel Island) Sanibel's first art gallery occupies an historic one-room schoolhouse with a modern sculpture on its lawn. Shelligrams are one of its specialties. Major wildlife artists, and other local and national artists, exhibit here.

Touch of Sanibel Pottery (472-4330; 1544 Periwinkle Way, Sanibel Island) Features utilitarian and decorative clayware, created both at the gallery and by guest artists. Its gladiolus vases, lighthouse lamps, and tropical designs make great souvenirs.

South Coast

Arsenault Gallery (263-1214; 385 Broad Ave. S., Old Naples) Changing exhibits and an eclectic selection of watercolors, acrylics, and oils depict historic Naples, Nantucket, and Caribbean scenes. Showcases the impressionistic work of my favorite local artist, Paul Arsenault.

The Darvish Collection (261-7581; 1199 Third St. S., Old Naples) Features the work of North American and European masters.

Gilded Gar Bage Gallery (261-7739; 1389 Third St. S., Old Naples) Modern funk to born-again junk by modern masters and emerging artists.

Harmon-Meek Gallery (261-2637; 386 Broad Ave. S., Old Naples) A most respected name in fine art, it hosts exhibitions for name artists.

Naples Art Gallery (262-4551; 275 Broad Ave. S., Windsor Plaza, Naples) This 25-year-old facility specializes in glass, representing 30 internationally known American studio glass artists. The spacious, stylish facility also exhibits paintings and sculptures with specially scheduled showings.

Sudderth Art International (261-6251; 1170 Third St. S., Unit B110, Old Naples) Classic and contemporary works from Asia, Europe, and North America.

GENERAL STORES

Charlotte Harbor Coast

Necessities General Store (964-2506; The Courtyard, 5800 Gasparilla Rd., Boca Grande) Beach needs, clothes, gifts, deli items.

Island Coast

Bailey's General Store (472-1516; Periwinkle Way and Tarpon Bay Rd., Sanibel Island) An island fixture for ages, it stocks mostly hardware, and fishing and kitchen supplies, with an attached grocery, bakery, and deli.

Island Store (472-2374; 11500 Andy Rosse Ln., Captiva Island) Buy those necessities you forgot here, but try not to forget too much because the prices reflect location, here at the ends of the earth.

GIFTS

Sarasota Bay Coast

Big Kids Toys (388-3555; 24 S. Blvd. of Presidents, St. Armands Circle) Small and major quirky gifts, such as juke boxes, games, antique-looking gas pumps, plus western and sports stuff.

Ethno Imports (951-1572; Southgate Mall, Sarasota) Handcrafted baskets, hammocks, jewelry, retablos, molas, pillows, handbags, nativities, cultural art, and T-shirts from Latin America and Africa.

Sea Chantey (349-6171; 5150 Ocean Blvd., Siesta Key) Among the riffraff of pink flamingos, T-shirts, and shell jewelry at Siesta Key Village, this shop stands out, with unusual objets d'art, boutique women's and children's clothes, jewelry, and imports. It seems incredible that so many fascinating gifts can be packed into one little shop: a department store of uniquities.

Triana (485-8582; Venice Center Mall, 222 W. Tampa Ave., Venice) Distinct ceramics, fans, tiles, cookware, fragrances, and paintings from Spain.

Charlotte Harbor Coast

Alexander's Imports (625-9918; Port Charlotte Center, Port Charlotte) Oriental decorative pieces and exotic costume jewelry.

Pirate's Ketch (637-0299; Fishermen's Village, Punta Gorda) Sandcast statues, nautical gifts, seashell kitsch, framed sea charts, and other art.

Island Coast

Animal Crackers (472-1935; 2075 Periwinkle Way, Sanibel Island) Take the kids — it's a carnival of walking toys, singing stuffed birds, tricks, T-shirts, and novelties.

Jerry's Bazaar (472-5636, Jerry's Shopping Center; 1700 Periwinkle Way, Sanibel Island) Collection of T-shirt, beach toy, shell, and candy shops, all under one roof, selling affordable mementos of the island.

Mr. McGregor's Garden (337-0087; 2310 McGregor Blvd., Fort Myers) Unique gift shop with a gardening orientation, located in a restored 1900s Cracker home near Edison Estate. Sample of wares: Irish herb-drying rack, English water cans, goatskin gardening gloves, wooden cow planters.

Pandora's Box (472-6263; 2075 Periwinkle Way) A seashell motif in decorative items, creative jewelry, potpourri, specialty children's gifts, and art greeting cards.

Swedish Affair (275-8004; Royal Palm Square, Fort Myers) Scandinavian gifts from funny to fine: Swedish joke books, lingonberry preserves, folk art, glassware, Christmas ornaments, and fine pewter serving pieces.

South Coast

Born To Be Wild (261-0560; Dockside Boardwalk, 1100 Sixth Ave. S., Naples) Stuffed toys, books, T-shirts, and gifts dedicated to promoting environmental awareness.

Conch Shelf (394-2511; 400 S. Collier Blvd., Marco Island) Florida specialty gifts — hand-carved herons, fish, and dolphins. Exclusive lines of crystal and glass.

Copán (642-1359; Tamiami Tr. and Route 92, south of Naples near entrance to Collier-Seminole State Park) Indian and Latin/South American arts-and-Native crafts, including Miccosukee feather-hangings and ethnic carved dolls.

El Condor (434-8548; Coconut Grove Marketplace, Naples) Features a collection of colorful folk art from Colombia, Latin America, and Haiti, including clay nativities and oil drum sculptures.

JEWELRY

Only in Naples: a boat-in jewelry store at Crayton Cove.

Sarasota Bay Coast

Jess Jewelers (756-5019; Orange Blossom Plaza, 409 Cortez Rd. W., Bradenton) Estate diamonds, beach-themed pieces, master goldsmiths.

Private Collections (346-3322; 5125 Ocean Blvd., The Village at Siesta Key) Beautiful specialty pieces, including unique Israeli jewelry, and estate jewelry. Master jeweler on staff.

Charlotte Harbor Coast

Al Morgan Jewelers (637-0946; 117 W. Marion Ave., downtown Punta Gorda) Fine custom work, exquisite ready-made pieces, sterling silver, and crystal.

Island Coast

Congress Jewelers (472-4177; Periwinkle Place, Sanibel Island) Dolphin, mermaid, and shell gold pendants, plus other fine jewelry.

Friday's Fine Jewelers (472-1454; Heart of the Island Center, 1620 Periwinkle Way, Sanibel Island) Fine watches, designer jewelry, tennis bracelets, and sea-themed pieces.

Thalheimer's Fine Jewelers (1-800-741-0141 or 489-0141; Bell Tower Shops, Fort Myers) The area's most reputable local jeweler, in a large shop carrying a full line of jewelry, Swiss watches, and other gifts.

The silver-lined streets of Naples.

South Coast

Images (394-3456; Port of Marco Shopping Village, Marco Island) Gold jewelry appropriate for Florida: bird-of-paradise pins, tennis pendants, starfish earrings; also, wood-sculptured fish and Swarovski crystal.

Thalheimer's Fine Jewelers (261-8422; 255 13th Ave. S., Old Naples) The most respected name in jewelers, carrying quality watches, diamond jewelry, crystal, and porcelain. Watchmaker, designer, and appraiser on premises. Art gallery upstairs.

William Phelps, Custom Jeweler (434-2233; Village on Venetian Bay, Naples) Fine crafted pendants, rings, earrings, and pins on display, plus colored stones and diamonds for customizing.

KITCHWARE & HOME DECOR

Sarasota Bay Coast

Architectural Imports (366-5766; 2258 6th St., Sarasota) Hand-crafted products for building and decorating.

Basketville (493-0007; 4011 S. Tamiami Tr., Venice) Region's widest selection of basketry, plus silk flowers, woodenware, and other items.

Kitchen Things (966-6156; Pelican Plaza, 8310 Tamiami Tr., Venice) Gourmet utensils, cutlery, kitchenware, and gadgets of all sorts.

The Lofty Lion (485-2588; 203 W. Venice Ave., Venice) A select collection of whimsical home decor items: shell appliqued pillows, bright fish mobiles, snail faucet handles, etc.

Longboat Interiors (383-2491; 12 Avenue of Flowers, Longboat Key) Rich Victorian parlor theme: heavy silver frames, silk flowers, antique pine, frilly and floral soft furnishings.

Shaman Imports (365-1855; 2065 12th St., Sarasota) Custom-painted pottery, pre-Colombian-style accessories, Equipale furniture, and Mexican handcrafts.

Charlotte Harbor Coast

Entertaining Thoughts (964-2209; Railroad Plaza, Boca Grande) Dishes, linens, and tabletop accessories.

Home Showcase (639-8882; 25173 Marion Ave., Punta Gorda) Florida-style decorations.

Santa Fe Accents (225-0233; 1381–D Market Circle, Port Charlotte) Custom furniture, clocks, chests, lamps, and accessories awash in Southwest colors and motifs; also, framed Native American art.

Island Coast

Countries Hurrah (482-3332; Bell Tower Shops, Fort Myers) Home accessories with a country and French provincial flavor.

Galloway's Clements & Assoc. (936-1231; Royal Palm Square, Fort Myers) Interior design elements with a tropical theme: beachscape watercolors, sea urchin sculptures, brass and enamel heron statues, shell appliqued pillows.

Island Style (472-6657; Periwinkle Place, Sanibel Island) Whimsical, artistic, and one-of-a-kind decorating elements with a sunbelt motif: hand-painted chairs, motion wood carvings, Caribbean-inspired pieces.

La Maison Marie-Claire (472-4421; The Village, 2340 Periwinkle Way, Sanibel Island) Stocks Mediterranean Coast items suitable to Florida lifestyles: Limoges porcelain, home fragrance lamps, French country furnishings, Quimper Faience dinnerware, and Biot handblown glassware.

Peel 'n Pare (433-3300; Bell Tower Shops, Fort Myers) Unique kitchen accents and implements.

Unpressured Cooker (472-2413; Periwinkle Place, Sanibel Island) Specialty Florida items: local cookbooks, alligator cutters, shell pie pans, sea-motif place mats.

South Coast

The Good Life (262-4355; 1170 Third St. S., Old Naples) Gourmet cookware, tabletops, serving pieces, imported Povtmeiron tableware, quality implements and floral designs.

Gattle's (262-4791; 1250 3rd St. S., Old Naples) Linens for the bed, bath, and table; fine home accessories and nursery items.

A Horse of a Different Color (261-1252; 355 13th Ave. So., Old Naples) One-of-a-kind and highly contemporary gifts, lamps, and accessories.

SHELL SHOPS

Sarasota Bay Coast

House of Shells (388-2880; 19 N. Blvd. of Presidents, St. Armands Circle) Unique tropical gifts, jewelry, and other souvenirs.

Sea Pleasures and Treasures (488-3510; 255 Venice Ave. W., Venice) Quantity — not necessarily quality — sea-themed gifts.

Island Coast

Island Shells and Gifts (283-8080; 4204–4206 Pine Island Road, Matlacha) Huge facility carrying an unusual stock of shells, shellcraft materials, jewelry, and other novelties.

Neptune's Treasures (472-3132; Treetops Center, 1101 Periwinkle Way, Sanibel Island) Along with the usual line of shell specimens and jewelry, this shop carries fossils and arrowheads.

The Shell Factory (995-2141; 2787 N. Tamiami Tr., North Ft. Myers) A palace of Florida funk and junk, The Shell Factory is built like a bazaar, with dozens of mini-shops within its 65,500 square feet. The main part displays specimen shells and shellcraft items of every variety. The children will like the mounted manatees and sharks, and aquariums. Jewelry, art, clothes, and knickknacks fill other nooks. Also at the complex (can't miss it, look for the giant conch shell on the sign), you will find restaurants, an arcade, and bumperboat rides.

Easy shell pickin' at this North Fort Myers landmark.

Showcase Shells (472-1971; Heart of the Islands Center, 1614 Periwinkle Way, Sanibel Island) As elegant as a jewelry store, this boutique adds a touch of class to sifting through specimen shells by putting them under glass and into artistic displays.

South Coast

Blue Mussel (262-4814; 478 Fifth Ave. S. Naples) Rare shells, jewelry, custom-designed mirrors, and other shellcrafts.

Shells by Emily (394-5575; 651 S. Collier Blvd., Marco Island) Shells from around the world, shellcraft accessories, and classes.

SHOPPING CENTERS AND MALLS

Mediterranean Revival architecture typifies Venice's buy-till-you-die scene.

Sarasota Bay Coast

De Soto Square (747-5868; Tamiami Tr. at Cortez Rd., Bradenton) 700,000 feet of shop-till-you-drop: over 100 stores including Sears, Burdines, and Dillards.

Downtown Sarasota One of the Gulf Coast's most successful downtown restoration projects has returned Sarasota's vitality to Main Street and environs. The area is also known as the Sarasota Theatre and Arts District. Rumors abound that Main Street may be converted into a walking mall but, for the time being, it encompasses approximately a 1.5 mile area, centered at Five Points, where Main Street intersects with four others. Old, renovated buildings house galleries (particularly along South Palm Avenue), book stores, clothing boutiques, antique shops, restaurants, sidewalk cafes, cabarets, clubs, and gift shops. The neighborhood seems fairly empty on weekdays, when parking is plentiful. Nights and weekends are a different story, however.

St. Armands Circle (388-1554; St. Armands Key) John Ringling envisioned a world-class shopping center upon one of the Sarasota barrier islands he owned, complete with park-lined walkways and baroque statuary. He would be gratified by St. Armands Circle. On a scale with Beverly Hill's Rodeo Drive and Palm Beach's Worth Avenue, it is named for developer Charles St. Amand. Its spin-off formation is suited geographically to the pancake shape of the island. Four sections arc off the circular center drive. "The Circle," as it is known in local shorthand, encompasses shops of the most upscale nature, galleries, restaurants, clubs, ice cream shops, and specialty boutiques. International style is well represented. The Circle is a hub of activity for the entire region. Horse-drawn carriages offer sunset rides and the Circus Ring of Fame honors distinguished Big Top entertainers. People dress in finery just to shop here, but don't feel obligated. Parking is free (but scarce), on the street and in the garage nearby.

Southgate Mall (951-0412; Siesta Rd. and S. Tamiami Tr., Sarasota) A major shopping mall, this one houses Burdines, Dillards, and a Publix supermarket.

Looping The Circle on St. Armand's Key, Sarasota's premier shoppers' haven.

Venice Centre Mall (226 Tampa Ave. W., Venice) Occupying the erstwhile winter quarters of the Kentucky Military Institute, the mall is listed on the National Register of Historic Buildings. It includes shops which specialize in unique gifts and clothing, which fall into formation along a spit-and-polish hall.

Venice Avenue (Venice Ave. W. and Tamiami Tr., Venice) Down a Mediterranean, date-palm-lined boulevard, you will find shops and restaurants of every style, to fit every budget.

The Village at Siesta Key (Ocean Blvd., Siesta Key) Refreshingly barefoot in style, this area mixes beach bawdy with an artistic temperament not quite as intense as that of downtown Sarasota.

Charlotte Harbor Coast

Fishermen's Village (637-0069; Maud St. and Marion Ave., Punta Gorda) Forty

Military students once marched the halls where today Venice shoppers troop.

shops and restaurants occupy a transformed marina. There's docking, lodging, charter boats, and fishing from the docks, besides shopping and dining. A preponderance of nautical clothing and gift ideas are reflective of the motif.

Port Charlotte Town Center (1441 Tamiami Tr., Port Charlotte) An indoor mega-mall with more than 100 commercial enterprises, including Burdines, Sears, and other chain outlets and specialty shops, such as Bombay Company and Victoria's Secrets.

Railroad Plaza (Park Ave., Boca Grande) Despite the millionaires and power-brokers who make Boca Grande their winter home, shopping here is low-key and affordable, with shades of historic quaintness. The restored railroad depot houses gift and apparel boutiques. Across the street, you will find an eccentric general store, and a department store that's been there forever, both of which set a somewhat funky tone.

Boca Grande shopping takes center stage at the renovated, circa-1910 train depot now known as Railroad Plaza.

Shopping made scenic at Fort Myers' Bell Tower Mall.

Island Coast

Bell Tower Shops (489-1221; Daniels Pkwy. and Tamiami Tr., Fort Myers)
Jacobson's, a small and exclusive department store, anchors this beautifully
landscaped, Mediterranean-style plaza of specialty shops, restaurants, and
movie theaters.

Captiva Island Like Captiva in general, the shopping scene here is quirky and
beach-oriented. Chadwick's Square, near the entrance to South Seas Plantation Resort, provides the best (if somewhat pricey) concentration of gifts and
fashion.

Coralwood Mall (574-1441; 2301 Del Prado Blvd., Cape Coral) An outdoor
mall of restaurants and chain stores, including Bealls Department Store.

Downtown Fort Myers (1st Street) Downtown is looking up slowly. Book
stores, street musicians, artists, and sweets shops appeal to the soft-core
shopper. On the fringes of the district you will find a scattering of small
antique dealers.

Edison Mall (939-5464; 4125 Cleveland Ave., Fort Myers) An entirely commercial, enclosed mall with major department stores such as Burdines, J. C. Pen-
neys, Sears, and Maas Brothers, plus about 150 smaller clothing and gift
shops, and a food court.

Matlacha (Pine Island) Sagging old fish houses, cracker-box shops, and fishing
motels heavily salt the flavor of this island village. Knickknack historic
structures painted in candy store colors give the town an artistic, Hansel-
and-Gretel feel. Sea-themed gifts, art, and jewelry comprise the majority of
merchandise.

Royal Palm Square (939-3900; Colonial Blvd. and Summerlin Rd., Fort Myers)
The ultimate outpost of Fort Myers chic, this alfresco mall takes you down
wooden walkways and past lush palms, exotic birds, fish ponds, and fountains.

Sanibel Island Periwinkle Way and Palm Ridge Road constitute the shopper's routes on Sanibel, which is known for its galleries (specializing in wildlife art), shell shops, and resort-wear stores. These are clustered in tastefully landscaped, nature-compatible, outdoor centers, the largest being Periwinkle Place. One of the most interesting, both architecturally and in terms of merchandise, is *The Village* on *Periwinkle Way*.

Times Square (At the foot of Mantanzas Pass Bridge, Fort Myers Beach) Shop in your bikini, if you wish, at this hub of ultra-casual island activity. You'll find a profusion of swimsuit boutiques, surf shops, and fast food outlets.

South Coast

Coastland Center (Tamiami Tr. N. and Golden Gate Pkwy., Naples) J. C. Penney, Burdines, Sears, and 110 other stores and eateries are gathered under one roof.

Coconut Grove Marketplace & Marina (1001 10th Ave. S., Naples) A pleasant contrast to the touristy character of Tin City and the expensive merchandise of Old Naples' plazas, Coconut Grove exudes a tropical temperament with its light wood interior, stylish wood signs fashioned by local artists, and a focus on things wild and islandy.

Fifth Avenue South (Naples) More plebeian than the Third Street scene, these nine blocks are devoted especially to antiques and gifts.

Never a leaf out of place along Naples' hallowed streets of wallet enticement.

Mission de San Marco Plaza (599 S. Collier Blvd., Marco Island) A modified strip mall, done in an interesting interpretation of Spanish style, holding specialty stores of all sorts.

Old Marine Marketplace (Tin City, Naples) I love the structure of this mall, which resurrects old, tin-roofed docks. Most commonly, you'll hear it called Tin City, because of its rustic demeanor. Its 40 shops tend to be ultra-

A mecca for tourist buys and kitsch decor.

touristy, selling mainly nautical gifts and resort wear, but it has enjoyable waterfront restaurants, and it's a good place to catch a fishing or sightseeing tour.

Lush and aromatic landscaping add a distinctly Florida dimer.sion to shopping in Naples' famed Third Street South district

Port of Marco Shopping Village (Royal Palm Dr., Marco Island) A small, comfortable, Old Florida-style center in the historical heart of Marco Island; gifts, clothes, and souvenirs on a mid-range scale.

Third Street South Plaza and the Avenues (Naples) A visit to this upscale shopping quarter in Old Naples, the heart of the arts scene, will reveal fine outdoor sculptures on loan from local galleries and fragrant foliage. This is window-shopping at its best (on my budget, anyway), displaying exquisite clothes, art, jewelry, and home decorations and furnishings.

The Village of Venetian Bay (Gulfshore Blvd. N. at Park Shore Dr., Naples) Upscale, Mediterranean-style domain of fashion, jewelry, and art; located on the waterfront.

Waterside Shops at Pelican Bay (598-1605; Seagate Dr. and Tamiami Tr. N., Pelican Bay, Naples) Naples' newest shopping enclave features the region's only Saks Fifth Avenue, located amidst cascading waters and lush foliage.

SPORTS STORES

Note: This listing includes general sports outlets only. To buy supplies and equipment for specific sports, please refer to *Recreation*.

Sarasota Bay Coast

Cook's Sportland (488-3516; 235 W. Venice Ave., Venice) Equipment for archery, golf, camping, and fishing; also, fishing licenses, tackle repair, sportswear, shoes, and western clothing.

Sarasota Outfitters (953-9591; 3540 Osprey Ave., Sarasota) Outdoors and camping gear and clothing.

Charlotte Harbor Coast

Champs Sports (627-5556; Port Charlotte, Port Charlotte) Clothes, shoes, and equipment for tennis, aerobics, weight-training, and all ball sports.

Island Coast

Kelly Mikes (772-3737; Del Prado Mall, 1410 S. Del Prado, Cape Coral) Shoes and equipment for all sports, especially bowling, tennis, and golf.

Ken's Sports (936-7106; 4600 S. Cleveland Ave., Fort Myers) Specializes in scuba, archery, tennis, darts, and shuffleboard.

South Coast

Beach Sports of Marco (642-4282; 571 Collier Blvd., Marco Island) Bikes, in-line skates, tackle, bait, surfboards, swimwear, fishing licenses.

Wright World of Sports (263-3070; 1450 Airport Rd. N., Naples) All ball sports, rentals, and trade-ins.

CHAPTER EIGHT

Practical Matters

INFORMATION

A comment on crime and humor on Anna Maria Island.

AMBULANCE/FIRE/POLICE

A ll four west coast counties have adopted the 911 emergency phone number system. Dial it for ambulance, fire, sheriff, and police. Listed below are non-emergency numbers for individual communities.

Town	Ambulance	Fire	Police/Sheriff
FOR EMERGENCY Anywhere in the region	911	911	911
SARASOTA BAY COAST			
Anna Maria			778-6621
Bradenton		747-1161	746-4111
Bradenton Beach		778-6621	778-6311
Cortez			778-6621
Holmes Beach		778-6621	778-2221
Longboat		383-1592	383-3726
Sarasota		364-2215	366-8000
Venice		492-3196	488-6711
Manatee County Sheriff			747-3011
Sarasota County Sheriff			951-5800
Florida Highway Patrol (Venice)			483-5911

CHARLOTTE COUNTY

Punta Gorda		639-3897
Charlotte County Sheriff		639-2101
Florida Highway Patrol (Venice)		483-5911

LEE COUNTY

Cape Coral	574-3223	574-3223
Fort Myers	334-6222	334-4155
Sanibel	472-1717	472-3111
Lee County Sheriff		332-3456
Florida Highway Patrol		278-7100

COLLIER COUNTY

Naples	434-4730	434-4844
Collier County Sheriff		774-4434
Florida Highway Patrol		455-3133

AREA CODE/TOWN GOVERNMENT & ZIP CODES

An apt reflection for the government center in "City of Palms."

AREA CODE

The area code for the Gulf Coast of Florida is 813. You must dial the area code for all long distance calls within the region.

GOVERNMENT

All incorporated cities on the West Coast are self-governing, with council-men, commissioners, mayors, and city managers in various roles. The unincorporated towns and communities are county-ruled.

Fort Myers is considered the region's major metropolis, though other cities are catching up in terms of population.

The incorporated cities of the Sarasota Bay Coast include Bradenton, Anna

Maria, Holmes Beach, Bradenton Beach, Sarasota, Longboat Key, and Venice. On the Charlotte Harbor Coast, North Port and Punta Gorda are incorporated.

Fort Myers, Cape Coral, and Sanibel make up the Island Coast's incorporated cities. Naples is Collier County's seat and the South Coast's only incorporated city.

ZIP CODES

Town	Government Center	Zip
SARASOTA BAY COAST		
Anna Maria	778-0781	34216
Bradenton	748-0800	34206
Bradenton Beach	778-1005	34217
Holmes Beach	778-2221	34217
Longboat Key	383-3721	34228
Sarasota	365-2200	34236
Venice	485-3311	34285
CHARLOTTE HARBOR COAST		
North Port	426-8484	34287
Punta Gorda	575-3302	33950
ISLAND COAST		
Cape Coral	574-040	33990
Fort Myers	332-6700	33902
Sanibel	472-370	33957
SOUTH COAST		
Naples	434-4701	33940

BANKS

S everal old and established banks have their branches located throughout Florida's Gulf Coast. Some are listed below, with toll-free information numbers, where available, and Instant Teller Machine Network Systems.

Bank	Number(s)	ITM Networks
Barnett		Honor, PLUS
Bradenton	755-0050	
Sarasota	953-6009	
Venice	474-9504	

Englewood	474-9504	
Charlotte County	743-1000	
Fort Myer	337-7770	
Naples	643-2265	
Nations Bank	1-800-367-6262	Cirrus, Plus, Honor, Nations 24

BIBLIOGRAPHY

Literary Souvenirs

BIOGRAPHY & REMINISCENCE

Captiva Civic Association. *True Tales of Old Captiva.* 1984. 353 pp., photos, $15.00. Transcripts from taped dialogues with the island's early settlers.

Levering, Ted. *The Other Side of the Bridge.* Fort Myers, FL: Willowmead Publishing Co., 1991. A folksy return to Captiva and Sanibel circa 1948.

Lindbergh, Anne Morrow. *Gift from the Sea.* New York: Pantheon, 1955. 142 pp., illust., hardcover $16.00. New York: Vintage Books. 138 pp., illust., paperback, $7.00. A small book packed with great sea-inspired wisdom, strong evidence points to Captiva as its inspiration.

Newton, James. *Uncommon Friends.* New York: Harcourt, Brace, Jovanovich, 1987. 368 pp., $10.95. Local man's memories of his friendships with Fort Myers' illustrious winterers: Thomas Edison, Henry Ford, Harvey Firestone and Charles Lindbergh.

Walton, Chelle Koster. *Sanibel Island Eyes (and other island afflictions and addictions).* Sanibel Island, FL: Island Eyes Press, 1989. 104 pp., $5.95. A five-year slice of irreverent insight into island living.

COOKBOOKS

The Best of Sanibel–Captiva Islands: Restaurants & Recipes. Sanibel, FL, 1992. 208 pp., illust., index, $14.95 A collection of histories and recipes of island restaurants, with introduction by part-time Captiva resident Willard Scott.

Caloosa Rare Fruit Exchange, Inc. *Tropical Fruit Cookbook.* Fort Myers, FL, 1991. 255 pp., illust., $12.00. Features the area's most unusual cultivated fruits (carambola, jaboticaba, black sapote, etc.) as well as its more usual ones (bananas, oranges and coconut.)

Grochowski, Nita. *Sunburst Tropical Fruit Co. Cookbook.* Pineland, FL: Mondongo Publishing Co., 1988. 80 pp., illust., index, $10.95. Recipes using mangoes, papayas, guava and other exotic fruit, written by a Pine Island commercial grove operator.

Junior League of Fort Myers. *Gulfshore Delights*. Fort Myers, FL, 1984. 286 pp., illust., index, $14.95.

Young, Joyce LaFray, *Seminole Indian Recipes*. Tampa, FL: Surfside Publishing, 1987. 24 pp. $4.95.

FICTION

Kallen, Lucille. *Piano Bird*. New York: Random House, 1984. 175 pp., $3.95. C.B. Greenfield mystery series with a Sanibel Island setting.

Macdonald, John D. Many of his Fibber McGee and other mysteries take place in a Sarasota Bay Coast setting, where he had a home.

Matthiessen, Peter. *Killing Mr. Watson*. New York: Random House, 1990. The parents of this author live on Sanibel Island. The subject of his novel was the posse-killing of Belle Star's murderer, back in the days of Jesse James.

White, Randy. *The Heat Islands*. New York: St. Martin's Press, 1992. 276 pp., $4.99. Mystery by a local fishing guide/journalist with local setting.

_____. *Sanibel Flats*. New York: St. Martin's Press, 1990. 307 pp., $3.95. His first Doc Ford mystery; set on Sanibel Island.

HISTORY & REMINISCENCE

Beater, Jack. *Pirates & Buried Treasure*. St. Petersburg: Great Outdoors Publishing, 1959. 118 pp., illust., $2.95. Somewhat factual, ever-colorful account of Gasparilla and cohorts, by the area's foremost legendaire.

Board, Prudy Taylor and Patricia Pope Bartlett. *Pictorial History of Lee County*. Virginia Beach, VA: The Donning Publishers, 1985. 192 pp., photos, index, $29.95.

Board, Prudy Taylor and Esther B. Colcord. *Historic Fort Myers*. Virginia Beach, VA: The Donning Publishers, 1992. 96 pp., photos, index, $15.95. Largely photographic treatment, written by two of the area's leading historians today.

_____. *Pages From the Past*. Virginia Beach, VA: The Donning Publishers, 1990. 192 pp., photos, index, $29.95. Largely photographic treatment of Fort Myers' history.

Dormer, Elinore M. *The Sea Shell Islands: A History of Sanibel and Captiva*. Tallahassee, FL: Rose Printing Co., 1987. 274 pp., illust., index, $16.00. The definitive work on island and regional history.

Hatton, Hap. *Tropical Splendor: An Architectural History of Florida*. New York: Alfred A. Knopf, 1987. 210 pp., illust., index, $40.00. Beautifully told and illustrated retrospective on the state's people and builders.

Jordan, Elaine Blohm. *Pine Island, the Forgotten Island*. Pine Island, FL: 1982. 186 pp., photos.

Matthews, Janet Snyder. *Edge of Wilderness: A Settlement History of Manatee*

River and Sarasota Bay. Sarasota, FL: Coastal Press, 1983. 464 pp., photos, index, $21.50.

_____. *Journey to Centennial Sarasota.* Sarasota, FL: Pine Level Press, 1989. 224 pp., photo, index, $29.95.

Schell, Rolfe F. *History of Fort Myers Beach.* Fort Myers Beach, FL: Island Press, 1980. 96 pp., photos, index, $6.95.

Zeiss, Betsy. *The Other Side of the River: Historical Cape Coral.* Cape Coral, FL, 1986. 215 pp., photos, index, $8.95.

NATURAL HISTORY

Campbell, George R. *The Nature of Things on Sanibel.* Fort Myers, FL: Press Printing, 1978. 174 pp., illust., index, $14.95. Factual, yet entertaining background on native fauna and flora.

Douglas, Marjory Stoneman. *The Everglades: River of Grass.* St. Simons, GA: Mockingbird Books, 1947. 308 pp., $4.95. The book that got the nation's attention on the developing plight of the pristine Everglades.

PHOTOGRAPHIC

Campen, Richard N. *Sanibel and Captiva Enchanting Islands.* Chagrin Falls, OH: West Summit Press, 1977. 96 pp., photos, $12.95. Old island style and faces preserved in black-and-white and color photos with journal description.

Capes, Richard. *Richard Capes' Drawings Capture Siesta Key.* Sarasota, FL, 1992. An artistic tour of the island in pen and ink, with handwritten description. 175 pp.

Stone, Lynn. *Sanibel Island.* Stillwater, MN: Voyageur Press, Inc., 1991. 96 pp., photos, $15.95. Sanibel's natural treasures in words and striking pictures.

RECREATION

Fuery, Captain Mike. *Florida Shelling Guide.* Captiva, FL: Sanibel Sandollar Publications, 1987. Features Sanibel, Captiva, and other Gulf Coast barrier islands.

_____. *South Florida Bay and Coastal Fishing.* Captiva, FL: Sanibel Sandollar Publications, 1987. Written by a Sanibel charter captain.

Greenberg, Margaret. *The Sanibel Shell Guide.* Orlando, FL: Anna Publishing, Inc., 1982. 117 pp., illust., photos, index, $5.95. Excellent resource for the beginning, but serious sheller.

TRAVEL

Buchan, Russell and Robert Tolf. *Florida: A Guide to the Best Restaurants, Resorts, and Hotels.* New York: Clarkson N. Potter, Inc., 1988. 259 pp., index.

Hupp, Susan and Laura Stewart. *Florida Historic Homes*. Orlando, FL: Orlando Sentinel Communications Co., 1988. 127 pp., illust, index, $9.95.

MacPerry, I. *Indian Mounds You Can Visit*. St. Petersburg, FL: Great Outdoors Publishing, 1993. 319 pp., photos, index, $12.95. Covers the entire West Coast of Florida, arranged by county.

Walton, Chelle Koster, et al. *Hidden Florida*. Berkeley, CA: Ulysses Press, 1993. 513 pp., illust., index. Focuses on outdoor recreation, adventure, and off-the-beaten-path travel.

Check It Out

HISTORY & REMINISCENCE

Bickel, Karl A. *The Mangrove Coast: The Story of the West Coast of Florida*. New York: Coward–McCann, 1942. 332 pp., photos, index. Vintage regional history of the area from Tampa Bay to Ten Thousand Islands, from the time of Ponce de Leon to 1885, spiced with romantic embellishments.

Briggs, Mildred. *Pioneers of Bonita Springs (Facts and Folklore)*. Florida, 1976. 100 pp., photos. Pirates, Indian healers, outlaws and more.

Fritz, Florence. *Unknown Florida*. Coral Gables, FL: University of Miami Press, 1963. 213 pp., photos, index. Focuses on southern-most Gulf Coast.

Gonzales, Thomas A. *The Caloosahatchee: History of the Caloosahatchee River and the City of Fort Myers Florida*. Fort Myers Beach, FL: Island Press Publishers, 1982. 134 pp. Memories of a native son, descendant of city's first settler.

Grismer, Karl H. *The Story of Fort Myers*. Fort Myers Beach, FL: The Island Press Publishers, 1982. 348 pp., photos, index.

_____. *The Story of Sarasota*. Tampa, FL: The Florida Grower Press, 1946. 376 pp., photos, index.

Marth, Del. *Yesterday's Sarasota*. Miami, FL: E.A. Seemann Publishing, Inc., 1977 (Updated). 160 pp., photos. Primarily pictorial history.

Matthews, Kenneth and Robert McDevitt. *The Unlikely Legacy*. Sarasota, FL: Aaron Publishers, Inc., 1980. 64 pp., illust. The story of John Ringling, the circus, and Sarasota.

Peeples, Vernon. *Punta Gorda and the Charlotte Harbor Area*. Norfolk, VA: The Donning Co., 1986. 208 pp., photos, index. Pictorial history authored by local politician.

Romans, Bernard. A *Concise Natural History of East and West Florida*. Gainesville, FL: University of Florida Press, 1962. 342 pp., index. A facsimile reproduction of the 1775 edition.

Schell, Rolfe F. *DeSoto Didn't Land at Tampa*. Fort Myers Beach, FL: Island Press, 1966. 96 pp., illust.

Tebeau, Charlton W. *Florida's Last Frontier: The History of Collier County*. Coral Gables FL: University of Miami Press, 1966. 278 pp., photos, index.

Widmer, Randolph J. *The Evolution of the Calusa*. Tuscaloosa: The University of

Alabama Press, 1988. 334 pp., index. Very technical discussion of the "nonagricultural chiefdom on the Southwest Florida Coast."

CLIMATE, SEASONS, AND WHAT TO WEAR

No fair-weather fisherman, this.

"The tropics brush the Mangrove Coast but do not overwhelm it."

— Karl Bickel, *The Mangrove Coast*, 1942.

Florida's nickname, the Sunshine State, once was as fresh as it was apt. Although overuse may have clouded somewhat the once-perfect image, Florida still remains the ultimate state of sunshine through the sheer power of statistics. The sun beams down on the Gulf Coast for nearly 75 percent of all daylight hours, and constitutes the one asset that locals can bank on. Businesses along the coast are known to promise free wares or substantial discounts on sunless days.

To residents, the sun's smile can seem more like a sneer as they await fall's begrudging permission to turn off air conditioners and open windows. They suffer their own brand of cabin fever during the summer months, which often seem to go on as long as a Canadian winter. Although visitors revel in the warmth and sunlight, they often wonder how residents endure the monotony of seasonal sameness.

The seasons do change along the southern Gulf Coast, although more subtly than "up north." Weather patterns vary within the region. The Sarasota Bay and Charlotte Harbor areas often get more rain. However, weather can be very localized — it may rain on the southern end of 12-mile-long Sanibel Island while the north end remains dry. Islands generally stay cooler than the mainland in summer, and warmer in winter, thanks to their insulating jacket of water. This is especially true where Charlotte Harbor runs wide and deep, creating a small pocket of tropical climate.

Winter is everyone's favorite time of year weather-wise, with temperatures along the coast reaching generally into the 70s during the day and dropping into the 50s at night. Visitors find green, balmy relief from snowblindness and frostbite. Floridians enjoy the relative coolness that brings with it a reprieve from sweltering days, steamy nights, and bloodthirsty insects. The fragrances of oranges, grapefruits, and key limes fill the air. It's a time for activity — resort areas fill up and migratory house guests from the north arrive.

Spring comes on tiptoe to the coast. No thaw-and-puddle barometer alerts us; the sense of spring giddiness affects only longtime residents. Floridians emerge from hibernation raring to leap and frolic, and perhaps do a little mischief. Gardenias and jasmine bloom, and everything that already looks green and alive bursts forth with an extra reserve of color. It's a time to celebrate the end of another season, and greedily to enjoy the domain that's been shared with visitors during the winter months.

Summers used to be reserved for die-hard Floridians. All but the most devoted residents boarded up their homes and businesses and headed somewhere — anywhere — cooler. Now there's a summer trade, composed of Floridians, Europeans, and northern families — enough to keep alive the resort communities through temperatures that snuggle up to 100 degrees.

An afternoon summer shower descends upon Sanibel Island.

Although technically classified sub-tropical, starting in June the region feels the bristles of that tropic brush. The pace of life slows, and late-afternoon rains suddenly and unpredictably revolt against the sun's constancy. Mangoes and guavas blush sweet temptation. Moonlit nights bring magic to the vining cereus, with its white, starburst blooms the size of a frisbee.

Fall appears in October, as a sharpening of vision after a blur of humidity. Residents don't exactly go out and buy wool plaids, but they do break out sweatshirts. Many build fires in hearths that have held dried floral arrangements for eight months. The leathery leaves of the sea grape tree turn red as the northern oak, and the gumbo limbo coaxes out rakes. The best part about a Gulf Coast fall, for those residents who once endured northern winters, is that it bodes not of rubber boots and long underwear.

Winter temperatures dip, albeit rarely, into the freezing range, so be prepared for just about any weather between December and February. Fortunately, swimsuits take up little room, so pack more than one of those (Florida's high humidity often denies anything from ever really drying out). Loose-fitting togs and cotton work best in any season. Long sleeves are welcome in the evenings during the winter. Summer showers require rain gear, especially if you plan on boating or playing outdoors.

Don't worry about dress codes in most restaurants. Ties and pantyhose are strictly for the office and, possibly, the theater. Worry more about comfort,

The silver cast of Gulf Coast sunsets.

especially if your skin burns easily. Pack lots of sunscreen, and hats. Bring insect repellent, too, especially if you plan on venturing into the jungle — or watching an island sunset, for that matter. Counties do spray for mosquitoes, but it has little effect on the tiny but prolific *no-see-um* (sand flea). Any DEET product repels mosquitoes. The best protection against both is sitting under a ceiling fan — practically standard equipment in homes and hotels.

On the cloudier side, Florida weather includes a high incidence of lightning, summer squalls, tornadoes, waterspouts, and the dreaded H-word. Hurricane season begins in June, but activity concentrates toward season's end in October. Watches and warnings alert you in plenty of time to head inland or north; to be safest, do so at first mention, especially if you are staying on an island.

Florida's celebrated sunshine is at its best on the Gulf Coast. Ol' Sol visits practically every day, and it's also where he slips into bed. Gulf Coast Florida boasts the most spectacular sunsets in the continental United States.

WEATHER LINES

Sarasota Bay Coast

Automated Weather Observation System 351-1655
Manatee County Emergency Management 748-5283
Sarasota County Emergency Management 951-5283
WWSB News 40 Weather Update Line 953-2900

Island Coast

News-Press Hurricane Hotline 332-5600, or 1-800-848-0515 (touch-tone only)

South Coast

Weather Service Forecast, Naples Beach Municipal Pier 262-2710
Weather Station WNOG 1270 AM 263-0101

AVERAGE GULF COAST FLORIDA AIR TEMPERATURES

Month Avg.	Max. Avg.	Min.
Jan.	72.8	52.8
Feb.	73.8	53.8
Mar.	78.3	57.8
Apr.	82.5	61.6
May	87.7	67.1
June	89.7	72.1
July	90.5	73.7
Aug.	90.9	73.8
Sept.	89.1	72.7
Oct.	84.9	66.8
Nov.	77.9	59.4
Dec.	74.1	53.8

Green Flash

The sun is setting, melting, golden, into the sea like a round pat of butter, balanced on its edge. Just as the final crescent of light disappears, it sends up on the horizon a final, green farewell flare.

What you've just witnessed is a tropical phenomenon called a "green flash". It occurs infrequently, and most people miss it — or only realize what they've seen, after the fact.

Skeptics will tell you that green flashes are just a good excuse to sit on the beach at sunset, perhaps with a celebratory glass of champagne or rum punch. The drinking part of the sunset ritual, they further theorize, may be more responsible for green flash sightings than reality.

Physics, however, backs up the notion that the sun emits a split-second green explosion as it winks below the sea's surface. It all has to do with the spectrum, wavelengths, refraction, and other terms you may remember from school science experiments.

Old Sol winks a brilliant farewell at his nightly Gulf Coast curtain call.

In short, it takes conditions like those we enjoy on the Gulf Coast to make the green flash happen: sunsets over the sea and near-tropical climes. Cloudless evening skies are also required, which occur more regularly during the cool months. Binoculars or a small telescope will help widen the band of refracted green light so it lasts longer. Patience and persistence are crucial. Once you've seen a green flash, some say, your trained eye is apt to spot more. With or without rum.

GULF COAST FLORIDA WATER TEMPERATURES

Annual average	77.5
Fall/winter average	70.8
Spring/summer average	84.1
Winter low	66.0
Summer high	87.0

HANDICAPPED SERVICES

Regulations concerning handicapped access vary, depending on locale. In general, most restaurants, attractions, and resorts provide physically impaired visitors with special ramps, bathroom stalls, and hotel rooms.

HOSPITALS

Visitors often mistake for a resort HealthPark, Fort Myers' new and stylish hospital.

Sarasota Bay Coast

BRADENTON

HCA L.W. Blake Hospital, 2020 59th St. W., Bradenton 34209; 792-6611; emergency room open 24 hours.

Manatee Memorial Hospital, 206 2nd St. E., Bradenton 34208; 746-5111; emergency room open 24 hours.

SARASOTA

HCA Doctors Hospital, 2750 Bahia Vista St., Sarasota 34239; 366-1411; emergency room open 24 hours.

Sarasota Memorial Hospital, 1700 So. Tamiami Trail, Sarasota 33580; 955-1111; emergency room open 24 hours.

VENICE

Venice Hospital, 540 The Rialto, Venice 33595; 485-7711; emergency room open 24 hours.

Charlotte Harbor Coast

ENGLEWOOD

Englewood Community Hospital, 700 Medical Blvd., Englewood 33533; 475-6571; emergency room open 24 hours.

PORT CHARLOTTE

Fawcett Memorial Hospital, 21298 Olean Blvd., Port Charlotte 33952; 629-1181; emergency room open 24 hours.

Bon Secours-St. Joseph Hospital, 2500 Harbor Blvd., Port Charlotte 33952; 625-4122; emergency room open 24 hours.

PUNTA GORDA

Medical Center Hospital, 809 E. Marion Ave., Punta Gorda 33950; 639-3131; emergency room open 24 hours.

Island Coast

CAPE CORAL

Cape Coral Hospital, 636 Del Prado Blvd, Cape Coral 33990; 574-2323; emergency room open 24 hours.

FORT MYERS

HealthPark Medical Center, 9981 HealthPark Circle, Fort Myers, 33908; 433-7799; emergency room open 24 hours.

Lee Memorial Hospital, 2776 Cleveland Ave., Fort Myers 33901; 332-1111; emergency room open 24 hours.

Southwest Florida Regional Medical Center, 2727 Winkler Ave., Fort Myers 33901; 939-1147; emergency room open 24 hours.

South Coast

NAPLES

Naples Community Hospital, 350 Seventh St. N., Naples 33940; 262-3131; emergency room open 24 hours.

North Collier Hospital, 1501 Immokalee Road, 33999; 597-1417; emergency room open 24 hours.

LATE NIGHT FOOD AND FUEL

Certain categories of Florida liquor licensing require bars to serve food, which provides a good source for late-night eating. Many chain restaurants located along major thoroughfares stay open late or all night, such as Grandma's Kitchen, Denny's, and Perkins.

Chain convenience stores, gas stations, and fuel/foodmarts also are open around the clock. Some of these include 7–11, Starvin' Marvin, Mobil Mart, and Circle K.

MEDIA

Media floods the Gulf Coast like high tide. Many publications are directed toward tourists, and some are only as permanent as the shoreline during a tidal surge. Magazines come and go, and radio stations often shift format.

Three daily newspapers stand out for their endurance and dependability: the *Sarasota Herald-Tribune*, the Fort Myers *News-Press*, and the *Naples Daily News*. Weeklies, also, stand firm ground in their respective communities, primarily because many are owned collectively by one corporation. Specialty tabloids inform seniors, shoppers, fishermen, women, and other groups.

Magazines show the most fluctuation. Traditionally, they were built to appeal to the region's upscale, mature population, which is concentrated in Naples. *Gulfshore Life* magazine has been the stalwart of regional lifestyle glossies, but even it shifts its focus to address changing populations and economic trends.

Fort Myers carries the crux of the region's broadcast media, which reach to the Charlotte Harbor and South coasts. Much of the Sarasota Bay Coast's TV comes from Tampa.

Sarasota Bay Coast

NEWSPAPERS

The Beachcomber, 5344 Gulf Dr. N., Holmes Beach 34217; 778-1003. Covers all of Anna Maria Island weekly.
The Bradenton Herald, P.O. Box 921, Bradenton 34206; 748-0411. Daily.
Longboat Key Observer, P. O. Box 8100, Longboat Key 34228; 383-5509. Weekly.

Sarasota Herald-Tribune, 801 S. Tamiami Trail, P.O. Box 1719, Sarasota FL 33577; 953-7755.

Venice Gondolier, 200 E. Venice Avenue, Venice 34285; 484-2611. Published twice weekly.

MAGAZINES

Business, 2201 Cantu Ct., Suite 102, Sarasota 34232; 378-9048.

Events, 47 S. Palm Ave., Suite 210, Sarasota 34236; 955-4464. Tabloid calendar listing.

Sarasota Arts Review, 1260 1st St., Suite 211, Sarasota 34236; 364-5825. Bi-monthly coverage of the area's lively arts scene.

Sarasota Magazine, P.O. Box 3312, Sarasota FL 34236; 366-8225. Lifestyle for upscale Sarasotans.

Sarasota Scene, Box 1418, Sarasota 34240-1418; 365-1119. Weekly covering the Sarasota–Bradenton area.

West Coast Woman, P.O. Box 3047, Sarasota 34230; 954-3300. Bi-weekly tabloid.

RADIO

WBRD-AM 1420; Bradenton. News/Talk.
WCTQ-FM 92; Venice. Country.
WDUV-FM 103.3; Bradenton. Music just for the two of us.
WJIS-FM 88.1; Bradenton. Contemporary Christian.
WKXY-AM 930; Sarasota. Adult Contemporary.
WKZM-FM 105; Sarasota. Christian.
WQSA-AM 1220; Sarasota. News/Talk.
WSPB-AM 1450; Sarasota. Classical.
WSRZ-FM 106.3; Sarasota. Oldies.

TELEVISION

WWSB Channel 40; Sarasota. ABC.

Charlotte Harbor Coast

NEWSPAPERS

Boca Beacon, P.O. Box 313, Boca Grande 33921; 964-2995.
Charlotte Herald, P.O. Box 2390, Port Charlotte 33949; 458-4544.
Englewood Sun Times, P.O. Box 1272, Englewood 34223; 474-5521. Bi-weekly.
Gasparilla Gazette, 375 Park Ave. Boca Grande 33921; 964-2728.
North Port Times, 13544A Tamiami Trail, North Port 34287; 426-9544.

RADIO

WEEJ-FM 100.1; Charlotte Harbor. Oldies.
WENG-AM 1530; Englewood. Pop Classics.

WKII-AM 1070; Punta Gorda. Hits Since the 50s.
WQLM-FM 92.9; Punta Gorda. Light Adult Contemporary.
WQLM-AM 1580; Punta Gorda. Talk/News.
WSEB-FM 91.3; Englewood. Christian.

Island Coast

Going my way?

NEWSPAPERS

Cape Coral Breeze, 2510 Del Prado Blvd., Cape Coral 33910; 574-1110. Daily.
Captiva Current, P.O. Box 549, Captiva 33924; 482-6860.
Fort Myers News-Press, P.O. Box 10, Fort Myers 33902; 335-0200. Publishes editions for Charlotte County and Bonita Springs.
Island Reporter, P.O. Box 809, Sanibel 33957; 472-1587. Weekly.
Observer Papers, 15501 McGregor Blvd., Fort Myers 33908; 482-7111. Publishes weekly editions for Fort Myers Beach and other neighborhoods.
Pine Island Eagle, 10700 Stringfellow Rd., Suite 60, Bokeelia 33922; 283-2260. Weekly.
Sanibel–Captiva Islander, P.O. Box 56, Sanibel 33957; 472-5185. Weekly.

MAGAZINES

Lee Business Digest, P.O. Box 639, Fort Myers 33902; 337-0755.
Lee Living, 6719 Winkler Rd., Suite 200, Fort Myers 33919; 433-2334.
Mature Lifestyles, 15951 McGregor Blvd., Suite 2D, Fort Myers 33908; 482-

7969. Free monthly tabloid with separate editions for Lee, Collier and Charlotte counties.

Nightlife News, P.O. Box 61233, Fort Myers 33906; 481-7931.

Southwest Florida Golf Reporter, P.O. Box 235, Cape Coral, FL 33910–0235; 458-2600.

RADIO

WAVV-FM 101.1; Fort Myers. Adult Contemporary.
WAYJ-FM 88.7; Fort Myers. Christian Contemporary.
WCKT-FM 107; Fort Myers. Country.
WCRM-AM 1350; Fort Myers. Spanish/Black Gospel.
WCVU-FM 94.5; Fort Myers. Easy Listening.
WDCQ-AM 1200; Fort Myers. Talk/Business.
WHEW-FM 102; Fort Myers. Country.
WINK-AM 1240; Fort Myers. News/Talk.
WINK-FM 96.9; Fort Myers. Adult Contemporary.
WMYR-AM 1410; Fort Myers. Country.
WOLZ-FM 95.3; Fort Myers. Oldies.
WRXK-FM 96; Estero. Adult Rock.
WSFP-FM 90.1; Fort Myers. Classical/Jazz/News
WSOR-FM 90.9; Fort Myers. Christian.
WSUV-FM 106.3; Fort Myers. Adult Contemporary.
WXKB-FM 103.7; North Fort Myers. Contemporary.
WWCL-AM 1440; Fort Myers. Spanish.
WWCN-AM 770; Estero. CNN/Talk.
WZCR-FM 99.3; Fort Myers Beach. Classic Rock.

TELEVISION

WBBH-TV Channel 20; Fort Myers. NBC.
WBR-TV Channel 7; Fort Myers. Independent.
WFTX-TV Channel 36; Cape Coral. Fox.
WINK-TV Channel 11; Fort Myers. CBS.

South Coast

NEWSPAPERS

Bonita Banner, P.O. Box 40, Bonita Springs 33959; 765-0110. Semi-weekly.
Naples Daily News, P.O. Box 7009, Naples 33941; 262-3161.

MAGAZINES

Florida Golfer Magazine, 201 S. Airport Rd., Naples 33942; 643-4994.
Gulfshore Life, 2900 S. Horseshoe Dr., Suite 400, Naples 33942; 643-3933.

Home & Condo, 2900 S. Horseshoe Dr., Suite 400, Naples 33942; 643-3933.
   Specifically addresses relocators.

RADIO

WAVV-FM 101.1, Naples. Easy Listening.
WGUF-FM 92.7; Naples. Beautiful Music.
WIXI-FM 105.5; Naples. Big Band.
WNOG-AM 1270; Naples. Talk.
WRGI-FM 93.5; Naples. Classics.
WSGL-FM 1031; Naples. Country.
WVIJ-FM 91.7; Naples. Christian.

TELEVISION

WEVU-TV Channel 26; Bonita Springs. ABC.
WNPL-TV Channel 46; Naples. Independent.
WSFP-TV Channel 30; Bonita Springs. PBS.

REAL ESTATE

Nature's intricate beach designs.

R eal estate prices run the gamut from reasonable to ultra-exclusive. In parts of Bradenton, Sarasota, and Fort Myers, planned communities cater to young families. Exclusive areas such as Longboat Key, Casey Key, Manasota Key, Sanibel Island, Captiva Island, and Naples are known for their pricey waterfront homes and golfing developments. Florida's $25,000 homestead exemption gives residents a break on first home purchases.

Most real estate publications can be found on the newsstands, or check local newspapers. Otherwise, contact the agencies listed below.

Florida Association of Realtors, P.O. Box 725025, Orlando 32872–5025; 407-438-1400.

Sarasota Board of Realtors, 3590 Tuttle Ave. S., Sarasota 33579; 923-2315.

Fort Myers Association of Realtors, Inc., 2840 Winkler Ave., Fort Myers 33916 936-3537.

Sanibel & Captiva Islands Association of Realtors, Inc., 695 Tarpon Bay Rd., Suite #10, Sanibel 33957; 472-9353.

ROAD SERVICE

AAA Auto Club

South Branch Offices
 3844 Bee Ridge Rd., Sarasota; 923-2525
 24-Hour Emergency Road Service 923-0933

 258 Ringling Shopping Center, Sarasota; 365-7540

 2516 Colonial Blvd., Fort Myers 33907; 939-6500
 24-Hour Emergency Road Service, 939-6585

 4910 North Tamiami Trail, Suite 120, Naples 33940; 263-0600
 24-Hour Emergency Road Service, 263-4910

TOURIST INFORMATION

Florida Tourism Bureau, 107 W. Gaines St., Suite 432, Tallahassee FL 32399-2000; 904-487-1462.

Sarasota Bay Coast

Anna Maria Island Chamber of Commerce, P.O. Box 1892, Holmes Beach 34218; 778-1541.

Longboat Key Chamber of Commerce, 5360 Gulf of Mexico Dr., Longboat Key 34228; 383-2466.

Manatee Chamber of Commerce, 222 Tenth St. W., Bradenton 34205; 729-9177.

Manatee County Convention & Visitors Bureau, P.O Box 1000, Bradenton 34206; 746-5989. Welcome center located off Interstate 75 exit number 43.

Sarasota Convention & Visitor Bureau, 655 N. Tamiami Trail, Sarasota 34236; 957-1877 or 1-800-522-9799.

Sarasota County Chamber of Commerce, P.O. Box 308, Sarasota 34230-0308; 955-8187.

Siesta Key Chamber of Commerce, 5263 Ocean Blvd., Sarasota 34242; 349-3800.

Venice Area Chamber of Commerce, 257 No. Tamiami Trail, Venice 34285-1534; 488-2236.

Charlotte Harbor Coast

Boca Grande Chamber of Commerce, P.O. Box 704, Boca Grande 33921; 964-0568. Information center located in Courtyard Plaza at the island's north end.

Charlotte County Chamber of Commerce, 2702 Tamiami Trail, Port Charlotte 33952; 627-2222.

Englewood Area Chamber of Commerce, 601 S. Indiana Ave., Englewood 34224; 474-5511.

North Port Area Chamber of Commerce, 12705 S. Tamiami Trail, North Port 34287; 426-0647.

Island Coast

Cape Coral Chamber of Commerce, P.O. 747, Cape Coral 33904; 549-6900 or 1-800-226-9609. Information center at 1625 Cape Coral Pkwy East.

Chamber cf Southwest Florida, 2051 Cape Coral Pkwy, Cape Coral 33904; 542-3721; or 8191 College Pkwy., Suite 306, Fort Myers 33919; 433-3321.

Fort Myers Beach Chamber of Commerce, 17200 San Carlos Blvd., Fort Myers Beach 33931; 454-7500.

Information Network for Southwest Florida Chamber of Commerce, 6361 Presidential Court, Fort Myers 33919; 433-INFO.

Greater Fort Myers Chamber of Commerce, P.O. Box 9289, Fort Myers 33902; 332-3624. Welcome center located downtown at 2310 Edwards Drive.

Greater Pine Island Chamber of Commerce, P.O. Box 525, Matlacha 33909; 283-0888. Information center located before the bridge to Matlacha on Pine Island Road.

Lee County Visitor & Convention Bureau, 2180 West 1st St., Suite 100, Fort Myers 33901; 335-2631 or 1-800-237-6444.

North Fort Myers Chamber of Commerce, 13180 No. Cleveland Ave., North Fort Myers 33903; 997-9111.

Sanibel–Captiva Islands Chamber of Commerce, 3422 Willard St., Fort Myers

33916; 227-2918. Information center located shortly after the causeway approach to Sanibel.

Southwest Florida Hispanic Chamber of Commerce, P.O. Box 1374, Cape Coral 33910–1374; 549-8701.

South Coast

Bonita Springs Area Chamber of Commerce, P.O. Box 1240, Bonita Springs 33959; 992-2943 or 1-800-226-2943. Welcome center located on Tamiami Trail across from entrance to Bonita Bay development.

Everglades Area Chamber of Commerce, P.O. Box 130, Everglades City 33929; 695-3941.

Marco Island Area Chamber of Commerce, 1102 North Collier Blvd., P.O. Box 913 Marco Island 33937; 394-7549.

Naples Chamber of Commerce, 3620 9th St. No., Naples 33940-3724; 262-6141.

Index

LODGING BY PRICE

Rate Categories:

Inexpensive	Up to $50
Moderate	$50-110
Expensive	$110-180
Very Expensive	$180 & up

INEXPENSIVE
Point Pleasant B&B
Rod & Gun Club

INEXPENSIVE–MODERATE
Beach & Tennis Club
Sea Grape Motel

MODERATE
Banyan House
Bonita Beach Resort Motel
Crescent House B&B
Duncan House B&B
Hampton Inn
Shangri-La

MODERATE—EXPENSIVE
Banana Bay Club
Cabbage Key Inn
Castaways
Days Inn at Lovers Key
Drum House Inn B&B
Harrington House B&B

Inn at the Beach
Inn by the Sea B&B
Island Inn
Sheraton Harbor Place

MODERATE–VERY EXPENSIVE
Naples Beach Hotel & Golf Club
Pink Shell Beach & Bay Resort

EXPENSIVE
Half Moon Beach Club

EXPENSIVE–VERY EXPENSIVE
Edgewater Beach
Gasparilla Inn
Holiday Inn, Longboat Key
Hyatt Sarasota
Keewaydin Island
Longboat Key Club
Manasota Beach Club
Radisson Suite Beach Resort
Safety Harbor Club
Sanibel Harbour Resourt & Spa
South Seas Plantation
Sundial Beach & Tennis Resort
'Tween Waters Inn

VERY EXPENSIVE
Clony Beach & Tennis Resort
Palm Island Resort
Registry Resort
Ritz-Carlton

RESTAURANTS BY PRICE

Price Categories

Inexpensive	Up to $15
Moderate	$15-25
Expensive	$25-35
Very Expensive	$35 or more

INEXPENSIVE
Barnacle Phil's
Emphasis Coffee House Cafe &
    Gallery
Guantanamera
Old Salty Dog
Snook Haven
Sugar & Spice

INEXPENSIVE–MODERATE
Alice's Flamingo
Casual Clam
Fernandez de Bull
Phillippi Creek Village Oyster Bar

MODERATE
Big Hickory Fishing Nook Restau-
    rant
Captain's Table
Coasters Seafood House
The Crow's Nest
Dock at Crayton Cove
Guadalajara
Lighthouse Hole
Mar-Vista Dockside Restaurant &
    Pub
Moore's Stone Crab Restaurant
Mucky Duck

Pelican Alley
Pier
Restaurant Tannengarten
Riverwalk Fish & Ale House
Rotten Ralph's
Runabouts Roadside Grille
Sandbar
Sharky's
Stan's Idle Hour Seafood restaurant

MODERATE–EXPENSIVE
Bangkok House
Bud's Any Fish You Wish
Snug Harbor
Tarwinkles Seafood Emporium
Through the Looking Glass

EXPENSIVE
Chophouse Grille
Lafayette Gourmet Seafood
Nicks on the Water
Olde Marco Inn
Theatre Restaurant
Veranda

EXPENSIVE–VERY EXPENSIVE
Carmichael's

VERY EXPENSIVE
Chef's Garden
Colony Restaurant
Greenhouse
L'Auberge du Bon Vivant
Lafite
Peter's La Cuisine

RESTAURANTS BY CUISINE

AMERICAN
Barnacle Phil's
Captain's Table
Casual Clam
Old Salty Dog, The
Pier, The
Runabouts Roadside Grille
Snook Haven
Snug Harbor
Tarwinkles Seafood Emporium
Theatre Restaurant
Through the Looking Glass

AMERICAN NOUVELLE
Carmichael's
Chophouse Grille
Emphasis Coffee House Cafe &
　　Gallery
Greenhouse, The
Lafite

AMISH
Sugar & Spice

BARBECUE
Snook Haven

CONTINENTAL
Chef's Garden, The
Colony Restaurant
Lafayette Gourmet Seafood
Lafite
Mucky Duck
Olde Marco Inn
Peter's La Cuisine
Pier, The
Through the Looking Glass

CUBAN
Fernandez de Bull
Guantanamera

ECLECTIC
Greenhouse, The

ENGLISH
Old Salty Dog, The

FLORIDA (Classic Southern)
Alice's Flamingo
Big Hickory Fishing Nook Restau-
　　rant
Dock at Crayton Cove
Lighthouse Hole
Phillippi Creek Village Oyster Bar
Rotten Ralph's
Stan's Idle Hour Seafood Restaurant
Veranda, The

FLORIDA (Nouvelle)
Tarwinkles Seafood Emporium

FRENCH
L'Auberge du Bon Vivant

GERMAN
Restaurant Tannengarten

ITALIAN
Nicks on the Water

MEXICAN
Guadalajara

SEAFOOD
Barnacle Phil's
Big Hickory Fishing Nook Restau-
　　rant
Bud's Any Fish You Wish
Captain's Table
Coasters Seafood House
Crow's Nest, The
Lighthouse Hole

About the Author

Robert Horvath

Chelle Koster Walton came to visit a friend on Sanibel Island in 1981. She's still there. As a writer, she specializes in Florida and Caribbean travel, food, and culture. Her *Caribbean Ways: A Cultural Guide* and *Hidden Florida: The Adventurer's Guide* have both won awards in Lowell Thomas Travel Journalism Competitions for Best Guidebook. A member of the Society of American Travel Writers, Walton is contributing editor for *Caribbean Travel and Life* and *Florida Travel and Life* magazines. Her work has appeared in numerous publications, including the *Miami Herald*, the Fort Lauderdale *Sun-Sentinel*, *Islands*, *Americana*, and the *Los Angeles Herald Examiner*.

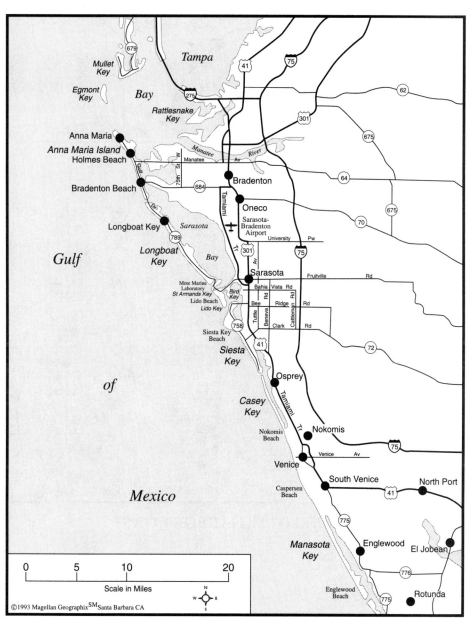

SARASOTA BAY COAST

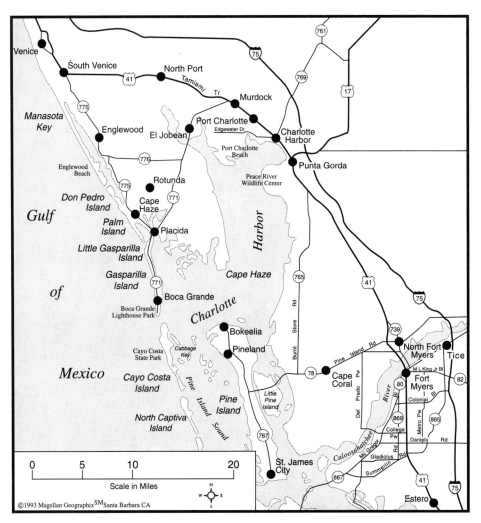

CHARLOTTE HARBOR COAST

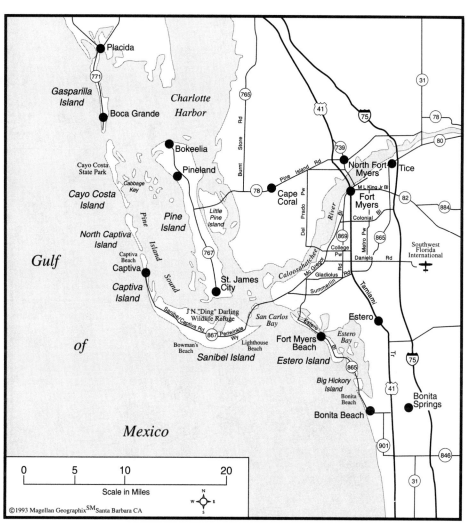

ISLAND COAST

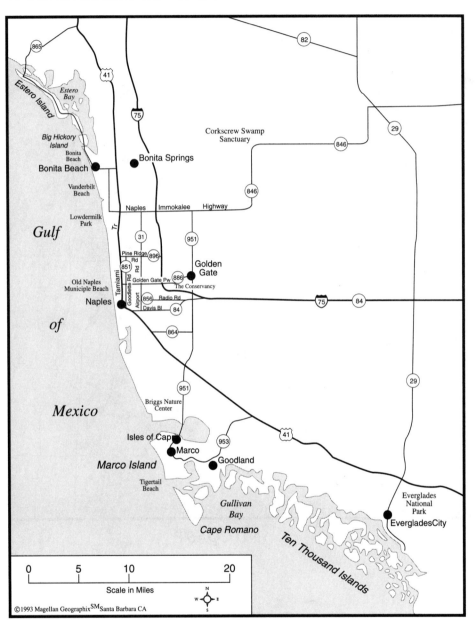

SOUTH COAST